ASTRONAUTS

ASTRONAUTS
Women on the Final Frontier

Written by
JIM OTTAVIANI

Artwork by
MARIS WICKS

First Second
New York

To the explorers—past and future—
of unpathed waters, undreamed shores.

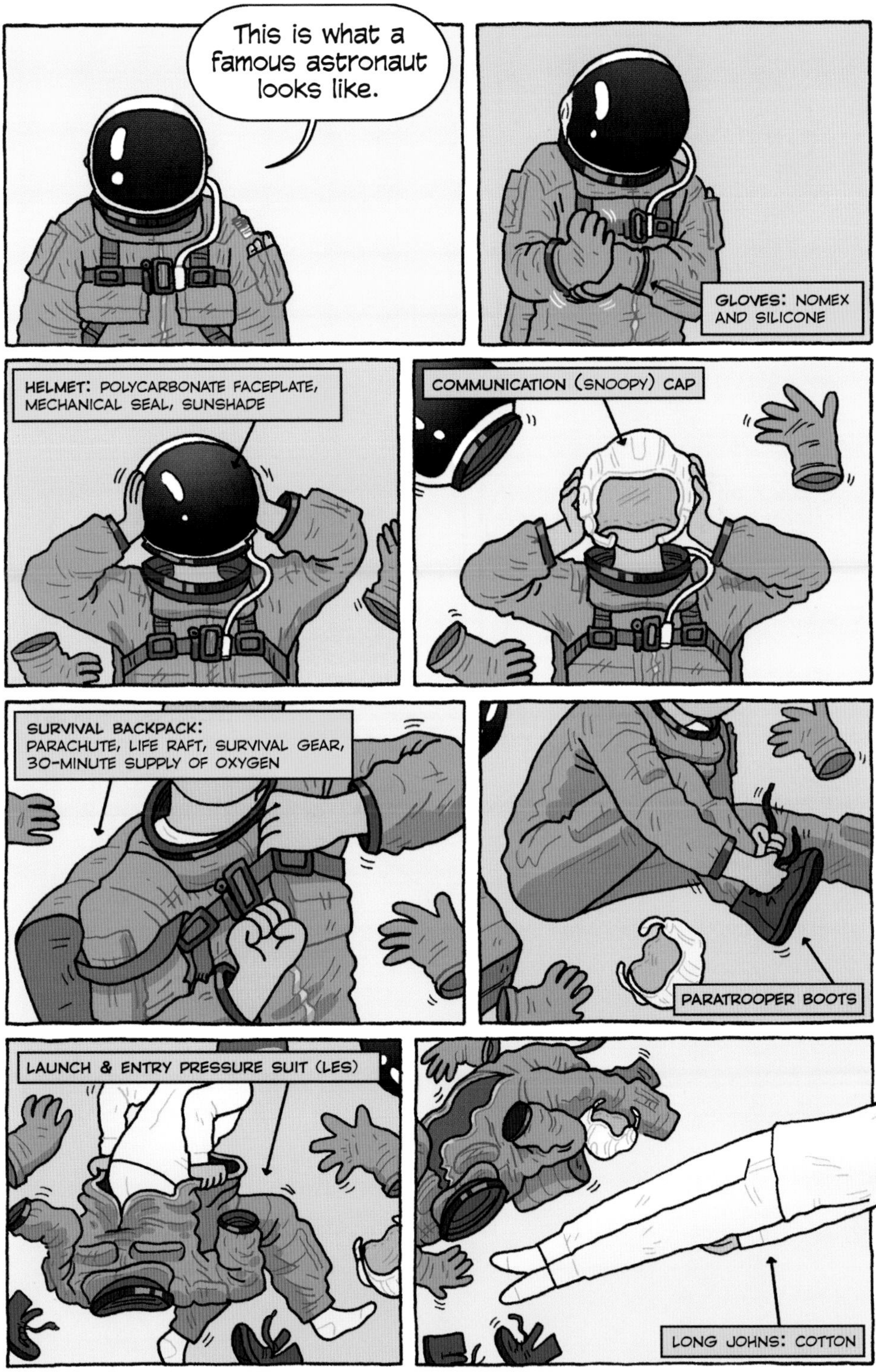
This is what a famous astronaut looks like.
GLOVES: NOMEX AND SILICONE
HELMET: POLYCARBONATE FACEPLATE, MECHANICAL SEAL, SUNSHADE
COMMUNICATION (SNOOPY) CAP
SURVIVAL BACKPACK: PARACHUTE, LIFE RAFT, SURVIVAL GEAR, 30-MINUTE SUPPLY OF OXYGEN
PARATROOPER BOOTS
LAUNCH & ENTRY PRESSURE SUIT (LES)
LONG JOHNS: COTTON

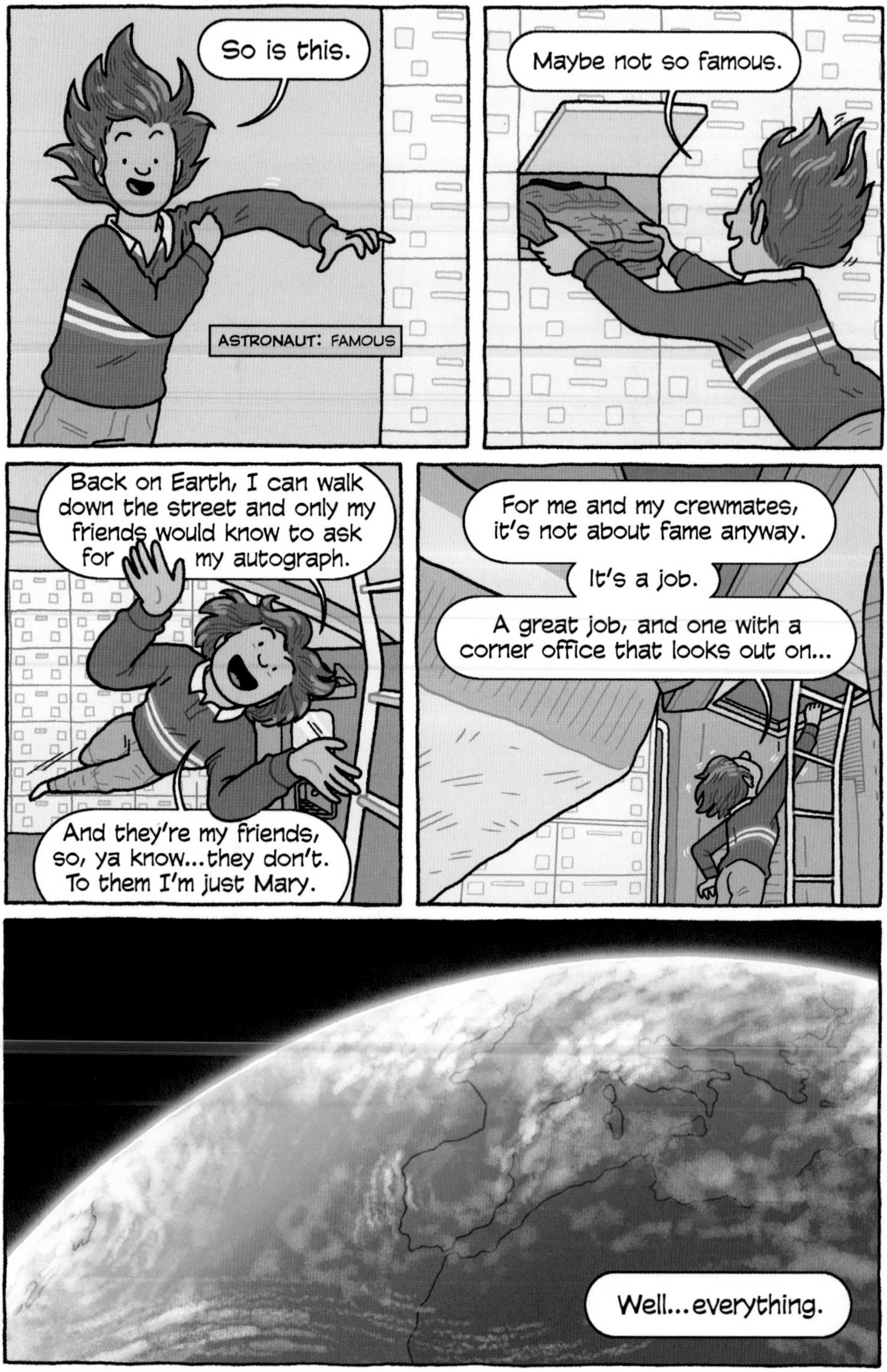

So is this.
ASTRONAUT: FAMOUS
Maybe not so famous.
Back on Earth, I can walk down the street and only my friends would know to ask for my autograph.
And they're my friends, so, ya know...they don't. To them I'm just Mary.
For me and my crewmates, it's not about fame anyway.
It's a job.
A great job, and one with a corner office that looks out on...
Well...everything.

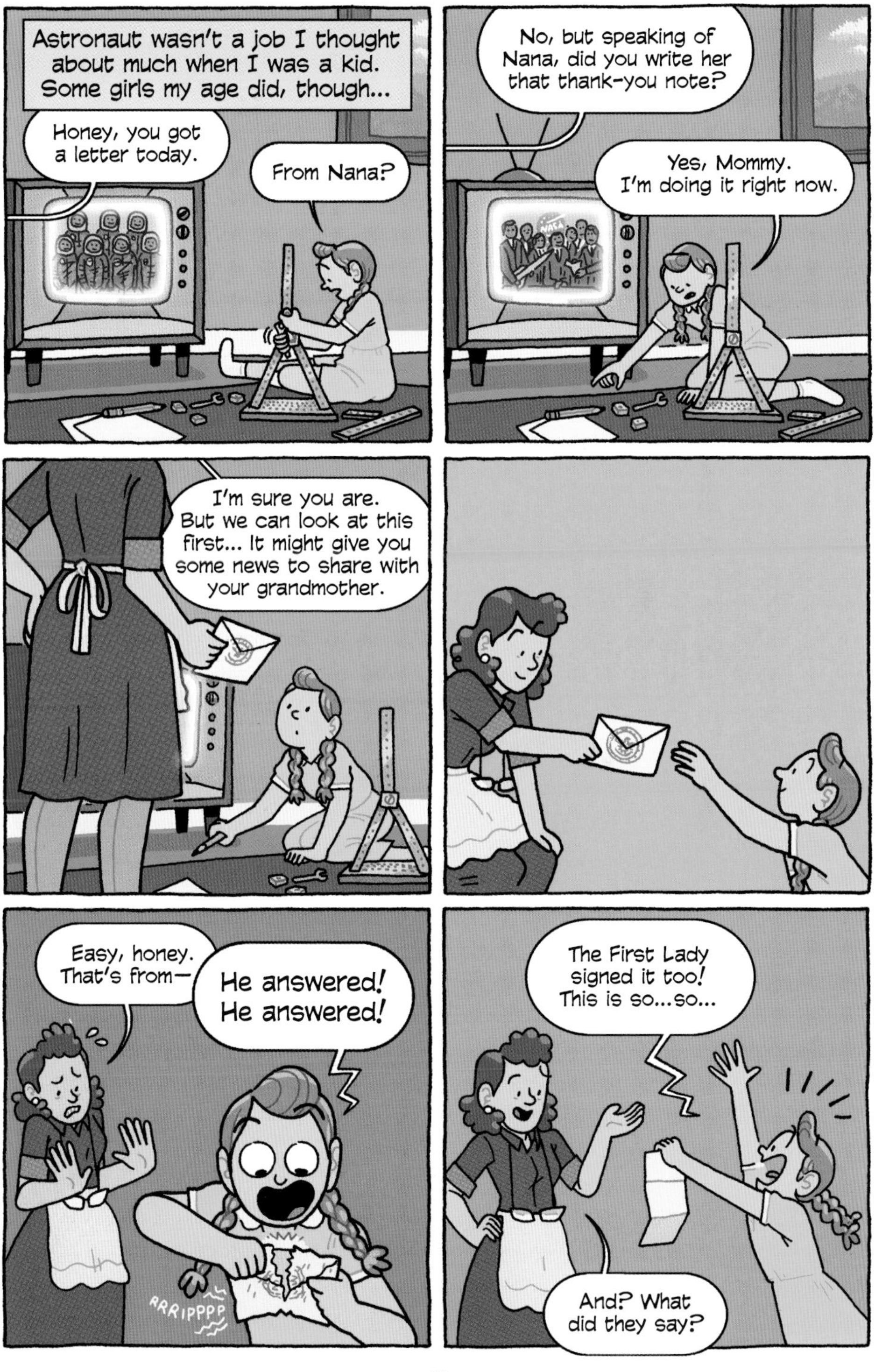
Astronaut wasn't a job I thought about much when I was a kid. Some girls my age did, though...
Honey, you got a letter today.
From Nana?
No, but speaking of Nana, did you write her that thank-you note?
Yes, Mommy. I'm doing it right now.
I'm sure you are. But we can look at this first... It might give you some news to share with your grandmother.
Easy, honey. That's from—
He answered! He answered!
RRRIPPPP
The First Lady signed it too! This is so...so...
And? What did they say?

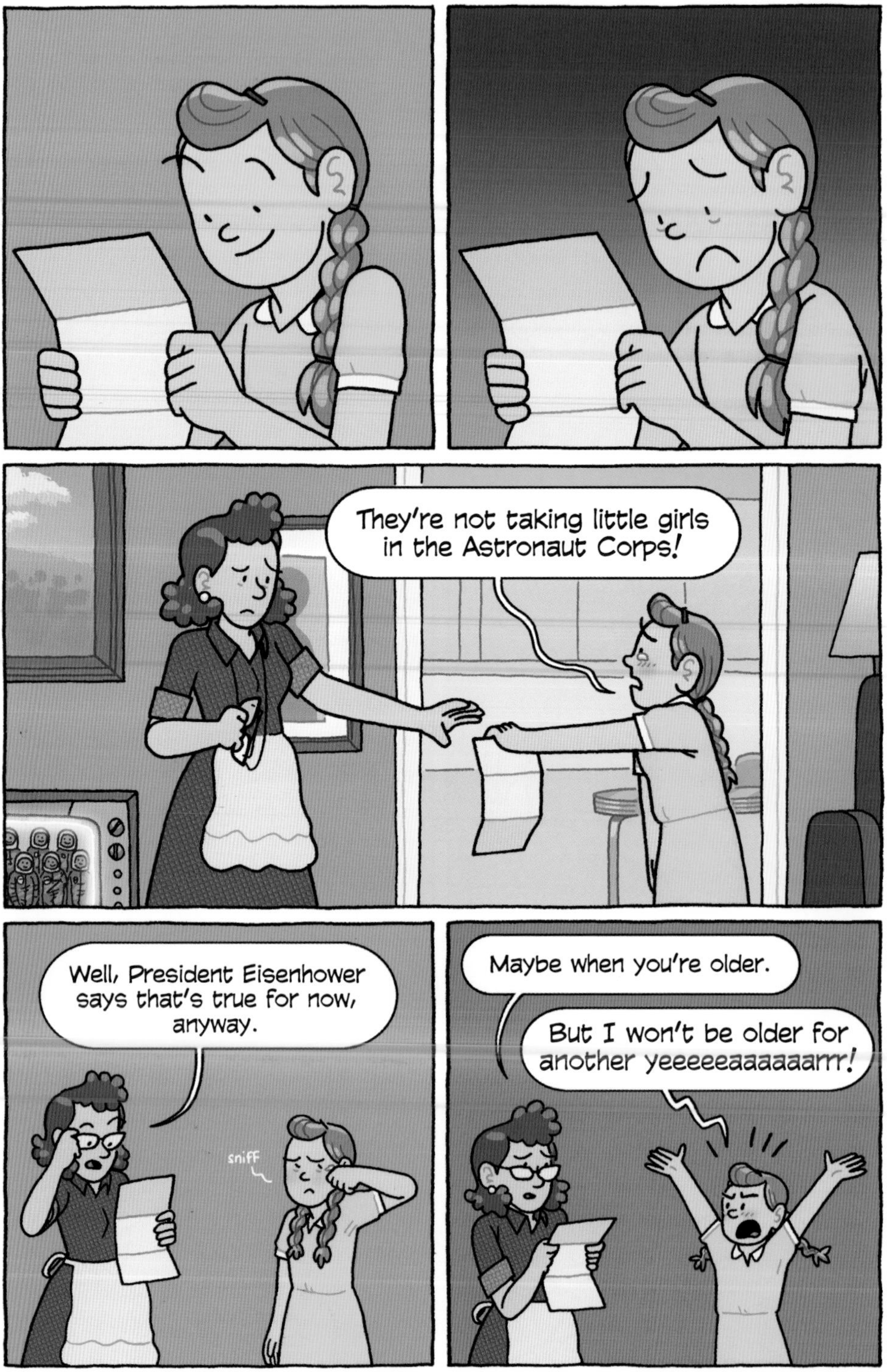

They're not taking little girls in the Astronaut Corps!
Well, President Eisenhower says that's true for now, anyway.
sniff
Maybe when you're older.
But I won't be older for another yeeeeeaaaaaarrr!

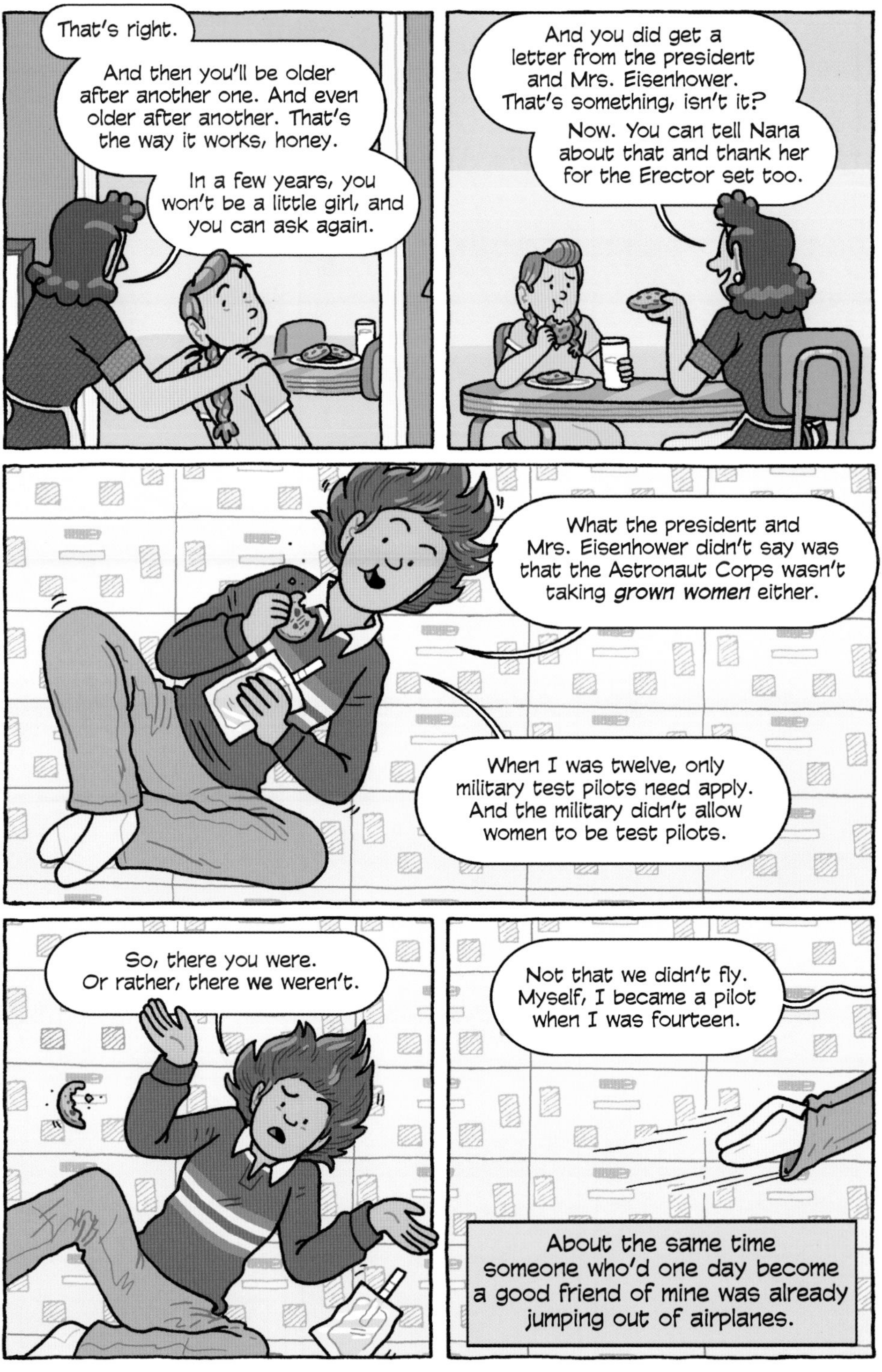
That's right.
And then you'll be older after another one. And even older after another. That's the way it works, honey.
In a few years, you won't be a little girl, and you can ask again.
And you did get a letter from the president and Mrs. Eisenhower. That's something, isn't it?
Now. You can tell Nana about that and thank her for the Erector set too.
What the president and Mrs. Eisenhower didn't say was that the Astronaut Corps wasn't taking *grown women* either.
When I was twelve, only military test pilots need apply. And the military didn't allow women to be test pilots.
So, there you were. Or rather, there we weren't.
Not that we didn't fly. Myself, I became a pilot when I was fourteen.
About the same time someone who'd one day become a good friend of mine was already jumping out of airplanes.

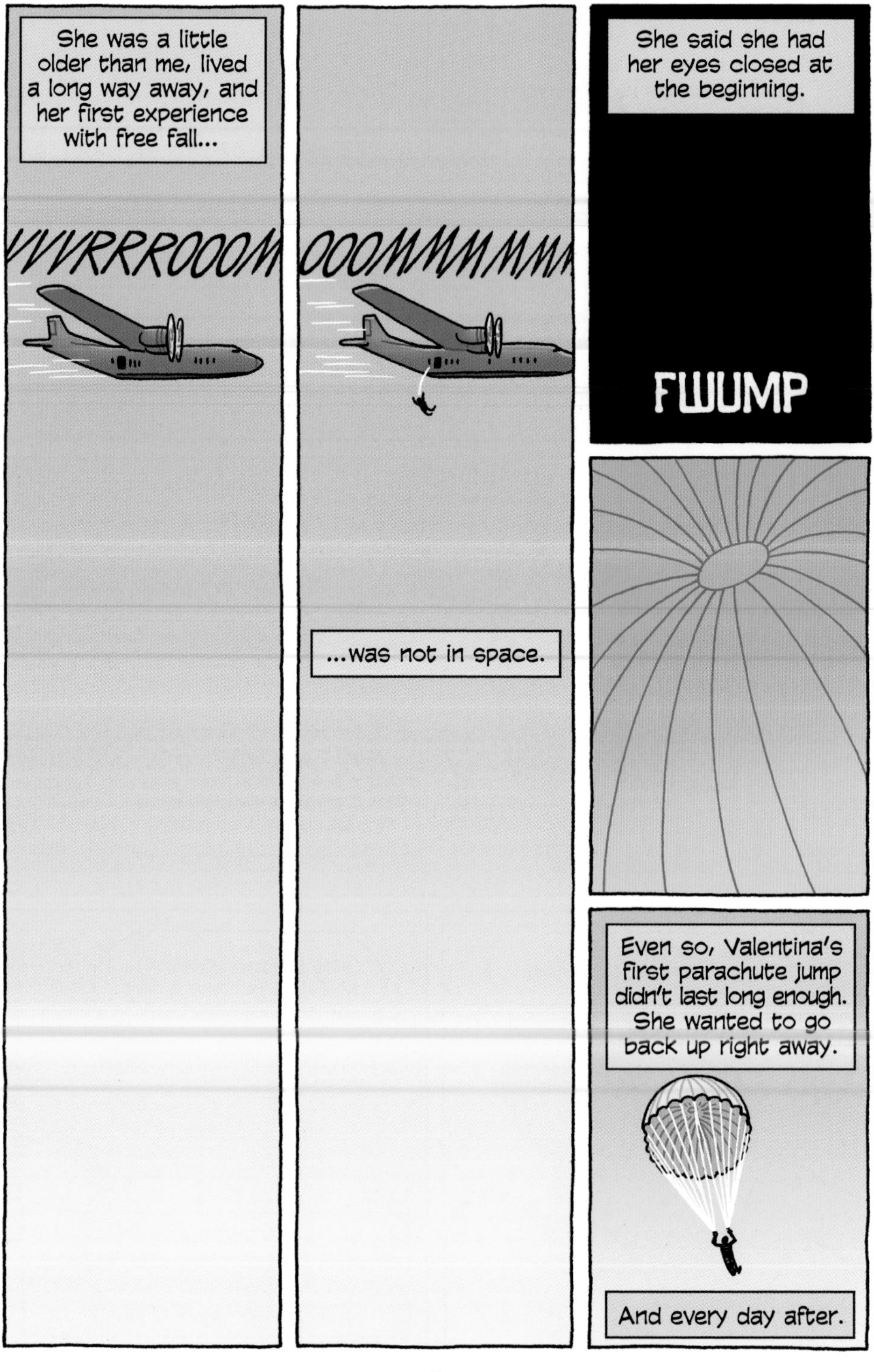
She was a little older than me, lived a long way away, and her first experience with free fall...
VVVRRROOOM
OOOMMMMMM
...was not in space.
She said she had her eyes closed at the beginning.
FWUMP
Even so, Valentina's first parachute jump didn't last long enough. She wanted to go back up right away.
And every day after.

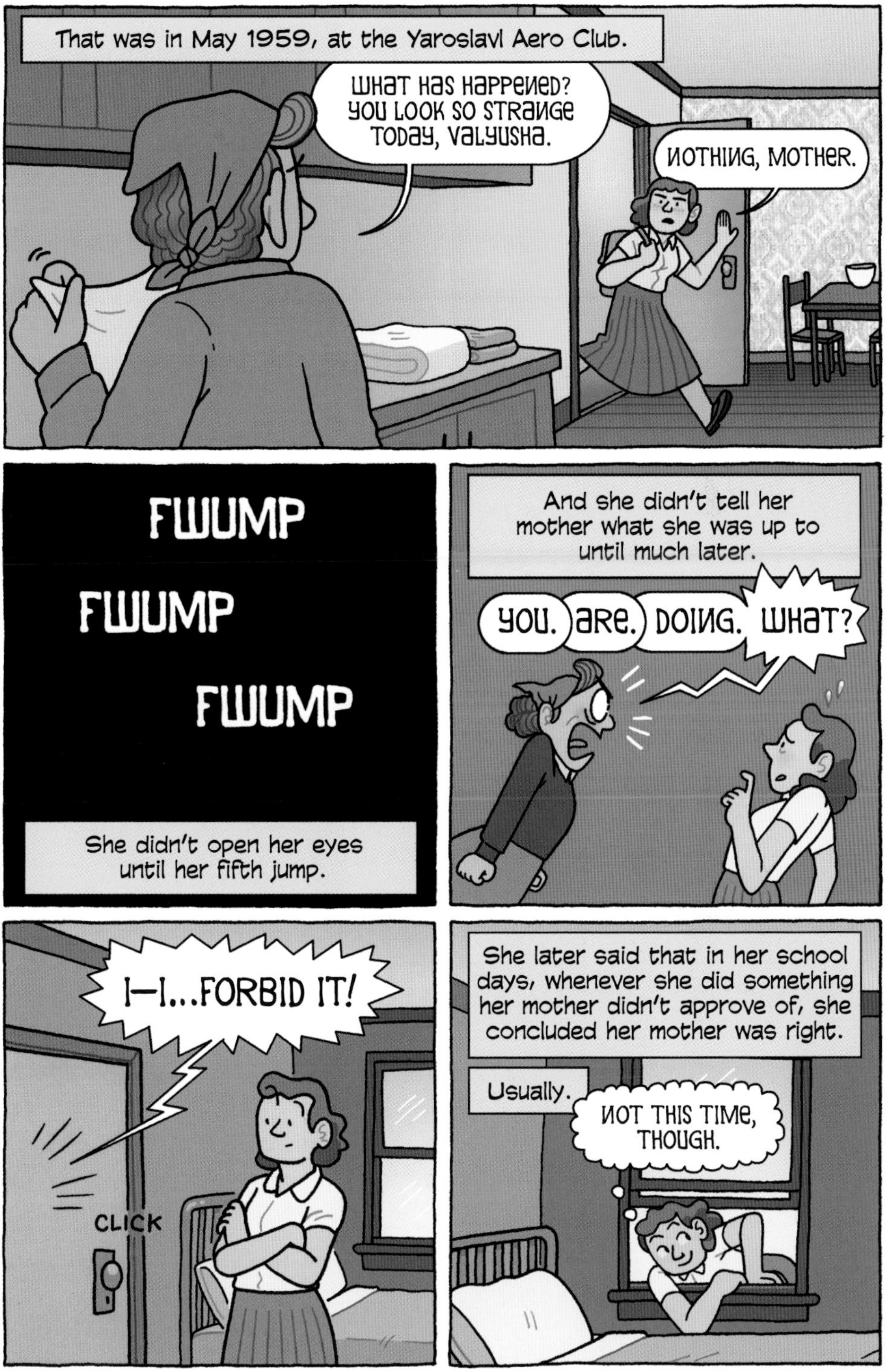

That was in May 1959, at the Yaroslavl Aero Club.
WHAT HAS HAPPENED? YOU LOOK SO STRANGE TODAY, VALYUSHA.
NOTHING, MOTHER.
FWUMP
FWUMP
FWUMP
She didn't open her eyes until her fifth jump.
And she didn't tell her mother what she was up to until much later.
YOU. ARE. DOING. WHAT?
I–I...FORBID IT!
CLICK
She later said that in her school days, whenever she did something her mother didn't approve of, she concluded her mother was right.
Usually.
NOT THIS TIME, THOUGH.

YOU ARE LATE, COMRADE TERESHKOVA.

YES, COMRADE KHAVRONIN! I'M SORRY, SIR, I WAS DETAINED!

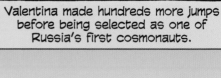

Valentina made hundreds more jumps before being selected as one of Russia's first cosmonauts.

The U.S. was selecting its first astronauts too right about then, and the doctor who was key to that selection process was Randy Lovelace.

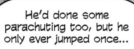

He'd done some parachuting too, but he only ever jumped once...

...and he did it from 40,200 feet, as a medical experiment in high-altitude escape.

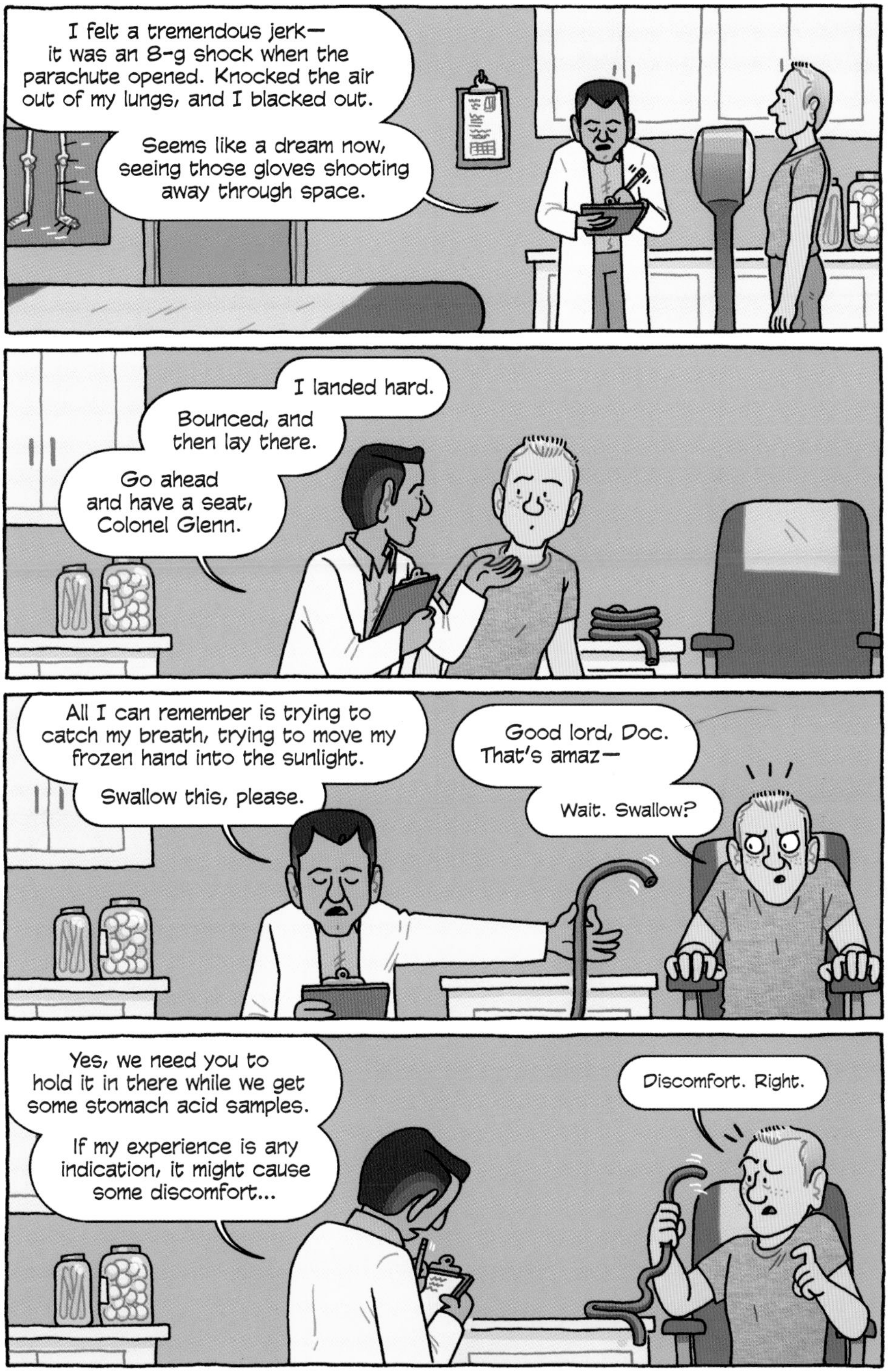
I felt a tremendous jerk— it was an 8-g shock when the parachute opened. Knocked the air out of my lungs, and I blacked out.
Seems like a dream now, seeing those gloves shooting away through space.
I landed hard.
Bounced, and then lay there.
Go ahead and have a seat, Colonel Glenn.
All I can remember is trying to catch my breath, trying to move my frozen hand into the sunlight.
Swallow this, please.
Good lord, Doc. That's amaz—
Wait. Swallow?
Yes, we need you to hold it in there while we get some stomach acid samples.
If my experience is any indication, it might cause some discomfort...
Discomfort. Right.

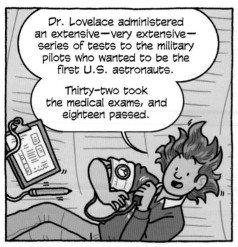

Dr. Lovelace administered an extensive—very extensive—series of tests to the military pilots who wanted to be the first U.S. astronauts.

Thirty-two took the medical exams, and eighteen passed.

In the end NASA selected seven to be America's first astronauts.

But Dr. Lovelace wasn't done with testing. He had a hunch...

Looking at the results all together, we can draw up a profile for the ideal astronaut.

Height, weight, stamina, tolerance for discomfort and isolation.

LOVELACE CLINIC

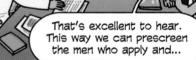

We now have a pretty good idea of the type of person NASA needs for the space program.

That's excellent to hear. This way we can prescreen the men who apply and...

That's the thing. Look at the data, and you'll see there's no reason to limit your candidate pool to men.

Women should be just as capable.

That's, um... interesting to hear. But...

Not that we've tested any.

That's great. But, I mean, there's no need to spend money on *that*.

Plenty of qualified candidates already, you know.

They're not wrong, I guess. But they're also not right.

I think we should find out for sure. I'm going to place a long-distance call to Flick.

NOD NOD

Brigadier General Don "Flick" Flickinger was part of the Air Force's Research and Development Command, and a friend of Dr. Lovelace's.

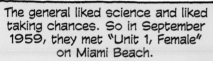

The general liked science and liked taking chances. So in September 1959, they met "Unit 1, Female" on Miami Beach.

Miss Cobb? Don Flickinger, USAF.

And I'm Randy Lovelace. I do aviation medicine.

Who are these...?

Wait, Lovelace.

That's the Mercury 7 doctor!

They were in town for an Air Force Association conference, and all had just been for a swim. Flickinger and Lovelace told her what they had in mind...

We'll need to confirm your credentials, Miss Cobb, but if you're interested...?

Don't have my credentials on me right now, but heck yes, I'm interested.

And call me Jerrie.

Jerrie Cobb had commercial flight experience and flying records (including an altitude record), and...

...has been the National Pilot's Association's "Pilot of the Year." There's more.

Nah, I'm sold.

I'll bring her in.

11

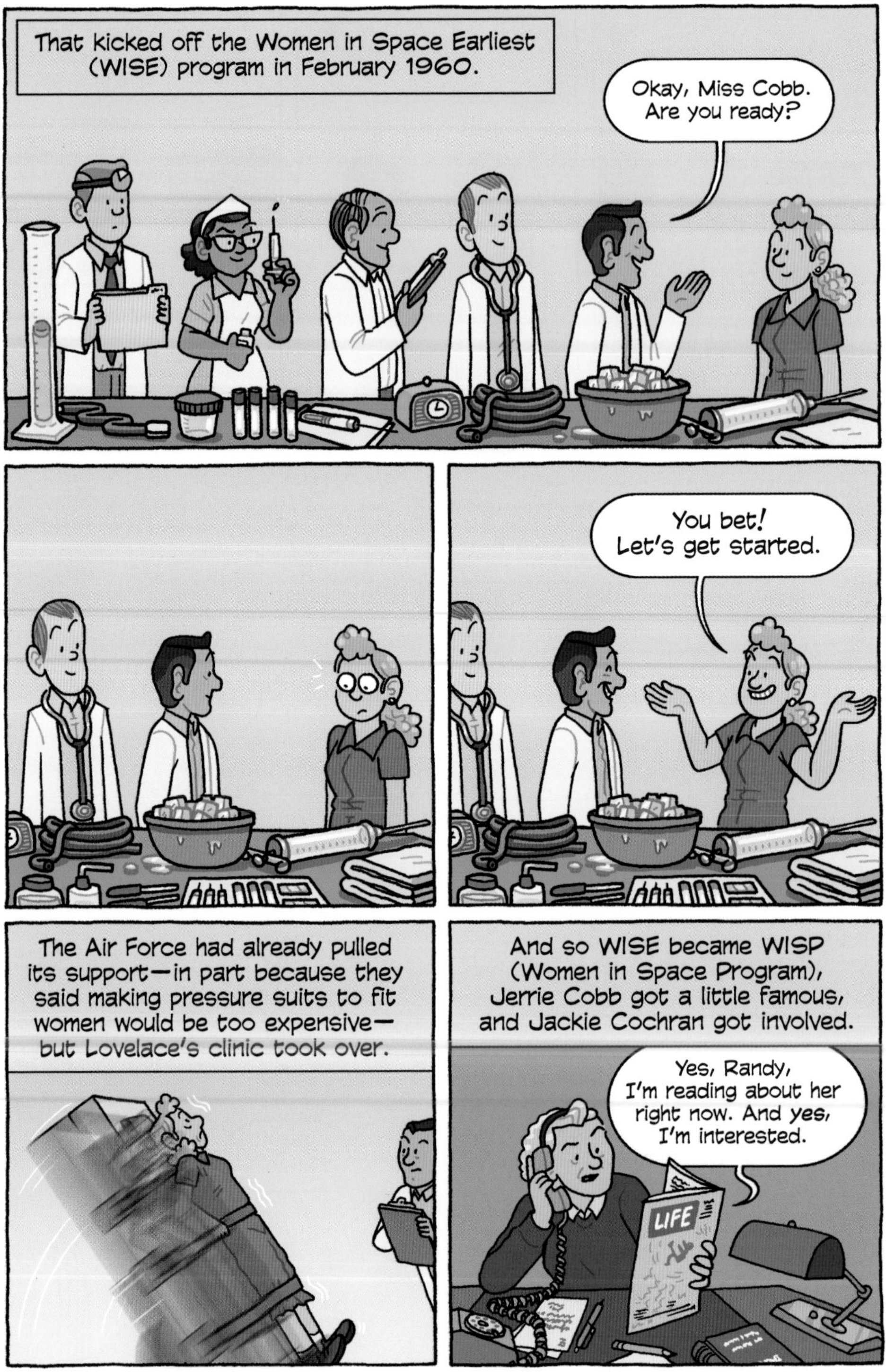
That kicked off the Women in Space Earliest (WISE) program in February 1960.
Okay, Miss Cobb. Are you ready?
You bet! Let's get started.
The Air Force had already pulled its support—in part because they said making pressure suits to fit women would be too expensive—but Lovelace's clinic took over.
And so WISE became WISP (Women in Space Program), Jerrie Cobb got a little famous, and Jackie Cochran got involved.
Yes, Randy, I'm reading about her right now. And *yes*, I'm interested.
LIFE

We can organize it like my Women Air Force Service Pilot training program.

Honey, I'm flying to Albuquerque.

Do you want to come with?

Jackie had piloting records herself, and training experience with the WASPs in the Second World War. She had fame, and money too.

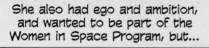

She also had ego and ambition, and wanted to be part of the Women in Space Program, but...

I've been your personal physician for a while, Jackie, and besides being too old for the job, there's your heart condition.

I can't approve you, Jackie. You're my friend and...but... well, I just can't.

She still agreed to supply funds for more women to undergo testing— most couldn't afford to take time away from their piloting and family to spend a week in the lab.

They came to the Lovelace Clinic separately and anonymously, but were tested in pairs.

MOTEL
Bel-Air
AIR CONDITIONED
TV POOL
NIGHTLY RATES
VACANCY
RECEPTION

Hi, you must be...

Yup. Here for the Lovelace tests. I'm "Unit 11, Female."

But you can call me Janey.

I'm Bernice. I mean, "Unit 10."

HA HA HA HA HA

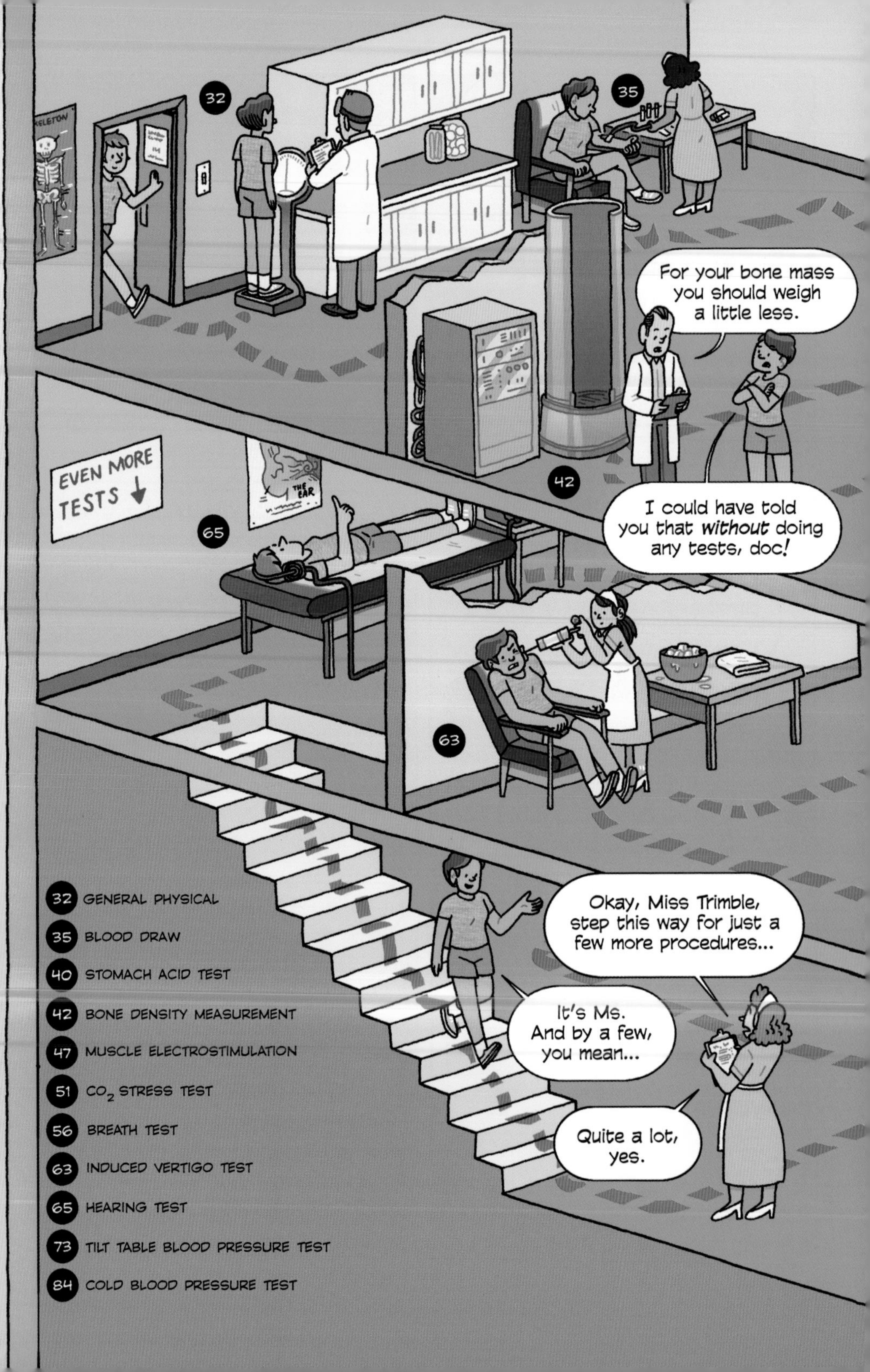

32
35
For your bone mass you should weigh a little less.
I could have told you that *without* doing any tests, doc!
42
EVEN MORE TESTS
THE EAR
65
63
Okay, Miss Trimble, step this way for just a few more procedures...
It's Ms. And by a few, you mean...
Quite a lot, yes.
32 GENERAL PHYSICAL
35 BLOOD DRAW
40 STOMACH ACID TEST
42 BONE DENSITY MEASUREMENT
47 MUSCLE ELECTROSTIMULATION
51 CO_2 STRESS TEST
56 BREATH TEST
63 INDUCED VERTIGO TEST
65 HEARING TEST
73 TILT TABLE BLOOD PRESSURE TEST
84 COLD BLOOD PRESSURE TEST

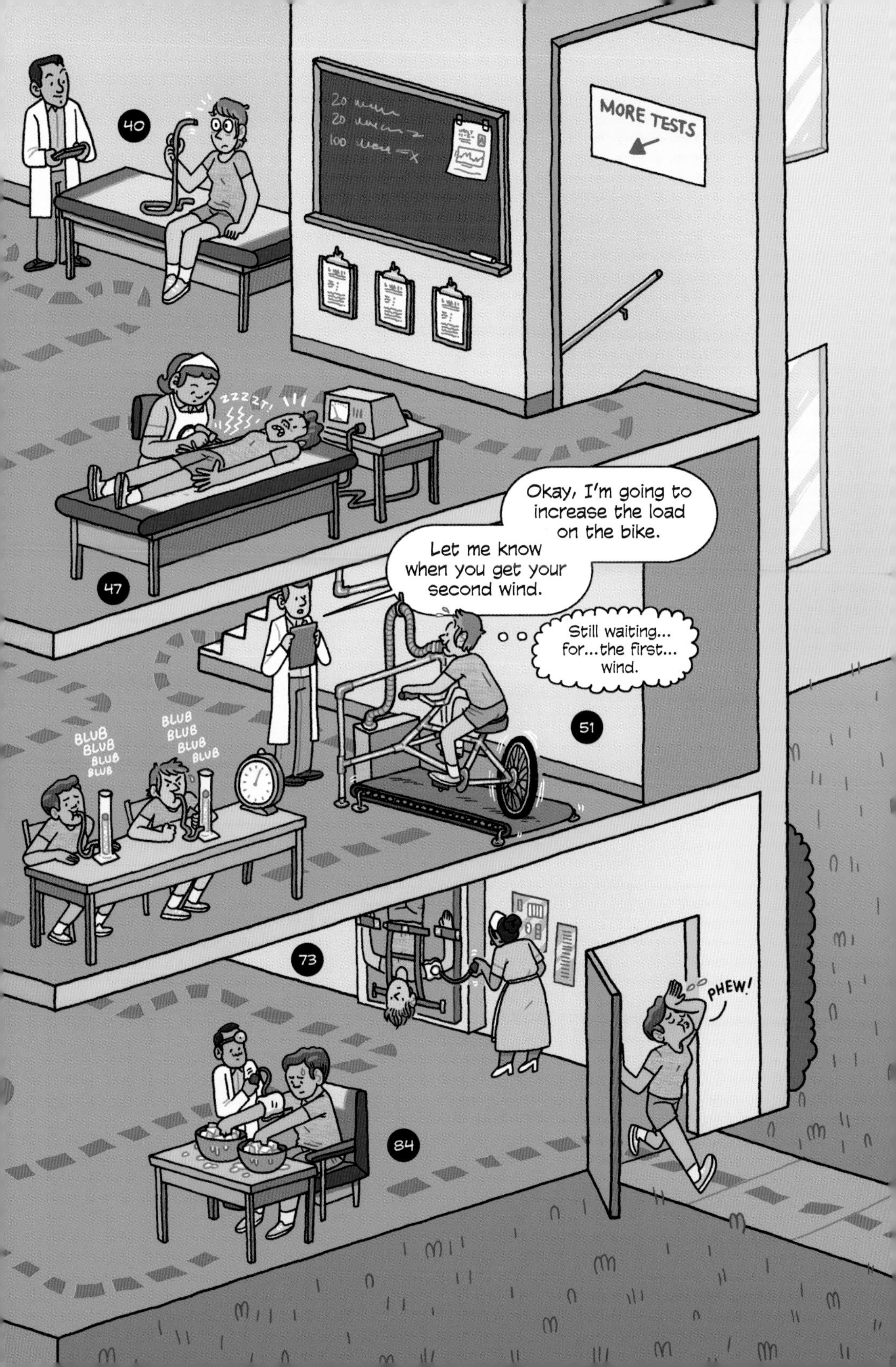
40
MORE TESTS
ZZZZT!
47
Okay, I'm going to increase the load on the bike.
Let me know when you get your second wind.
Still waiting... for...the first... wind.
51
BLUB BLUB BLUB BLUB
BLUB BLUB BLUB BLUB
73
PHEW!
84

Two of the women gave up their jobs, and one ended up getting a divorce because of the testing.

They all thought it was worth it— if they passed, they'd have a chance to fly jets, and maybe even more.

MYRTLE CAGLE | JERRIE COBB | JANET DIETRICH | MARION DIETRICH | WALLY FUNK | SARAH GORELICK | JANEY HART

JEAN HIXSON | RHEA HURRLE | GENE NORA STUMBOUGH | IRENE LEVERTON | JERRIE SLOAN | BERNICE TRIMBLE

And thirteen did pass. But the jets?

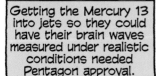

That's not what happened.

You want to determine the...

Getting the Mercury 13 into jets so they could have their brain waves measured under realistic conditions needed Pentagon approval.

...the *difference* between male and female astronauts?

First, *astronauts*?

Second, if you don't know the difference *already*, we refuse to put money into the project.

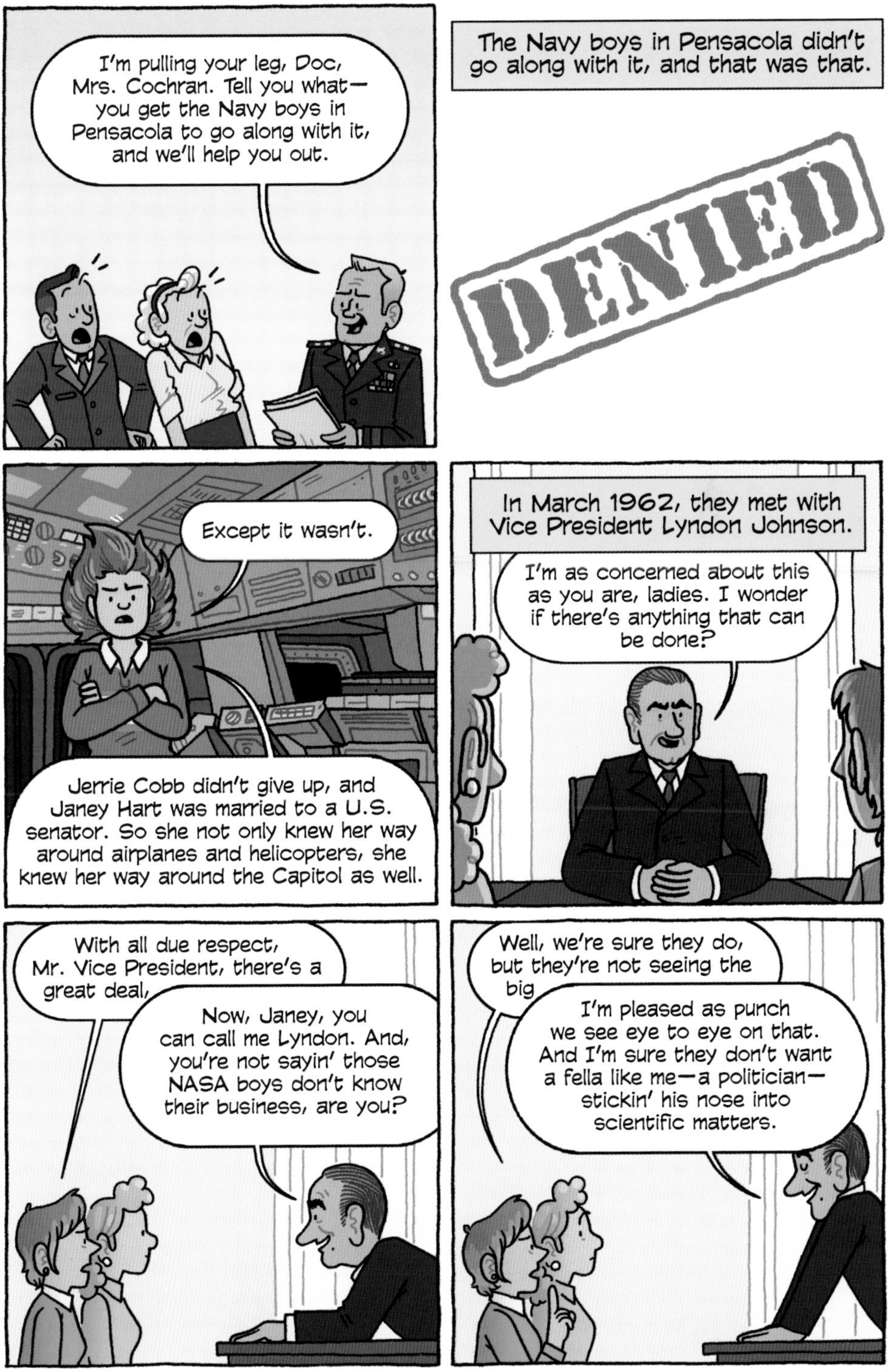

I'm pulling your leg, Doc, Mrs. Cochran. Tell you what—you get the Navy boys in Pensacola to go along with it, and we'll help you out.
The Navy boys in Pensacola didn't go along with it, and that was that.
DENIED
Except it wasn't.
Jerrie Cobb didn't give up, and Janey Hart was married to a U.S. senator. So she not only knew her way around airplanes and helicopters, she knew her way around the Capitol as well.
In March 1962, they met with Vice President Lyndon Johnson.
I'm as concerned about this as you are, ladies. I wonder if there's anything that can be done?
With all due respect, Mr. Vice President, there's a great deal,
Now, Janey, you can call me Lyndon. And, you're not sayin' those NASA boys don't know their business, are you?
Well, we're sure they do, but they're not seeing the big
I'm pleased as punch we see eye to eye on that. And I'm sure they don't want a fella like me—a politician—stickin' his nose into scientific matters.

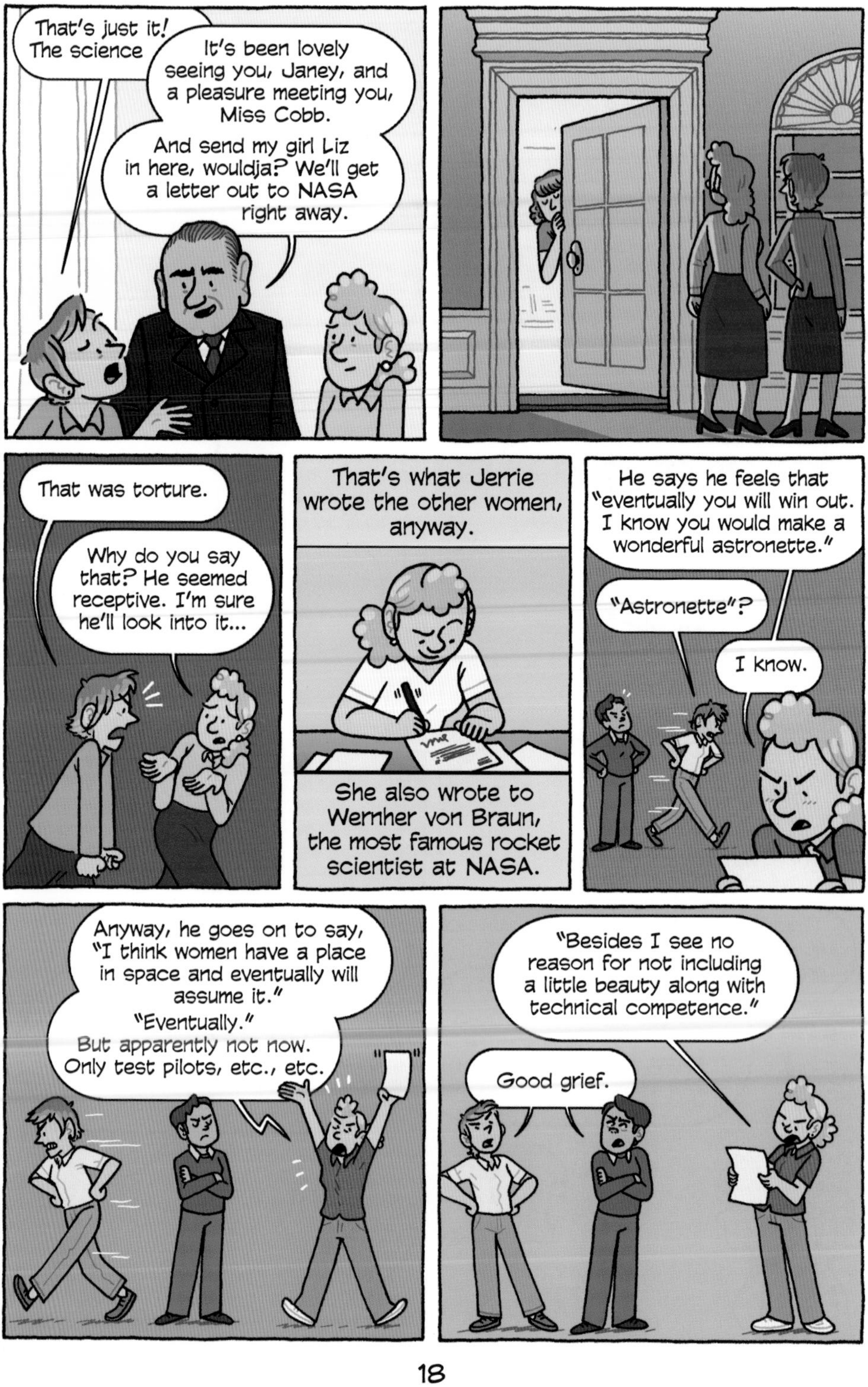
That's just it! The science
It's been lovely seeing you, Janey, and a pleasure meeting you, Miss Cobb.
And send my girl Liz in here, wouldja? We'll get a letter out to NASA right away.
That was torture.
Why do you say that? He seemed receptive. I'm sure he'll look into it...
That's what Jerrie wrote the other women, anyway.
She also wrote to Wernher von Braun, the most famous rocket scientist at NASA.
He says he feels that "eventually you will win out. I know you would make a wonderful astronette."
"Astronette"?
I know.
Anyway, he goes on to say, "I think women have a place in space and eventually will assume it."
"Eventually." But apparently not now. Only test pilots, etc., etc.
"Besides I see no reason for not including a little beauty along with technical competence."
Good grief.

They weren't done. In July 1962 they got themselves a congressional hearing. This was their big chance to make the case for women astronauts.

What does your husband, Senator Phil Hart, think about your petition to Congress?

I've never asked him. Now, if you'll please—

...excuse us?

The topic of the hearing was "Qualifications for Astronauts."

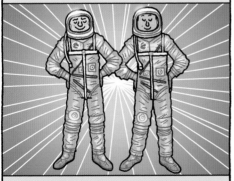

There were other special guests.

John Glenn and Scott Carpenter had both just flown in space. They were Famous American Heroes, and that's with a capital F, capital A, and capital H!

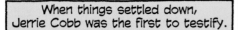

When things settled down, Jerrie Cobb was the first to testify.

A-almost three years ago, Dr. Randolph Lovelace and Air Force Brig. Gen. Donald Flickinger asked me to be the first woman to undergo the Mercury astronaut tests at the Lovelace Clinic.

When my qualifications checked out, I passed them all, and as a result, it was decided to test a whole, um, group of woman pilots.

Famed pilot Jacqueline Cochran paid the expenses of many of us who underwent these tests.

After twelve other women had p-passed, I was sort of, well, drafted to be spokesperson for all of us. As you can tell, it certainly wasn't because of my speaking ability.

HA HA HA HA HA HEH HEH HEH HEH HA HA HA

Now, there are sound reasons for using women as astronauts.

Women weigh less and consume less food and oxygen than men, important when every pound of humanity and life support systems is a grave obstacle in the cost of space vehicles.

Women are more radiation-resistant and less prone to heart attacks, and are less susceptible to monotony, loneliness, heat, cold, pain, and noise.

We have seen the pride of the entire free world in U.S. astronauts like Glenn and Carpenter.

UNDER NO CIRCUMSTANCES SHOULD AN AMERICAN BECOME THE FIRST WOMAN IN SPACE. THAT WOULD BE AN INSULT TO THE FEELINGS OF SOVIET WOMEN.

But no nation has yet sent a human female into space.

Miss Cobb, that was an excellent statement. I think we can safely say that the purpose of space exploration is to someday colonize other planets.

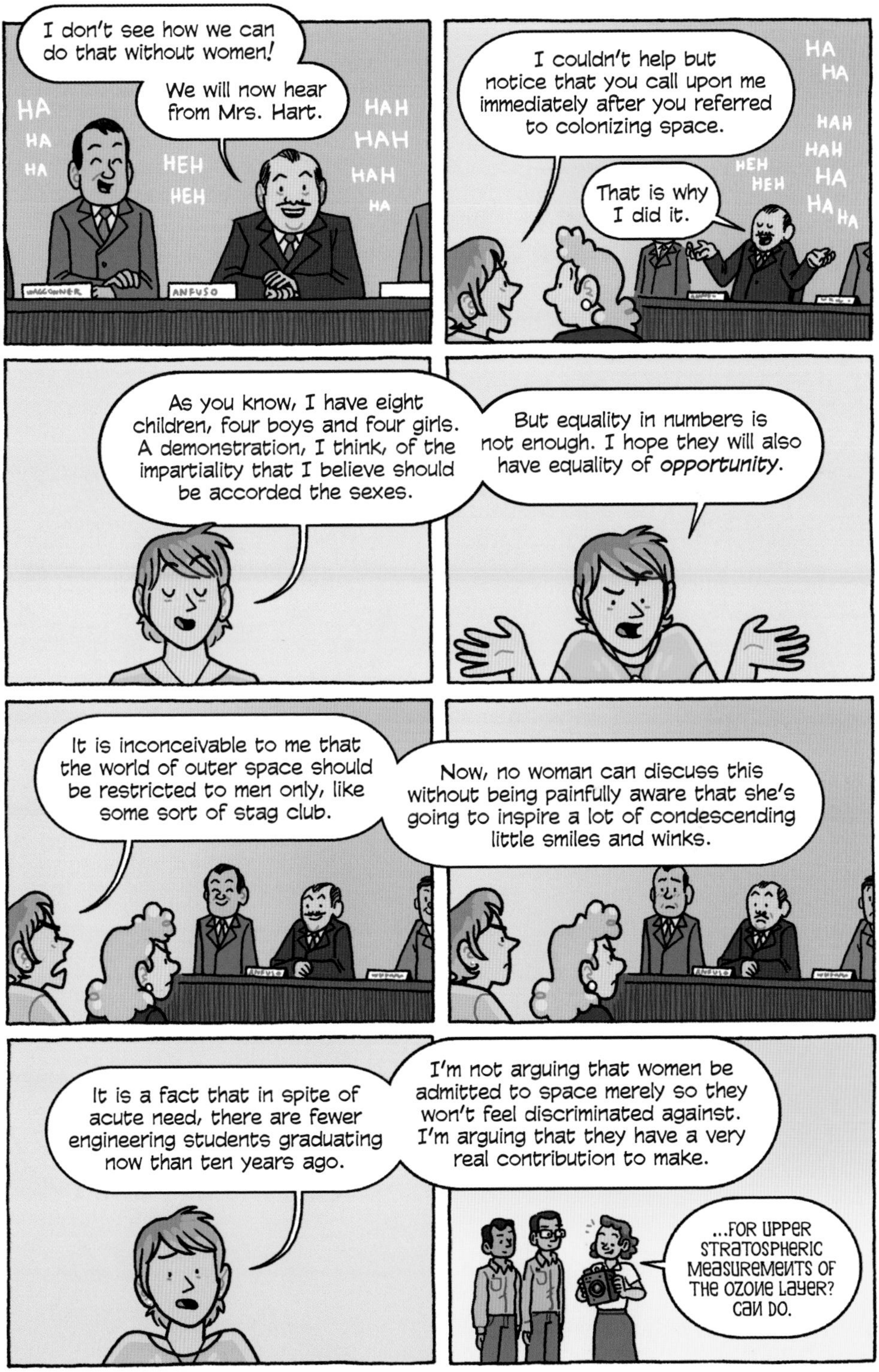
I don't see how we can do that without women!
HA HA HA
HEH HEH
We will now hear from Mrs. Hart.
HAH HAH HAH HA
WAGGONER
ANFUSO
I couldn't help but notice that you call upon me immediately after you referred to colonizing space.
That is why I did it.
HEH HEH
HA HA HAH HAH HA HA HA
As you know, I have eight children, four boys and four girls. A demonstration, I think, of the impartiality that I believe should be accorded the sexes.
But equality in numbers is not enough. I hope they will also have equality of *opportunity*.
It is inconceivable to me that the world of outer space should be restricted to men only, like some sort of stag club.
Now, no woman can discuss this without being painfully aware that she's going to inspire a lot of condescending little smiles and winks.
It is a fact that in spite of acute need, there are fewer engineering students graduating now than ten years ago.
I'm not arguing that women be admitted to space merely so they won't feel discriminated against. I'm arguing that they have a very real contribution to make.
...FOR UPPER STRATOSPHERIC MEASUREMENTS OF THE OZONE LAYER? CAN DO.

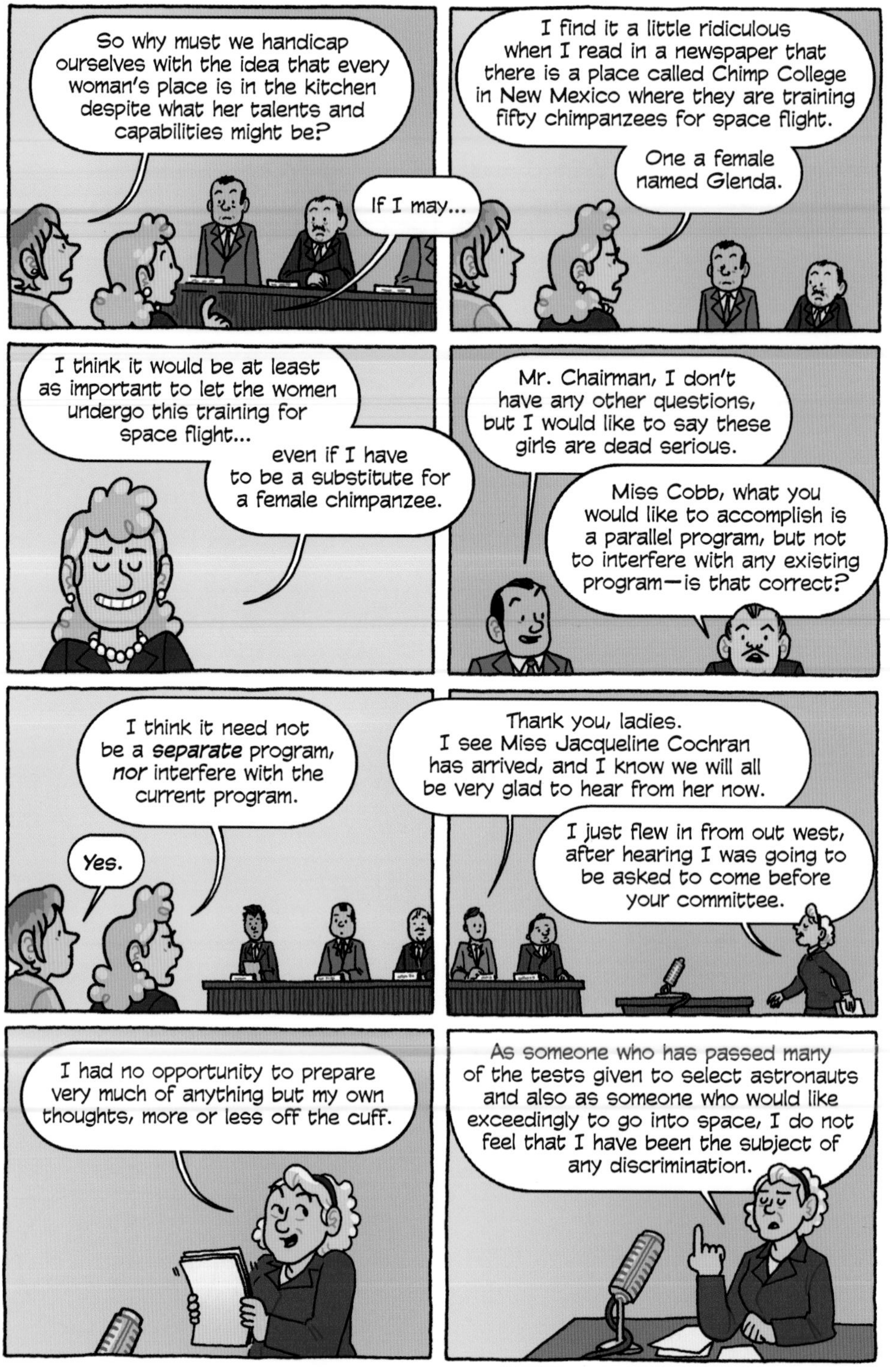
So why must we handicap ourselves with the idea that every woman's place is in the kitchen despite what her talents and capabilities might be?
If I may...
I find it a little ridiculous when I read in a newspaper that there is a place called Chimp College in New Mexico where they are training fifty chimpanzees for space flight.
One a female named Glenda.
I think it would be at least as important to let the women undergo this training for space flight...
even if I have to be a substitute for a female chimpanzee.
Mr. Chairman, I don't have any other questions, but I would like to say these girls are dead serious.
Miss Cobb, what you would like to accomplish is a parallel program, but not to interfere with any existing program—is that correct?
I think it need not be a *separate* program, *nor* interfere with the current program.
Yes.
Thank you, ladies. I see Miss Jacqueline Cochran has arrived, and I know we will all be very glad to hear from her now.
I just flew in from out west, after hearing I was going to be asked to come before your committee.
I had no opportunity to prepare very much of anything but my own thoughts, more or less off the cuff.
As someone who has passed many of the tests given to select astronauts and also as someone who would like exceedingly to go into space, I do not feel that I have been the subject of any discrimination.

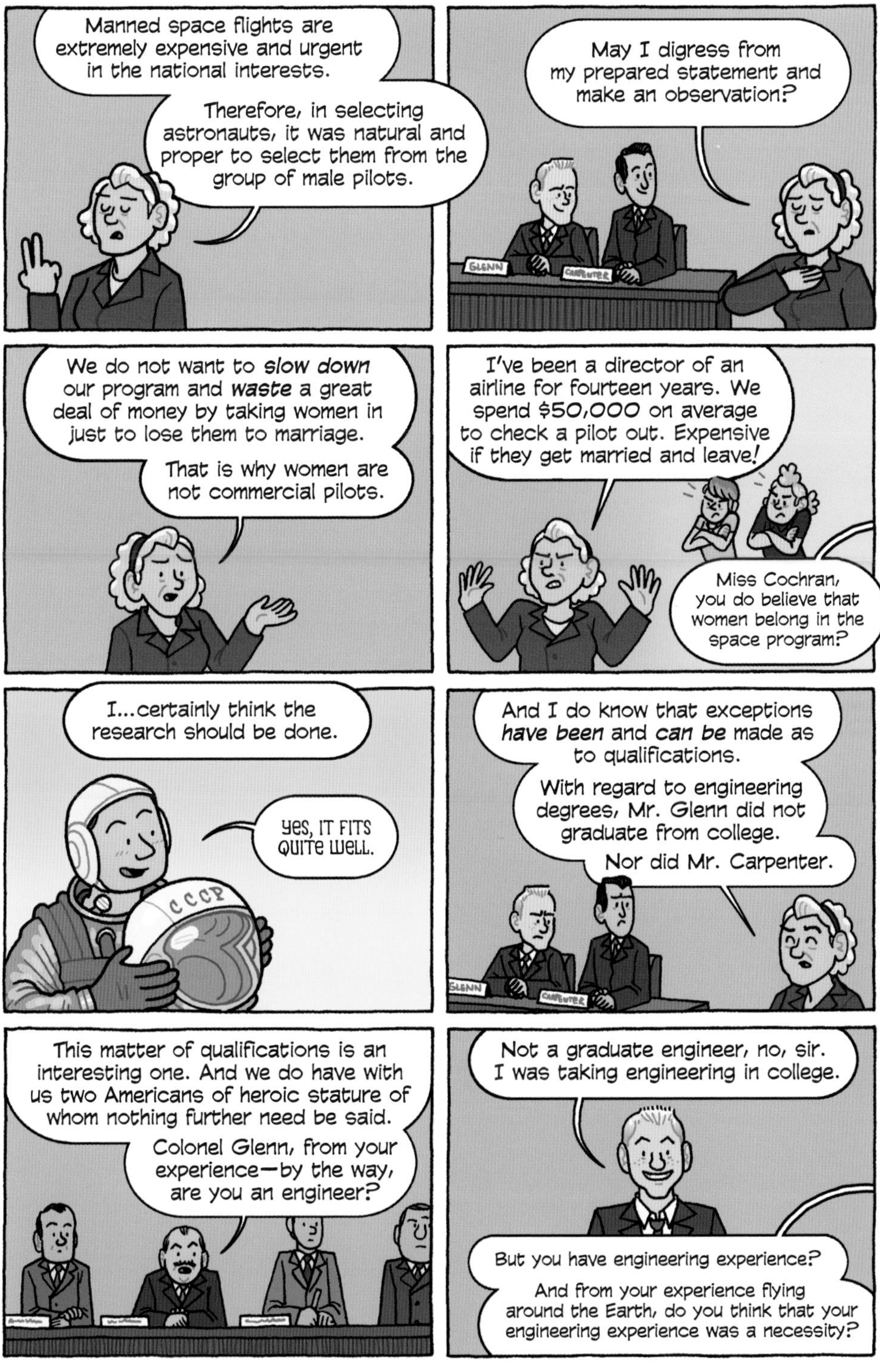
Manned space flights are extremely expensive and urgent in the national interests.
Therefore, in selecting astronauts, it was natural and proper to select them from the group of male pilots.
May I digress from my prepared statement and make an observation?
GLENN
CARPENTER
We do not want to *slow down* our program and *waste* a great deal of money by taking women in just to lose them to marriage.
That is why women are not commercial pilots.
I've been a director of an airline for fourteen years. We spend $50,000 on average to check a pilot out. Expensive if they get married and leave!
Miss Cochran, you do believe that women belong in the space program?
I...certainly think the research should be done.
YES, IT FITS QUITE WELL.
CCCP
And I do know that exceptions *have been* and *can be* made as to qualifications.
With regard to engineering degrees, Mr. Glenn did not graduate from college.
Nor did Mr. Carpenter.
GLENN
CARPENTER
This matter of qualifications is an interesting one. And we do have with us two Americans of heroic stature of whom nothing further need be said.
Colonel Glenn, from your experience—by the way, are you an engineer?
Not a graduate engineer, no, sir. I was taking engineering in college.
But you have engineering experience?
And from your experience flying around the Earth, do you think that your engineering experience was a necessity?

Oh, yes, sir.

More than just in orbit, but prior to flight, to understand all the systems, to work in the design areas to ferret out trouble, to analyze them in flight, and to make the best contribution following the flight.

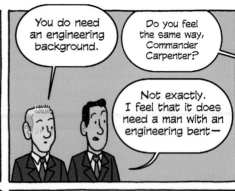

You do need an engineering background.

Do you feel the same way, Commander Carpenter?

Not exactly. I feel that it does need a man with an engineering bent—

You said a "man." Don't you mean a "person"?

I stand corrected.

Are you an engineer?

HEH HEH

Yes, sir, I am now a graduate engineer.

HAH HA HA

Why are they laughing?

Because he didn't graduate.

But he did receive an "earned" degree in aeronautical engineering in May.

Right after his flight.

What?!

Well, now. Regarding this physical examination program. It isn't that it qualifies anybody for anything. It just shows that they are a good, healthy person.

If we can find any women that demonstrate that they have better all-around *qualifications* for going into a program than we have, we would welcome them.

With open arms.

For the purposes of my going home this afternoon, I think that should be stricken from the record.

I think we will let the record stand, Colonel.

Okay, then. I think this gets back to the way our social order is organized, really.

The fact that women are not in this field is a fact of our social order. It may be undesirable.

It obviously is, but...

I am not anti-anybody— I am just pro-space.

Let's face this. It's obvious that the present training structure and standards effectively eliminate women.

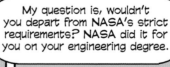

FULTON   WAGGONNER   ANFUSO

My question is, wouldn't you depart from NASA's strict requirements? NASA did it for you on your engineering degree.

25

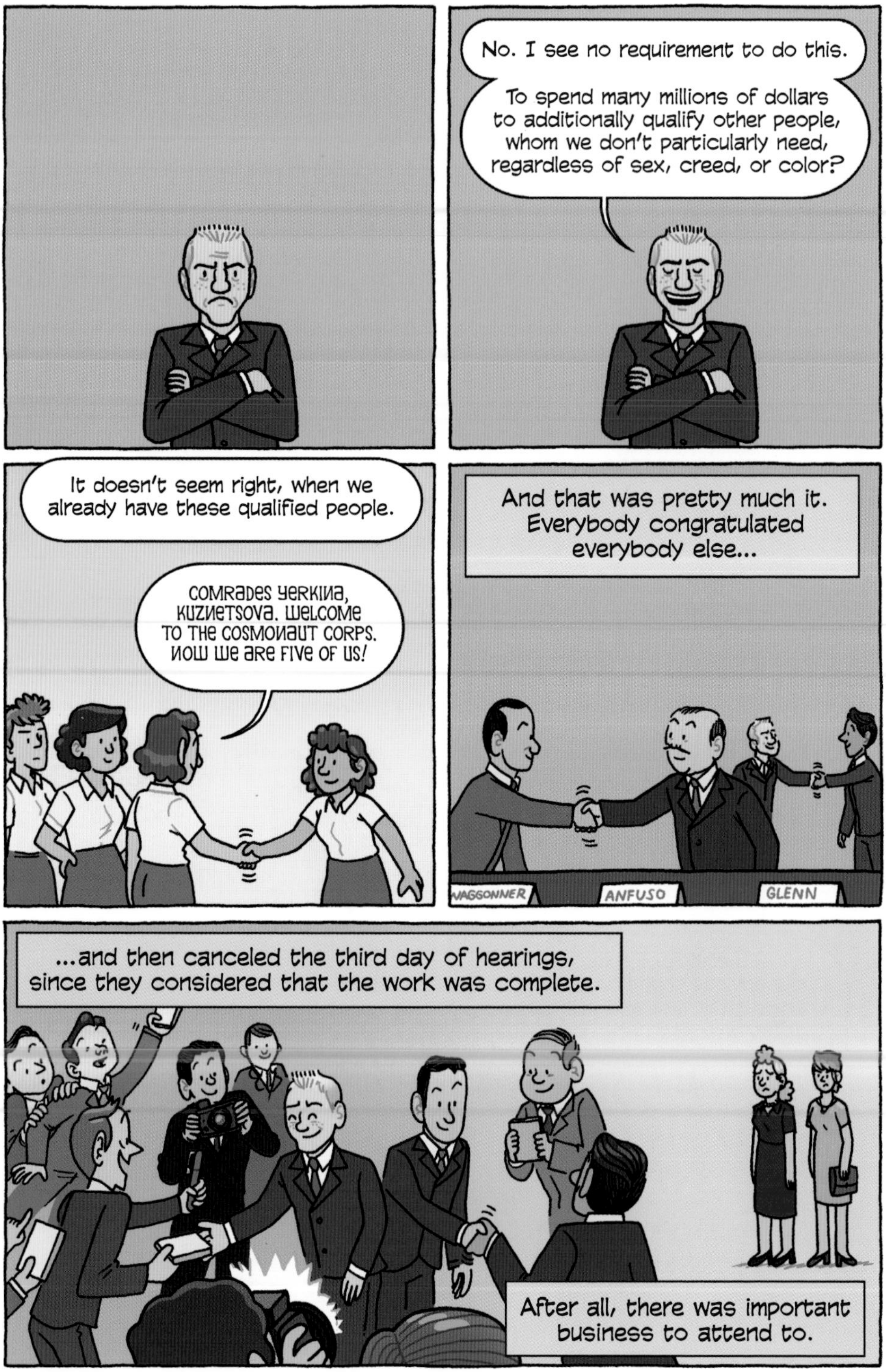

No. I see no requirement to do this.
To spend many millions of dollars to additionally qualify other people, whom we don't particularly need, regardless of sex, creed, or color?
It doesn't seem right, when we already have these qualified people.
COMRADES YERKINA, KUZNETSOVA. WELCOME TO THE COSMONAUT CORPS. NOW WE ARE FIVE OF US!
And that was pretty much it. Everybody congratulated everybody else...
WAGGONNER
ANFUSO
GLENN
...and then canceled the third day of hearings, since they considered that the work was complete.
After all, there was important business to attend to.

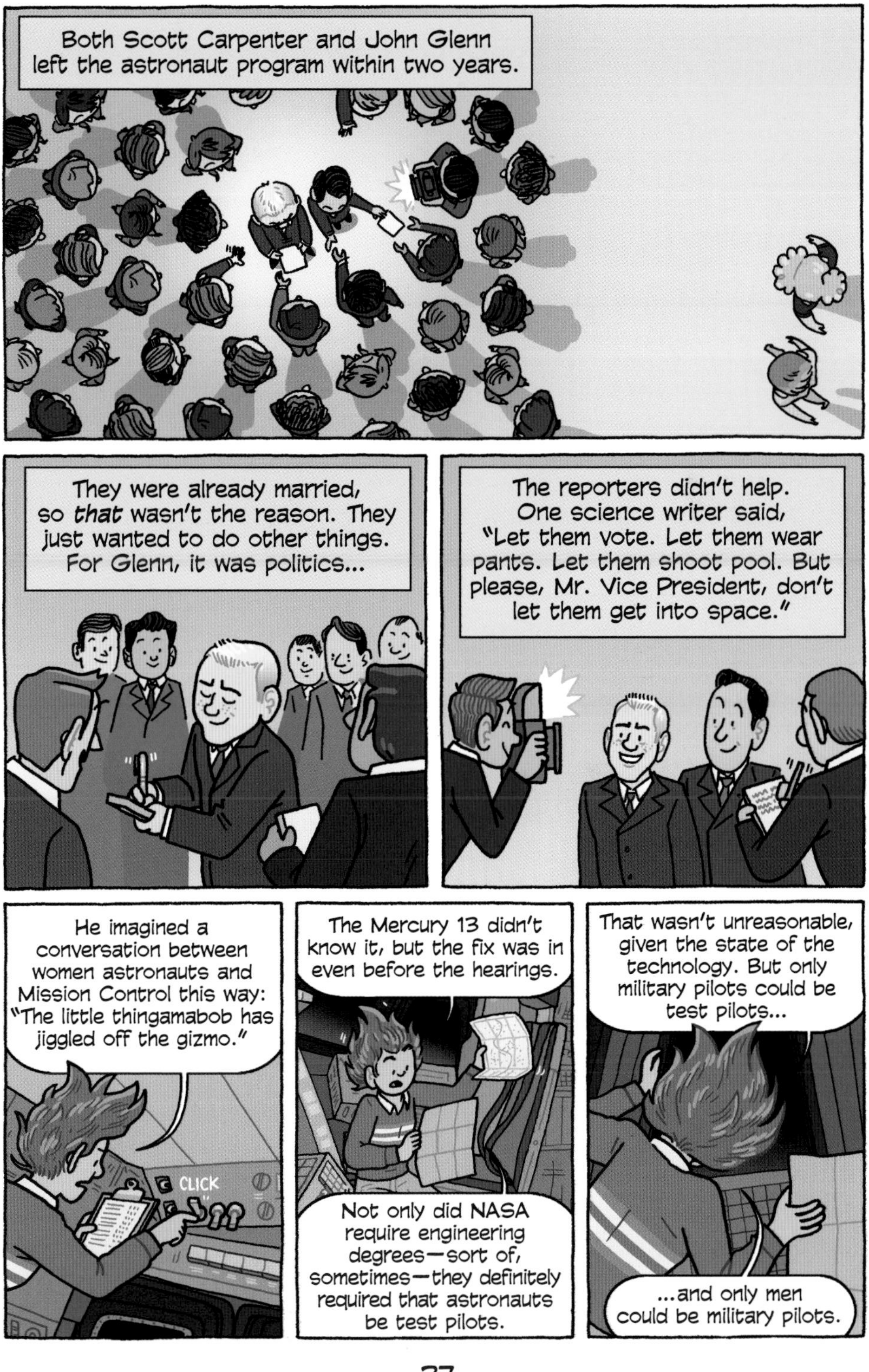
Both Scott Carpenter and John Glenn left the astronaut program within two years.
They were already married, so *that* wasn't the reason. They just wanted to do other things. For Glenn, it was politics...
The reporters didn't help. One science writer said, "Let them vote. Let them wear pants. Let them shoot pool. But please, Mr. Vice President, don't let them get into space."
He imagined a conversation between women astronauts and Mission Control this way: "The little thingamabob has jiggled off the gizmo."
CLICK
The Mercury 13 didn't know it, but the fix was in even before the hearings.
Not only did NASA require engineering degrees—sort of, sometimes—they definitely required that astronauts be test pilots.
That wasn't unreasonable, given the state of the technology. But only military pilots could be test pilots...
...and only men could be military pilots.

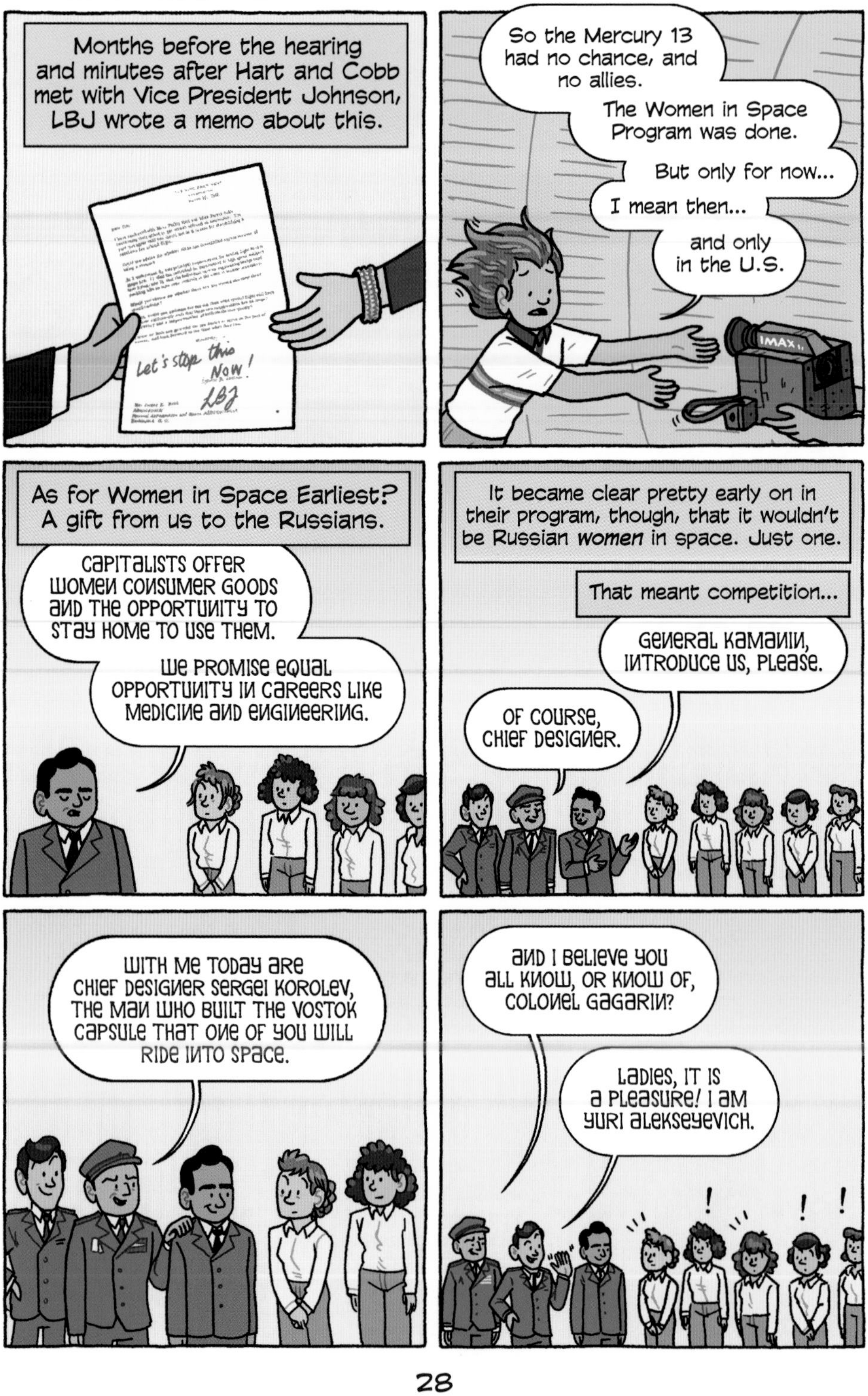

Months before the hearing and minutes after Hart and Cobb met with Vice President Johnson, LBJ wrote a memo about this.
Let's stop this Now!
LBJ
So the Mercury 13 had no chance, and no allies.
The Women in Space Program was done.
But only for now...
I mean then...
and only in the U.S.
IMAX
As for Women in Space Earliest? A gift from us to the Russians.
CAPITALISTS OFFER WOMEN CONSUMER GOODS AND THE OPPORTUNITY TO STAY HOME TO USE THEM.
WE PROMISE EQUAL OPPORTUNITY IN CAREERS LIKE MEDICINE AND ENGINEERING.
It became clear pretty early on in their program, though, that it wouldn't be Russian *women* in space. Just one.
That meant competition...
GENERAL KAMANIN, INTRODUCE US, PLEASE.
OF COURSE, CHIEF DESIGNER.
WITH ME TODAY ARE CHIEF DESIGNER SERGEI KOROLEV, THE MAN WHO BUILT THE VOSTOK CAPSULE THAT ONE OF YOU WILL RIDE INTO SPACE.
AND I BELIEVE YOU ALL KNOW, OR KNOW OF, COLONEL GAGARIN?
LADIES, IT IS A PLEASURE! I AM YURI ALEKSEYEVICH.

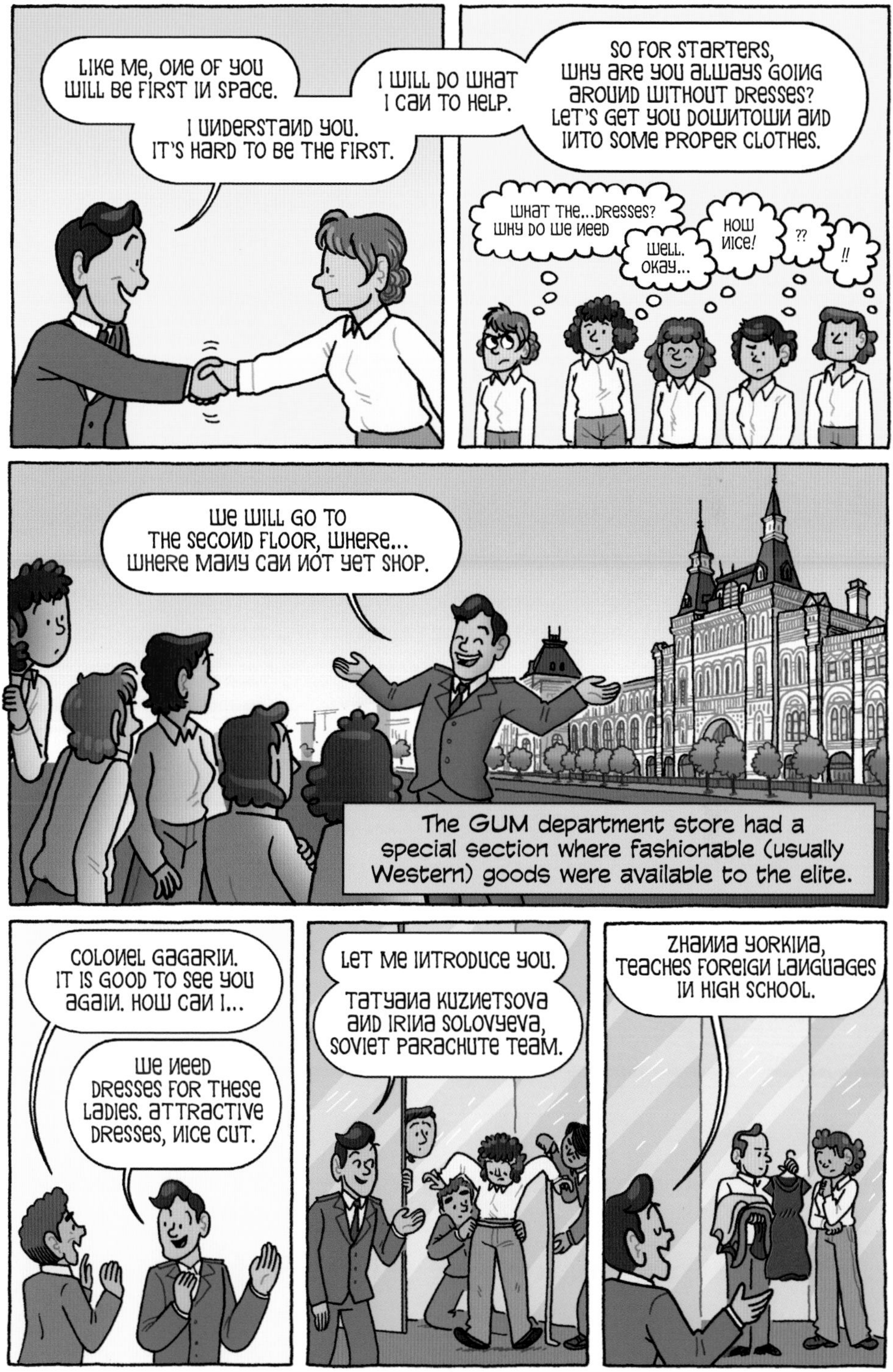
LIKE ME, ONE OF YOU WILL BE FIRST IN SPACE.
I UNDERSTAND YOU. IT'S HARD TO BE THE FIRST.
I WILL DO WHAT I CAN TO HELP.
SO FOR STARTERS, WHY ARE YOU ALWAYS GOING AROUND WITHOUT DRESSES? LET'S GET YOU DOWNTOWN AND INTO SOME PROPER CLOTHES.
WHAT THE...DRESSES? WHY DO WE NEED
WELL. OKAY...
HOW NICE!
??
!!
WE WILL GO TO THE SECOND FLOOR, WHERE... WHERE MANY CAN NOT YET SHOP.
The GUM department store had a special section where fashionable (usually Western) goods were available to the elite.
COLONEL GAGARIN. IT IS GOOD TO SEE YOU AGAIN. HOW CAN I...
WE NEED DRESSES FOR THESE LADIES. ATTRACTIVE DRESSES, NICE CUT.
LET ME INTRODUCE YOU.
TATYANA KUZNETSOVA AND IRINA SOLOVYEVA, SOVIET PARACHUTE TEAM.
ZHANNA YORKINA, TEACHES FOREIGN LANGUAGES IN HIGH SCHOOL.

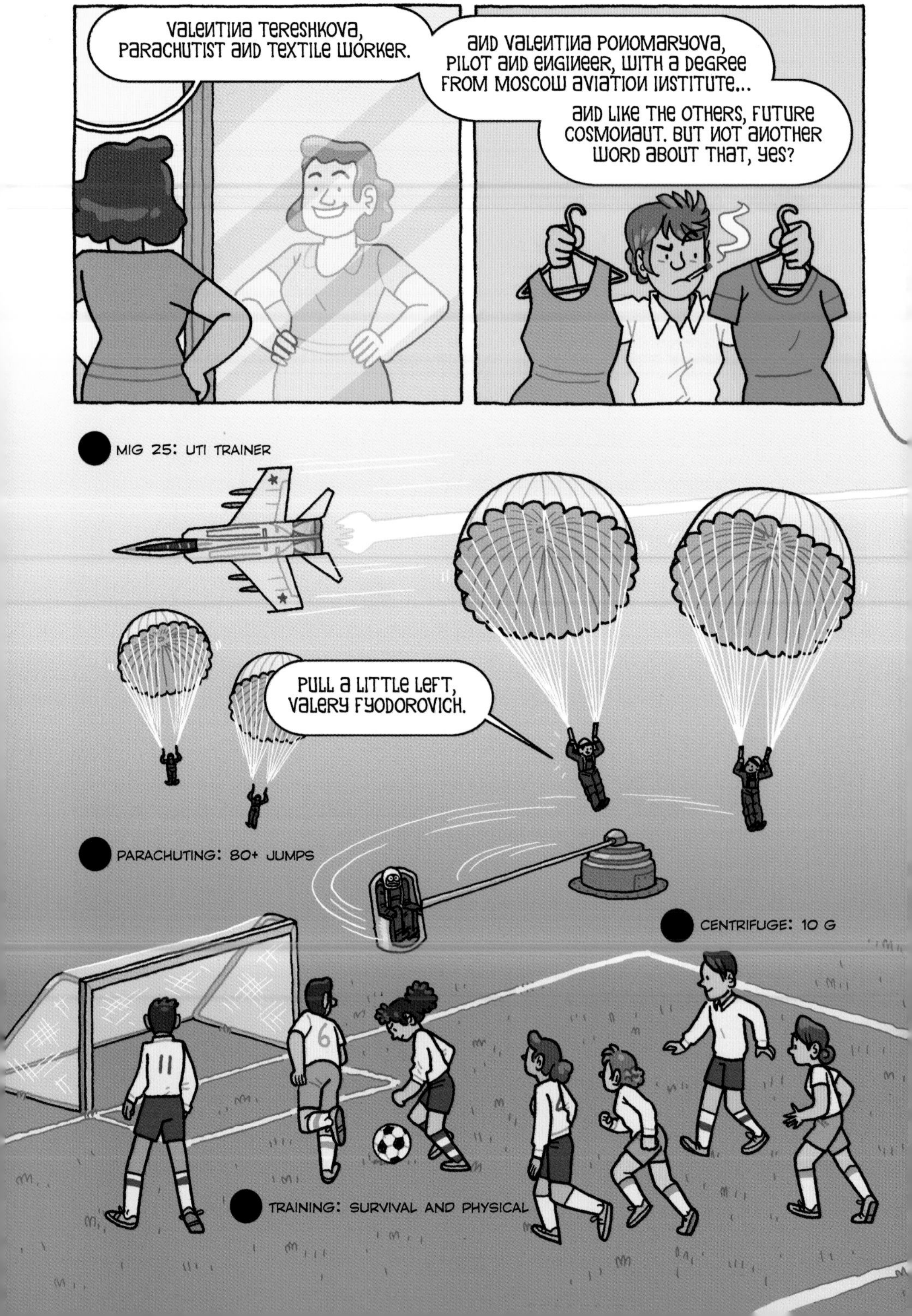
VALENTINA TERESHKOVA, PARACHUTIST AND TEXTILE WORKER.
AND VALENTINA PONOMARYOVA, PILOT AND ENGINEER, WITH A DEGREE FROM MOSCOW AVIATION INSTITUTE...
AND LIKE THE OTHERS, FUTURE COSMONAUT. BUT NOT ANOTHER WORD ABOUT THAT, YES?
MIG 25: UTI TRAINER
PULL A LITTLE LEFT, VALERY FYODOROVICH.
PARACHUTING: 80+ JUMPS
CENTRIFUGE: 10 G
TRAINING: SURVIVAL AND PHYSICAL

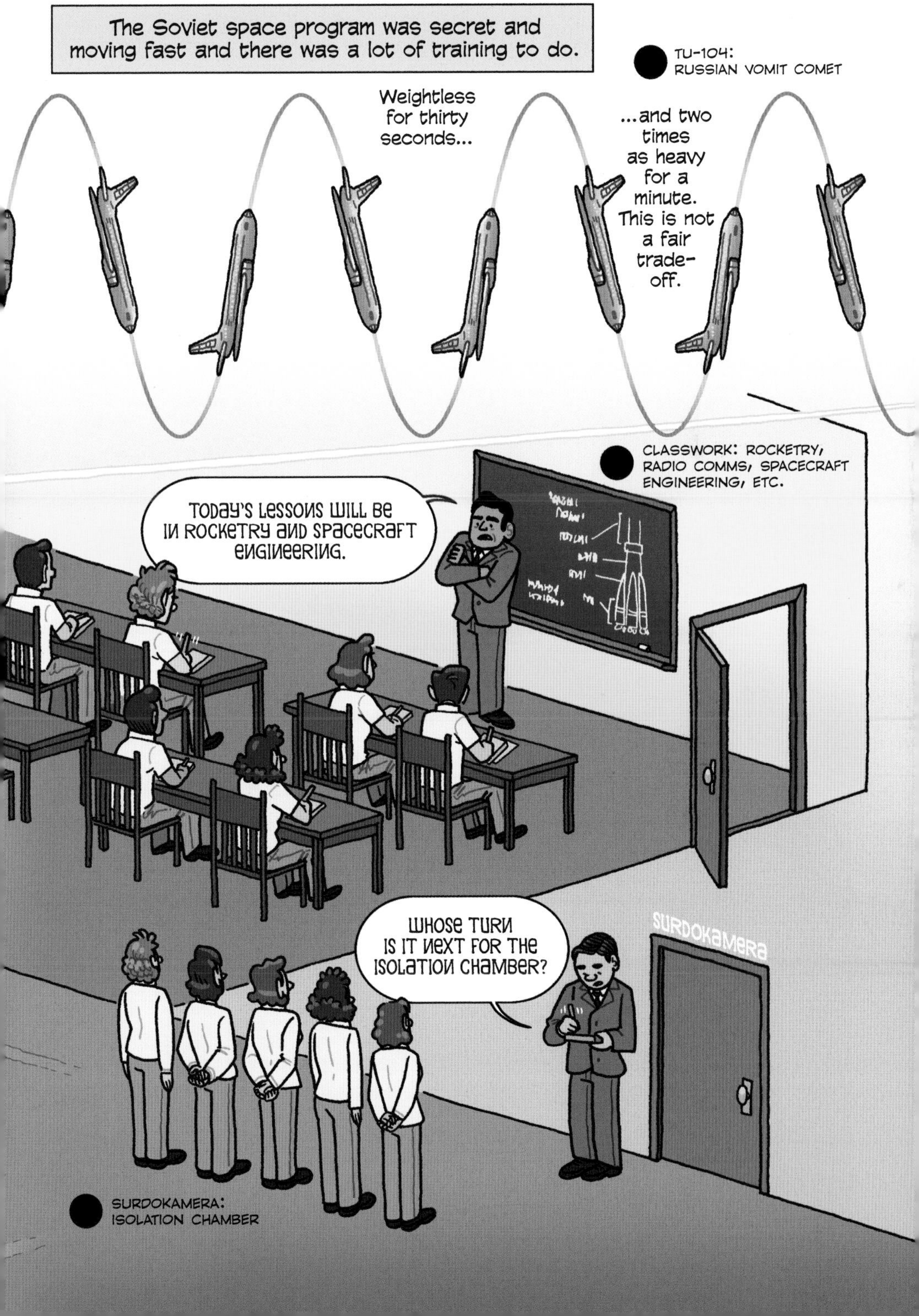

The Soviet space program was secret and moving fast and there was a lot of training to do.
TU-104: RUSSIAN VOMIT COMET
Weightless for thirty seconds...
...and two times as heavy for a minute. This is not a fair trade-off.
CLASSWORK: ROCKETRY, RADIO COMMS, SPACECRAFT ENGINEERING, ETC.
TODAY'S LESSONS WILL BE IN ROCKETRY AND SPACECRAFT ENGINEERING.
SURDOKAMERA
WHOSE TURN IS IT NEXT FOR THE ISOLATION CHAMBER?
SURDOKAMERA: ISOLATION CHAMBER

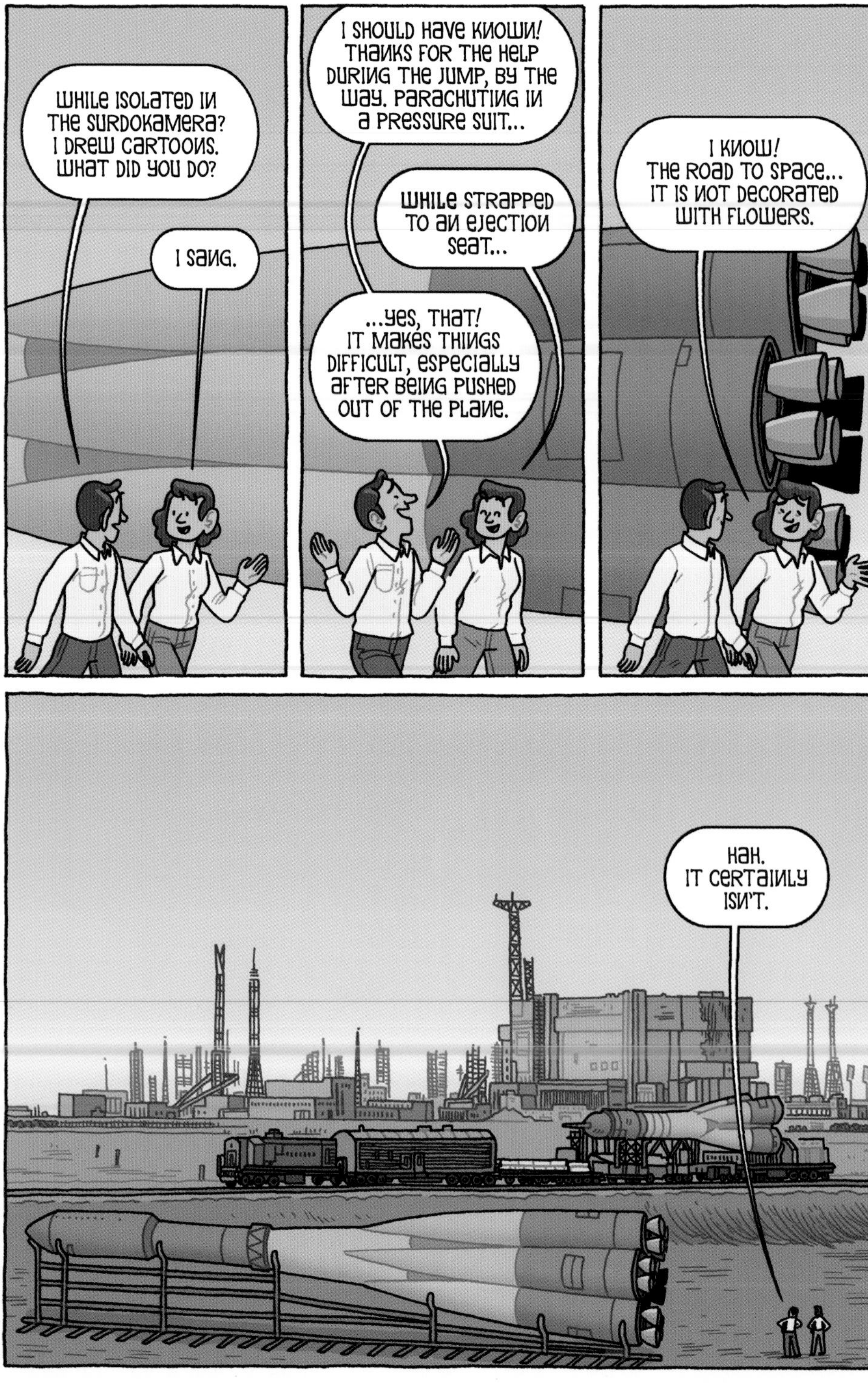
WHILE ISOLATED IN THE SURDOKAMERA? I DREW CARTOONS. WHAT DID YOU DO?
I SANG.
I SHOULD HAVE KNOWN! THANKS FOR THE HELP DURING THE JUMP, BY THE WAY. PARACHUTING IN A PRESSURE SUIT...
WHILE STRAPPED TO AN EJECTION SEAT...
...YES, THAT! IT MAKES THINGS DIFFICULT, ESPECIALLY AFTER BEING PUSHED OUT OF THE PLANE.
I KNOW! THE ROAD TO SPACE... IT IS NOT DECORATED WITH FLOWERS.
HAH. IT CERTAINLY ISN'T.

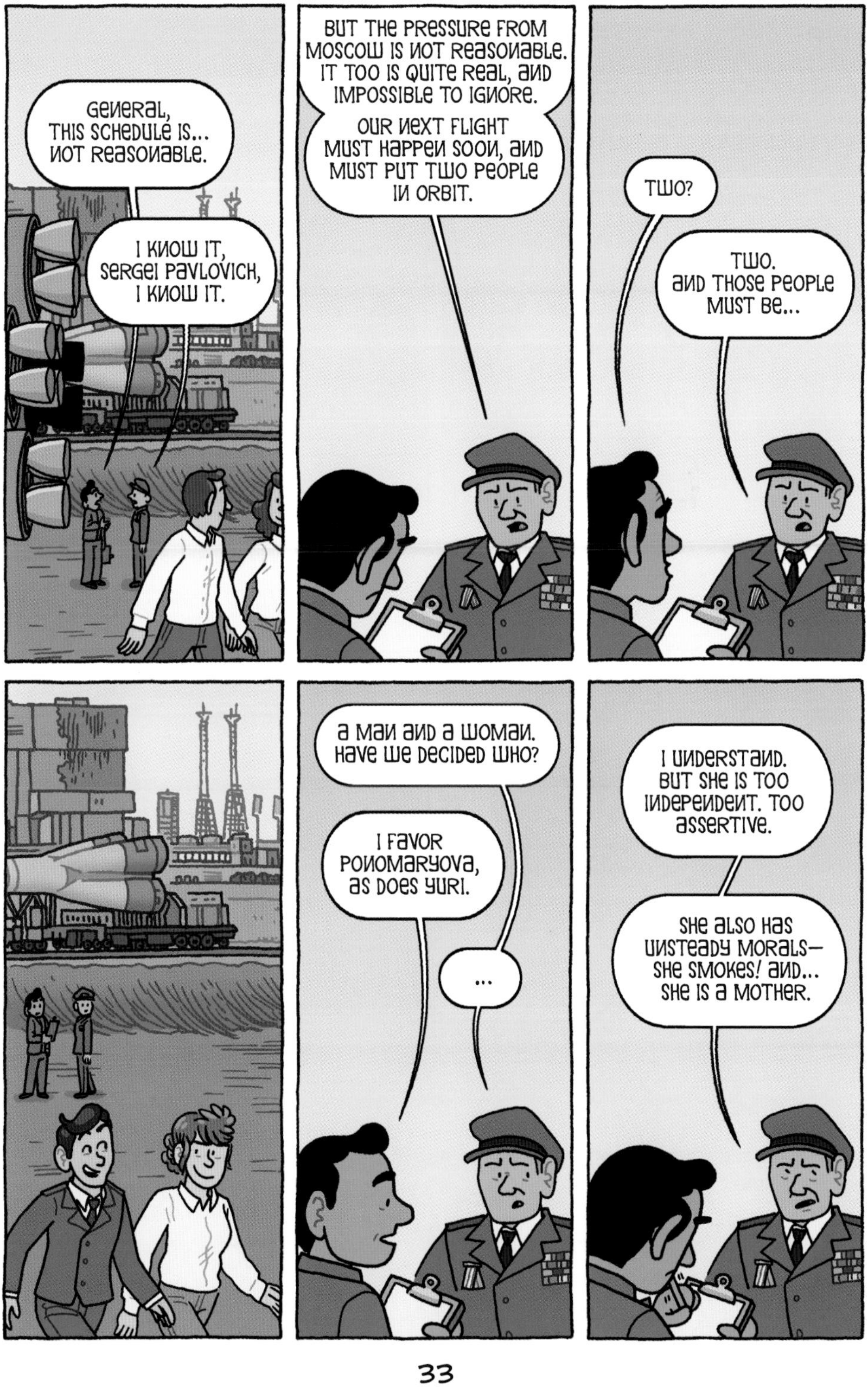
GENERAL, THIS SCHEDULE IS... NOT REASONABLE.
I KNOW IT, SERGEI PAVLOVICH, I KNOW IT.
BUT THE PRESSURE FROM MOSCOW IS NOT REASONABLE. IT TOO IS QUITE REAL, AND IMPOSSIBLE TO IGNORE.
OUR NEXT FLIGHT MUST HAPPEN SOON, AND MUST PUT TWO PEOPLE IN ORBIT.
TWO?
TWO. AND THOSE PEOPLE MUST BE...
A MAN AND A WOMAN. HAVE WE DECIDED WHO?
I FAVOR PONOMARYOVA, AS DOES YURI.
...
I UNDERSTAND. BUT SHE IS TOO INDEPENDENT. TOO ASSERTIVE.
SHE ALSO HAS UNSTEADY MORALS— SHE SMOKES! AND... SHE IS A MOTHER.

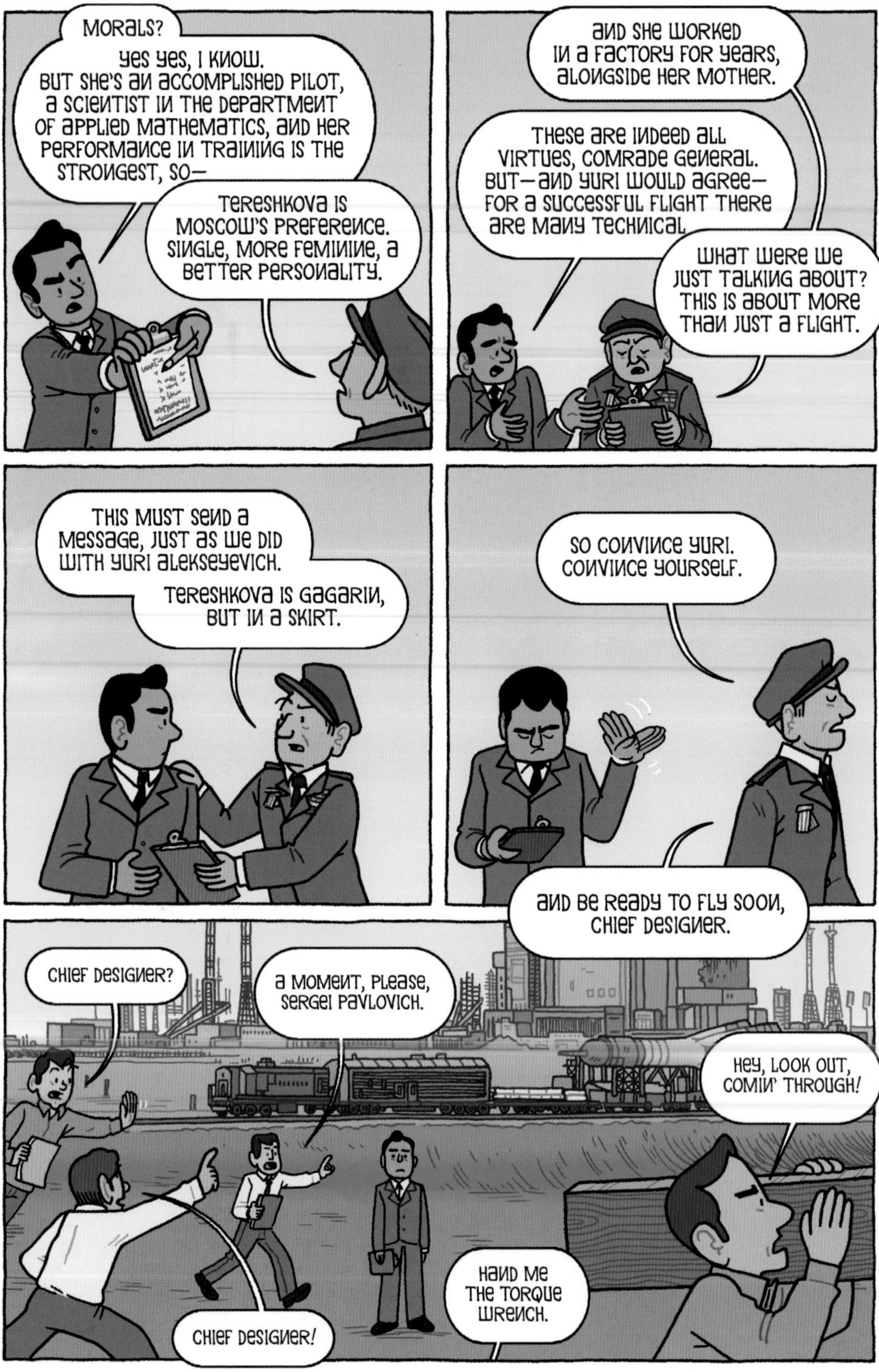
MORALS?
YES YES, I KNOW. BUT SHE'S AN ACCOMPLISHED PILOT, A SCIENTIST IN THE DEPARTMENT OF APPLIED MATHEMATICS, AND HER PERFORMANCE IN TRAINING IS THE STRONGEST, SO—
TERESHKOVA IS MOSCOW'S PREFERENCE. SINGLE, MORE FEMININE, A BETTER PERSONALITY.
AND SHE WORKED IN A FACTORY FOR YEARS, ALONGSIDE HER MOTHER.
THESE ARE INDEED ALL VIRTUES, COMRADE GENERAL. BUT—AND YURI WOULD AGREE—FOR A SUCCESSFUL FLIGHT THERE ARE MANY TECHNICAL
WHAT WERE WE JUST TALKING ABOUT? THIS IS ABOUT MORE THAN JUST A FLIGHT.
THIS MUST SEND A MESSAGE, JUST AS WE DID WITH YURI ALEKSEYEVICH.
TERESHKOVA IS GAGARIN, BUT IN A SKIRT.
SO CONVINCE YURI. CONVINCE YOURSELF.
AND BE READY TO FLY SOON, CHIEF DESIGNER.
CHIEF DESIGNER?
A MOMENT, PLEASE, SERGEI PAVLOVICH.
HEY, LOOK OUT, COMIN' THROUGH!
HAND ME THE TORQUE WRENCH.
CHIEF DESIGNER!

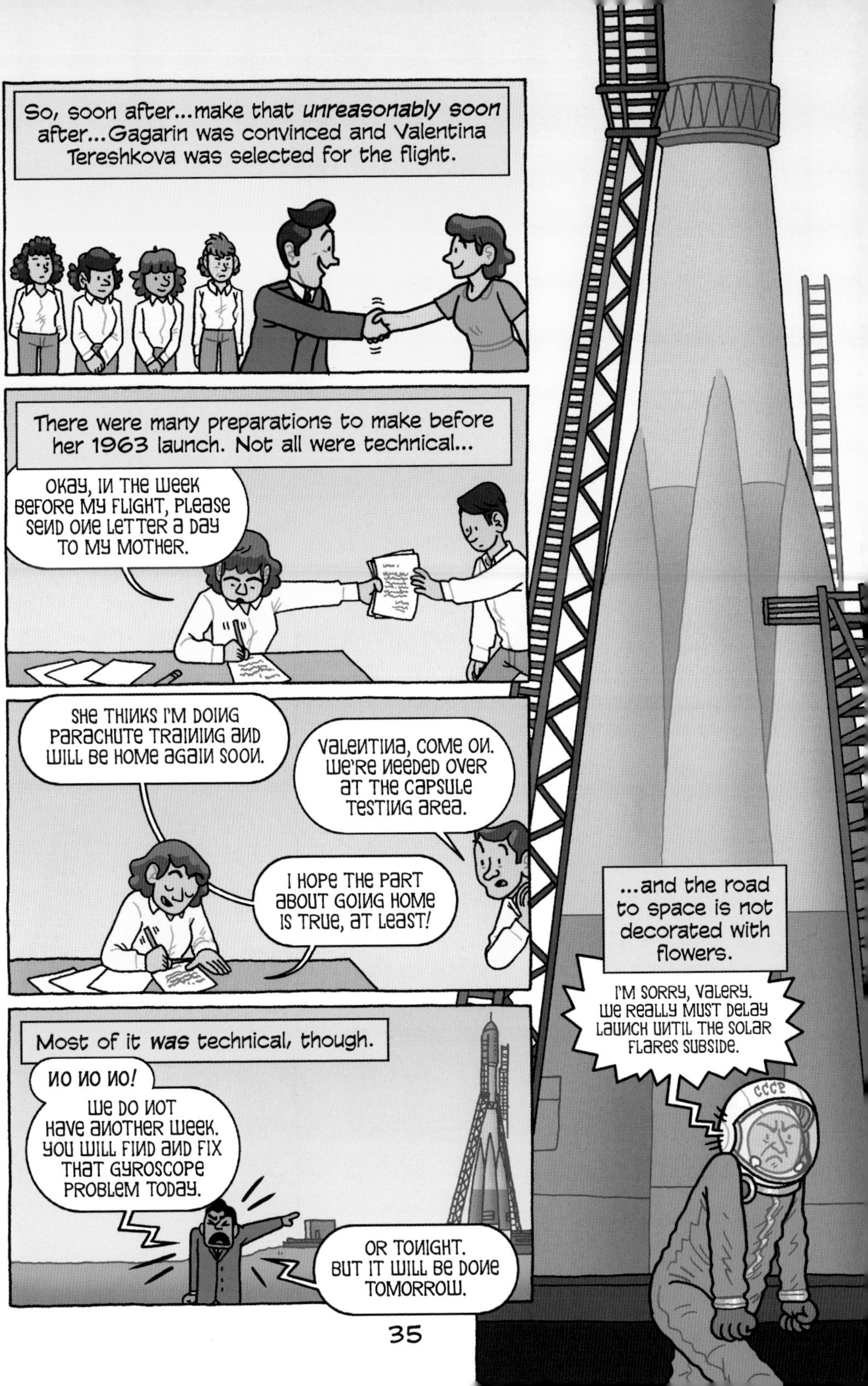

So, soon after...make that *unreasonably* soon after...Gagarin was convinced and Valentina Tereshkova was selected for the flight.
There were many preparations to make before her 1963 launch. Not all were technical...
OKAY, IN THE WEEK BEFORE MY FLIGHT, PLEASE SEND ONE LETTER A DAY TO MY MOTHER.
SHE THINKS I'M DOING PARACHUTE TRAINING AND WILL BE HOME AGAIN SOON.
VALENTINA, COME ON. WE'RE NEEDED OVER AT THE CAPSULE TESTING AREA.
I HOPE THE PART ABOUT GOING HOME IS TRUE, AT LEAST!
Most of it *was* technical, though.
NO NO NO!
WE DO NOT HAVE ANOTHER WEEK. YOU WILL FIND AND FIX THAT GYROSCOPE PROBLEM TODAY.
OR TONIGHT. BUT IT WILL BE DONE TOMORROW.
...and the road to space is not decorated with flowers.
I'M SORRY, VALERY. WE REALLY MUST DELAY LAUNCH UNTIL THE SOLAR FLARES SUBSIDE.
CCCP

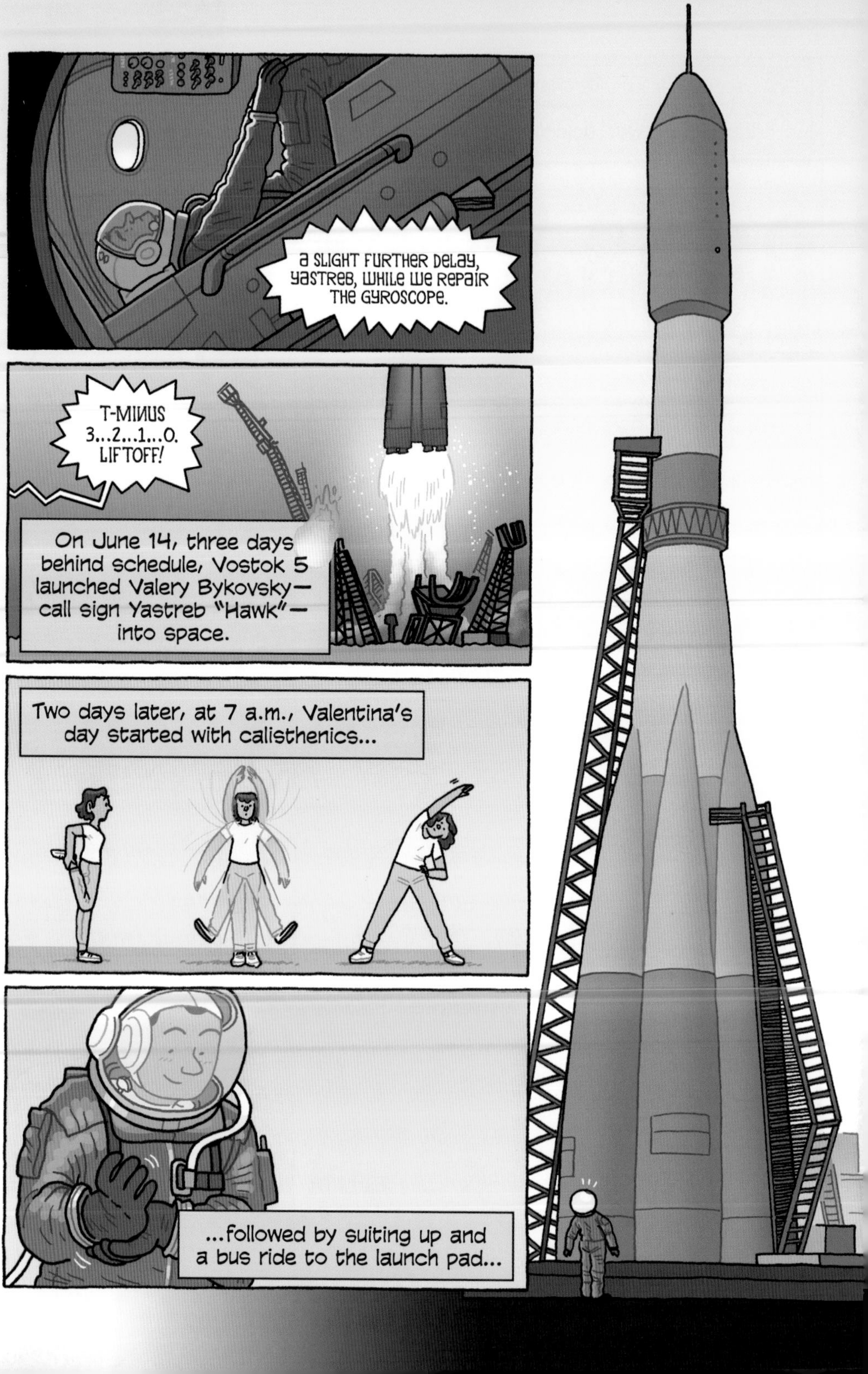
A SLIGHT FURTHER DELAY, YASTREB, WHILE WE REPAIR THE GYROSCOPE.
T-MINUS 3...2...1...0. LIFTOFF!
On June 14, three days behind schedule, Vostok 5 launched Valery Bykovsky—call sign Yastreb "Hawk"—into space.
Two days later, at 7 a.m., Valentina's day started with calisthenics...
...followed by suiting up and a bus ride to the launch pad...

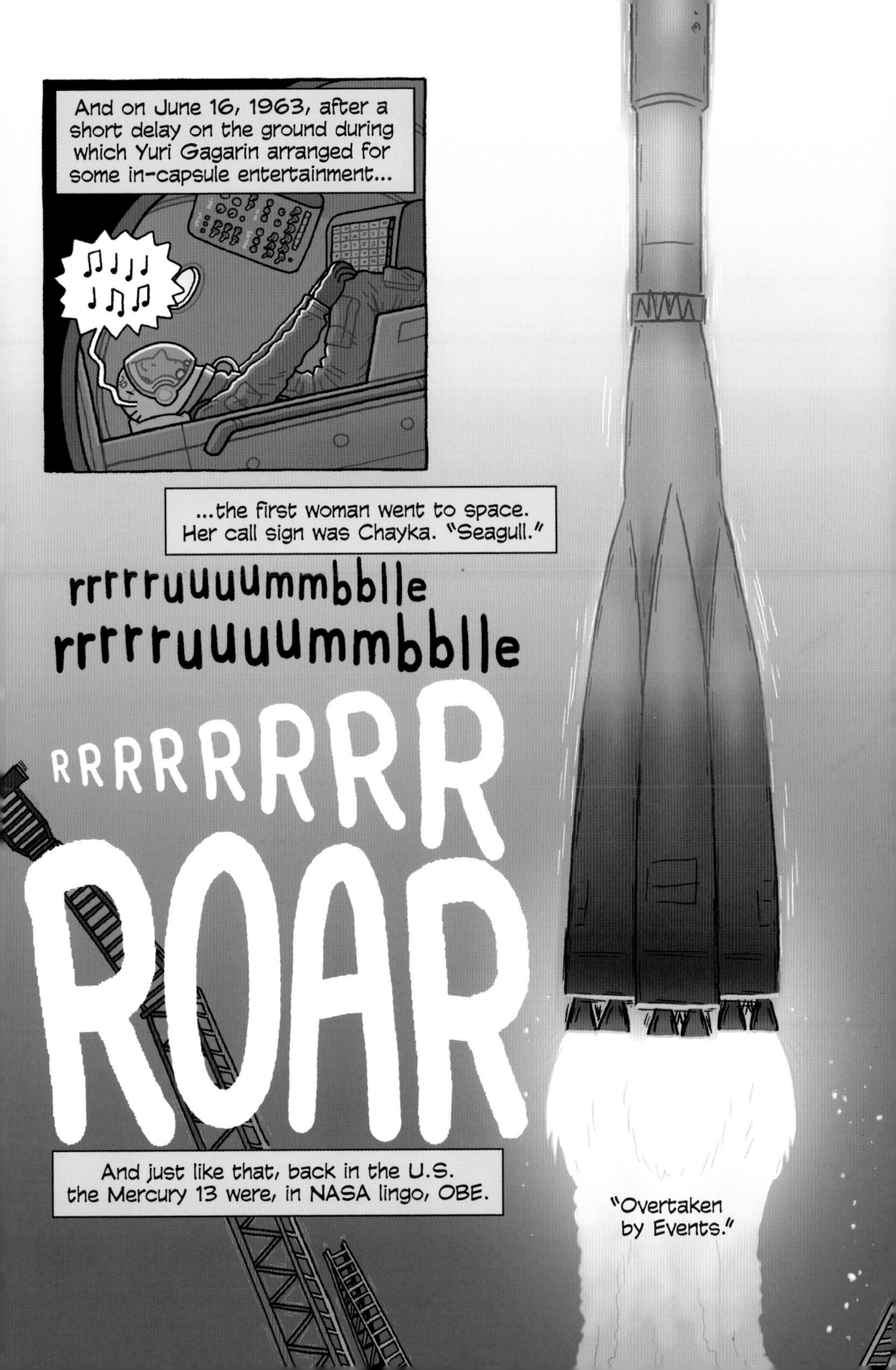
And on June 16, 1963, after a short delay on the ground during which Yuri Gagarin arranged for some in-capsule entertainment...
...the first woman went to space. Her call sign was Chayka. "Seagull."
rrrrruuuummbblle
rrrrruuuummbblle
RRRRRRRR
ROAR
And just like that, back in the U.S. the Mercury 13 were, in NASA lingo, OBE.
"Overtaken by Events."

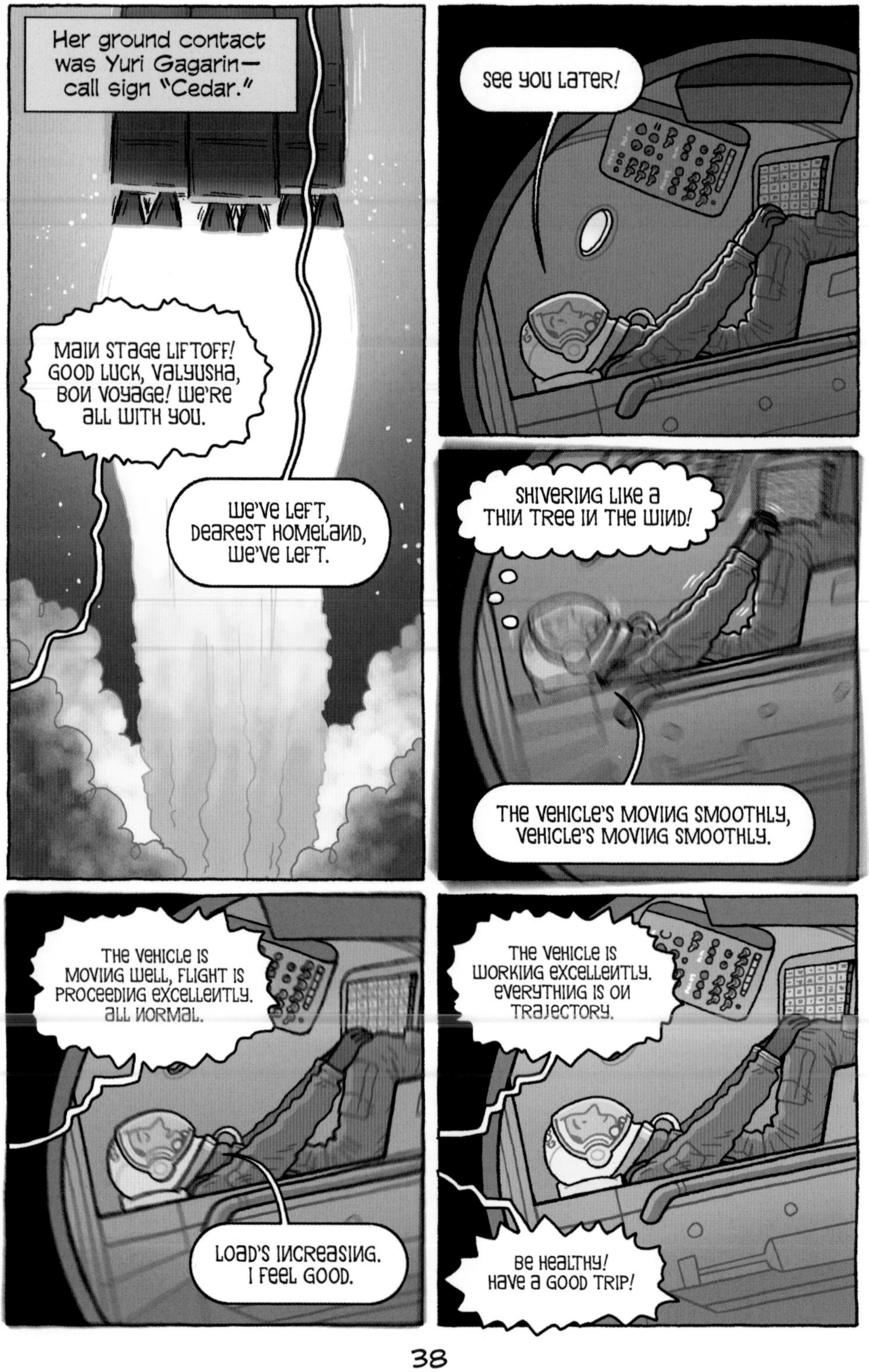
Her ground contact was Yuri Gagarin—call sign "Cedar."
MAIN STAGE LIFTOFF! GOOD LUCK, VALYUSHA, BON VOYAGE! WE'RE ALL WITH YOU.
WE'VE LEFT, DEAREST HOMELAND, WE'VE LEFT.
SEE YOU LATER!
SHIVERING LIKE A THIN TREE IN THE WIND!
THE VEHICLE'S MOVING SMOOTHLY, VEHICLE'S MOVING SMOOTHLY.
THE VEHICLE IS MOVING WELL, FLIGHT IS PROCEEDING EXCELLENTLY. ALL NORMAL.
LOAD'S INCREASING. I FEEL GOOD.
THE VEHICLE IS WORKING EXCELLENTLY. EVERYTHING IS ON TRAJECTORY.
BE HEALTHY! HAVE A GOOD TRIP!

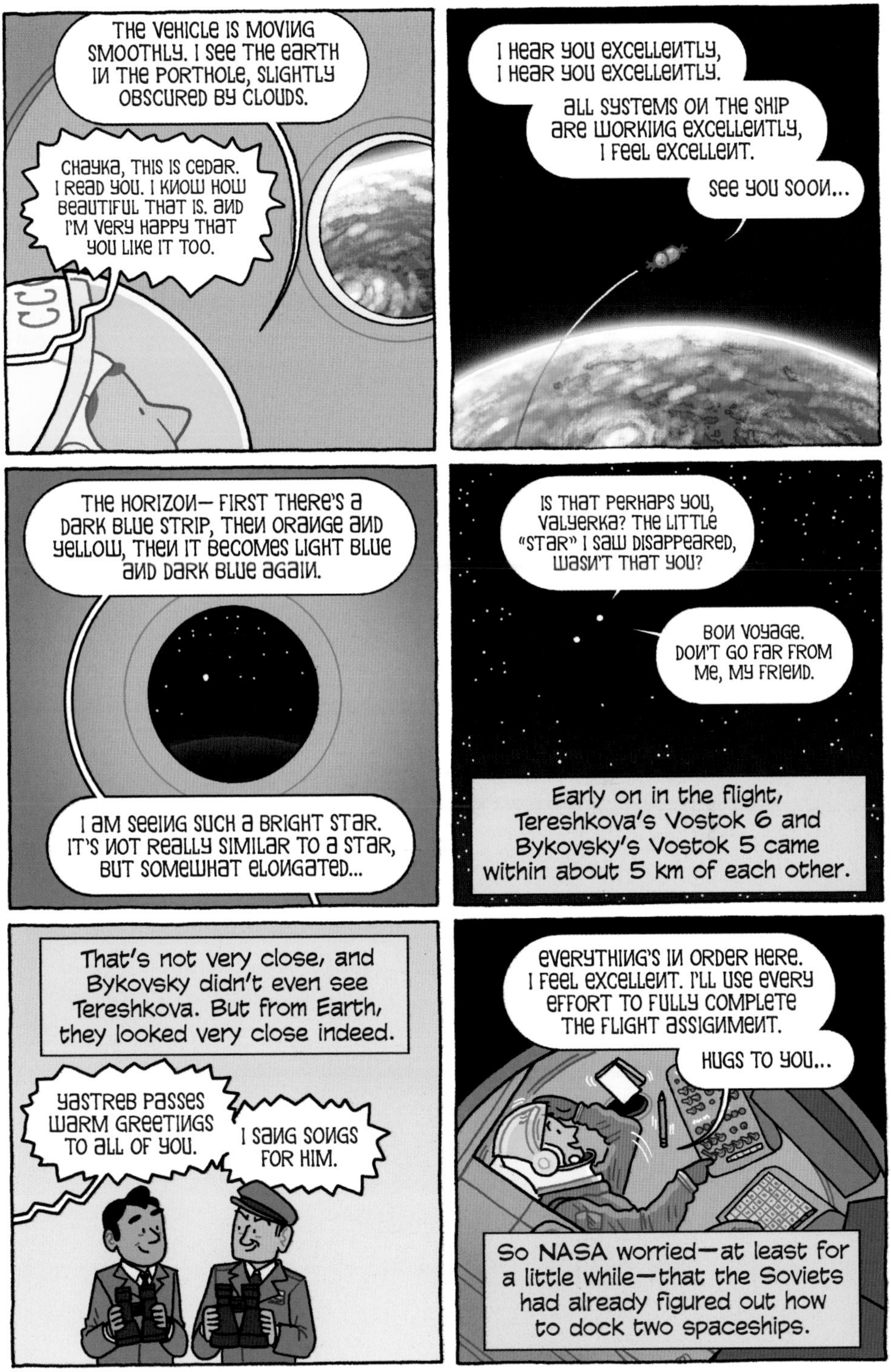
THE VEHICLE IS MOVING SMOOTHLY. I SEE THE EARTH IN THE PORTHOLE, SLIGHTLY OBSCURED BY CLOUDS.
CHAYKA, THIS IS CEDAR. I READ YOU. I KNOW HOW BEAUTIFUL THAT IS. AND I'M VERY HAPPY THAT YOU LIKE IT TOO.
I HEAR YOU EXCELLENTLY, I HEAR YOU EXCELLENTLY.
ALL SYSTEMS ON THE SHIP ARE WORKING EXCELLENTLY, I FEEL EXCELLENT.
SEE YOU SOON...
THE HORIZON— FIRST THERE'S A DARK BLUE STRIP, THEN ORANGE AND YELLOW, THEN IT BECOMES LIGHT BLUE AND DARK BLUE AGAIN.
I AM SEEING SUCH A BRIGHT STAR. IT'S NOT REALLY SIMILAR TO A STAR, BUT SOMEWHAT ELONGATED...
IS THAT PERHAPS YOU, VALYERKA? THE LITTLE "STAR" I SAW DISAPPEARED, WASN'T THAT YOU?
BON VOYAGE. DON'T GO FAR FROM ME, MY FRIEND.
Early on in the flight, Tereshkova's Vostok 6 and Bykovsky's Vostok 5 came within about 5 km of each other.
That's not very close, and Bykovsky didn't even see Tereshkova. But from Earth, they looked very close indeed.
YASTREB PASSES WARM GREETINGS TO ALL OF YOU.
I SANG SONGS FOR HIM.
EVERYTHING'S IN ORDER HERE. I FEEL EXCELLENT. I'LL USE EVERY EFFORT TO FULLY COMPLETE THE FLIGHT ASSIGNMENT.
HUGS TO YOU...
So NASA worried—at least for a little while—that the Soviets had already figured out how to dock two spaceships.

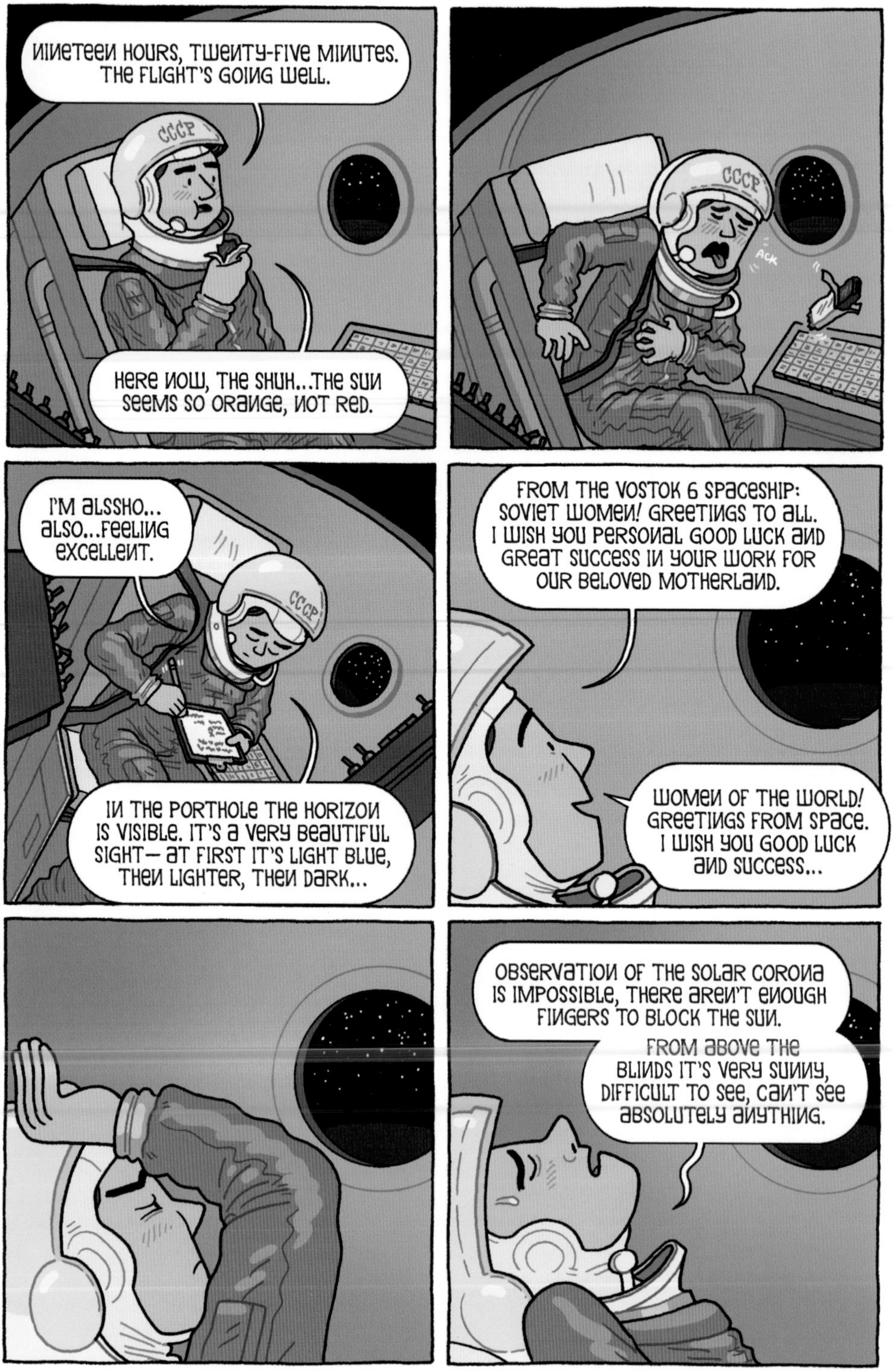
NINETEEN HOURS, TWENTY-FIVE MINUTES. THE FLIGHT'S GOING WELL.
HERE NOW, THE SHUH...THE SUN SEEMS SO ORANGE, NOT RED.
ACK
I'M ALSSHO... ALSO...FEELING EXCELLENT.
IN THE PORTHOLE THE HORIZON IS VISIBLE. IT'S A VERY BEAUTIFUL SIGHT— AT FIRST IT'S LIGHT BLUE, THEN LIGHTER, THEN DARK...
FROM THE VOSTOK 6 SPACESHIP: SOVIET WOMEN! GREETINGS TO ALL. I WISH YOU PERSONAL GOOD LUCK AND GREAT SUCCESS IN YOUR WORK FOR OUR BELOVED MOTHERLAND.
WOMEN OF THE WORLD! GREETINGS FROM SPACE. I WISH YOU GOOD LUCK AND SUCCESS...
OBSERVATION OF THE SOLAR CORONA IS IMPOSSIBLE, THERE AREN'T ENOUGH FINGERS TO BLOCK THE SUN.
FROM ABOVE THE BLINDS IT'S VERY SUNNY, DIFFICULT TO SEE, CAN'T SEE ABSOLUTELY ANYTHING.

On the second day, she had more work to do, but...

PARAMETERSSSSH: CABIN PRESSURE 1.15; HUMIDITY 61 PERCENT, TEMPERATURE 23 DEGREES C.

THE TEMPERATURE SWITCH ISSSS IN POSITION... CARBON DIOXIDE 0.1; OXYGEN 250.

NAGGING PAIN IN RIGHT SHIN. HELMET OBSTRUCTS ME AND PRESSES AGAINST SHOULDER. EARPIECE PRESSES AGAINST LEFT EAR AND SENSOR ON MY HEAD MAKES ME ITCH AND GIVES ME HEADACHES.

SNAP

CHYORT!

YURI— I MEAN, CEDAR—

I HOPE TO FULLY COMPLETE THE FLIGHT ASSSSH PER THE PLAN... I DON'T FEEL TIRED BECAUSE I'VE TAKEN FREQUENT BREAKS.

AMMM NOT GETTING THE PHOTOMETER TO WORK. I'VE ATTEMPTED SSSHSEVERAL TIMESSSSSH.

DON'T WORRY, I'LL DO EVERYTHING IN THE MORNING. DON'T WORRY ABOUT ME.

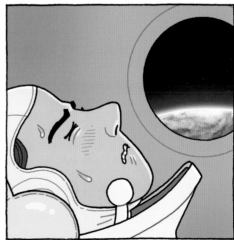

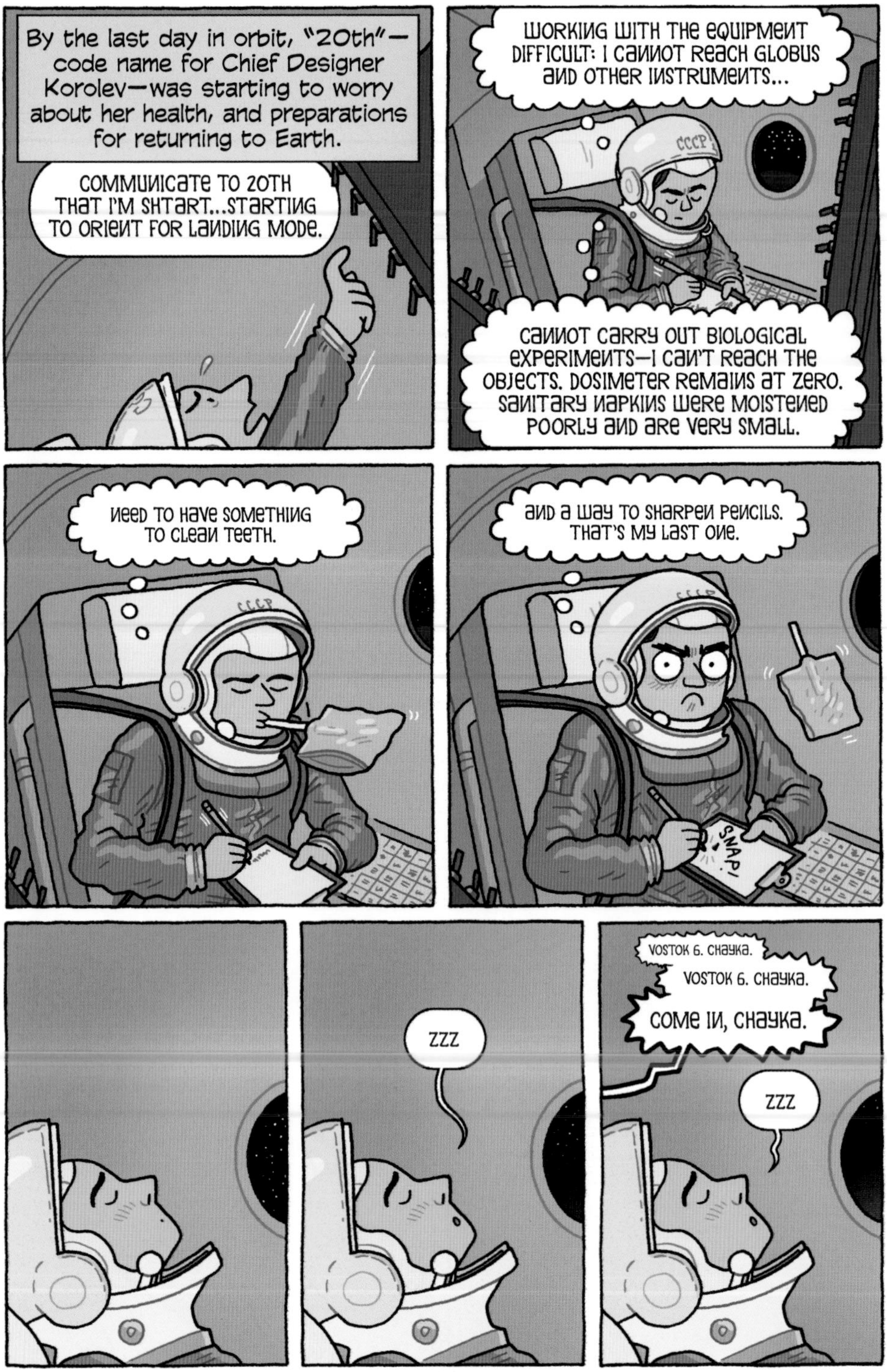
By the last day in orbit, "20th"—code name for Chief Designer Korolev—was starting to worry about her health, and preparations for returning to Earth.
COMMUNICATE TO 20TH THAT I'M SHTART...STARTING TO ORIENT FOR LANDING MODE.
WORKING WITH THE EQUIPMENT DIFFICULT: I CANNOT REACH GLOBUS AND OTHER INSTRUMENTS...
CCCP
CANNOT CARRY OUT BIOLOGICAL EXPERIMENTS—I CAN'T REACH THE OBJECTS. DOSIMETER REMAINS AT ZERO. SANITARY NAPKINS WERE MOISTENED POORLY AND ARE VERY SMALL.
NEED TO HAVE SOMETHING TO CLEAN TEETH.
CCCP
AND A WAY TO SHARPEN PENCILS. THAT'S MY LAST ONE.
SNAP!
ZZZ
VOSTOK 6. CHAYKA.
VOSTOK 6. CHAYKA.
COME IN, CHAYKA.
ZZZ

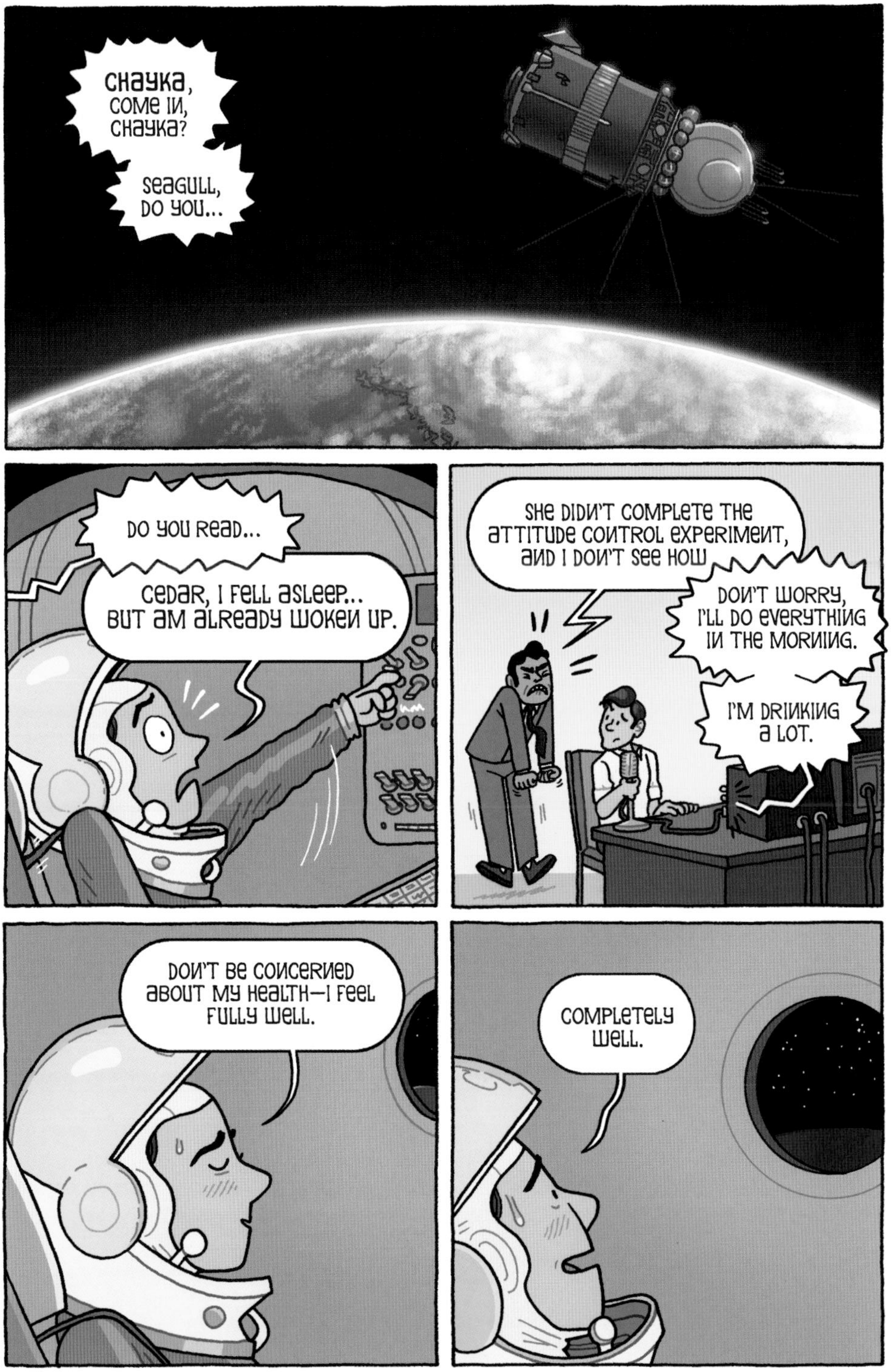
Chayka, come in, Chayka?
Seagull, do you...
Do you read...
Cedar, I fell asleep... but am already woken up.
She didn't complete the attitude control experiment, and I don't see how
Don't worry, I'll do everything in the morning.
I'm drinking a lot.
Don't be concerned about my health—I feel fully well.
Completely well.

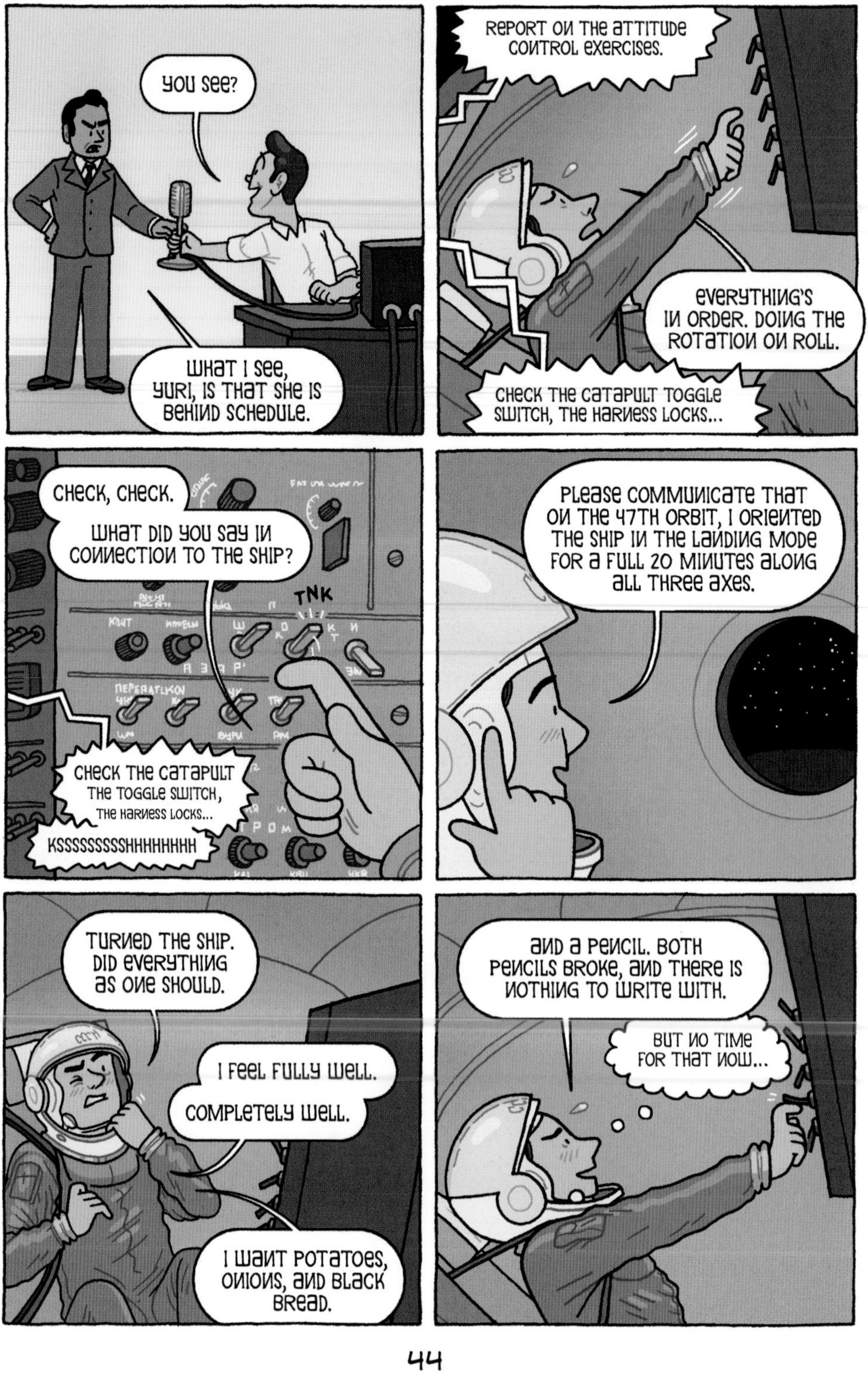
YOU SEE?
WHAT I SEE, YURI, IS THAT SHE IS BEHIND SCHEDULE.
REPORT ON THE ATTITUDE CONTROL EXERCISES.
EVERYTHING'S IN ORDER. DOING THE ROTATION ON ROLL.
CHECK THE CATAPULT TOGGLE SWITCH, THE HARNESS LOCKS...
CHECK, CHECK.
WHAT DID YOU SAY IN CONNECTION TO THE SHIP?
TNK
CHECK THE CATAPULT THE TOGGLE SWITCH, THE HARNESS LOCKS...
KSSSSSSSSSHHHHHHHH
PLEASE COMMUNICATE THAT ON THE 47TH ORBIT, I ORIENTED THE SHIP IN THE LANDING MODE FOR A FULL 20 MINUTES ALONG ALL THREE AXES.
TURNED THE SHIP. DID EVERYTHING AS ONE SHOULD.
I FEEL FULLY WELL.
COMPLETELY WELL.
I WANT POTATOES, ONIONS, AND BLACK BREAD.
AND A PENCIL. BOTH PENCILS BROKE, AND THERE IS NOTHING TO WRITE WITH.
BUT NO TIME FOR THAT NOW...

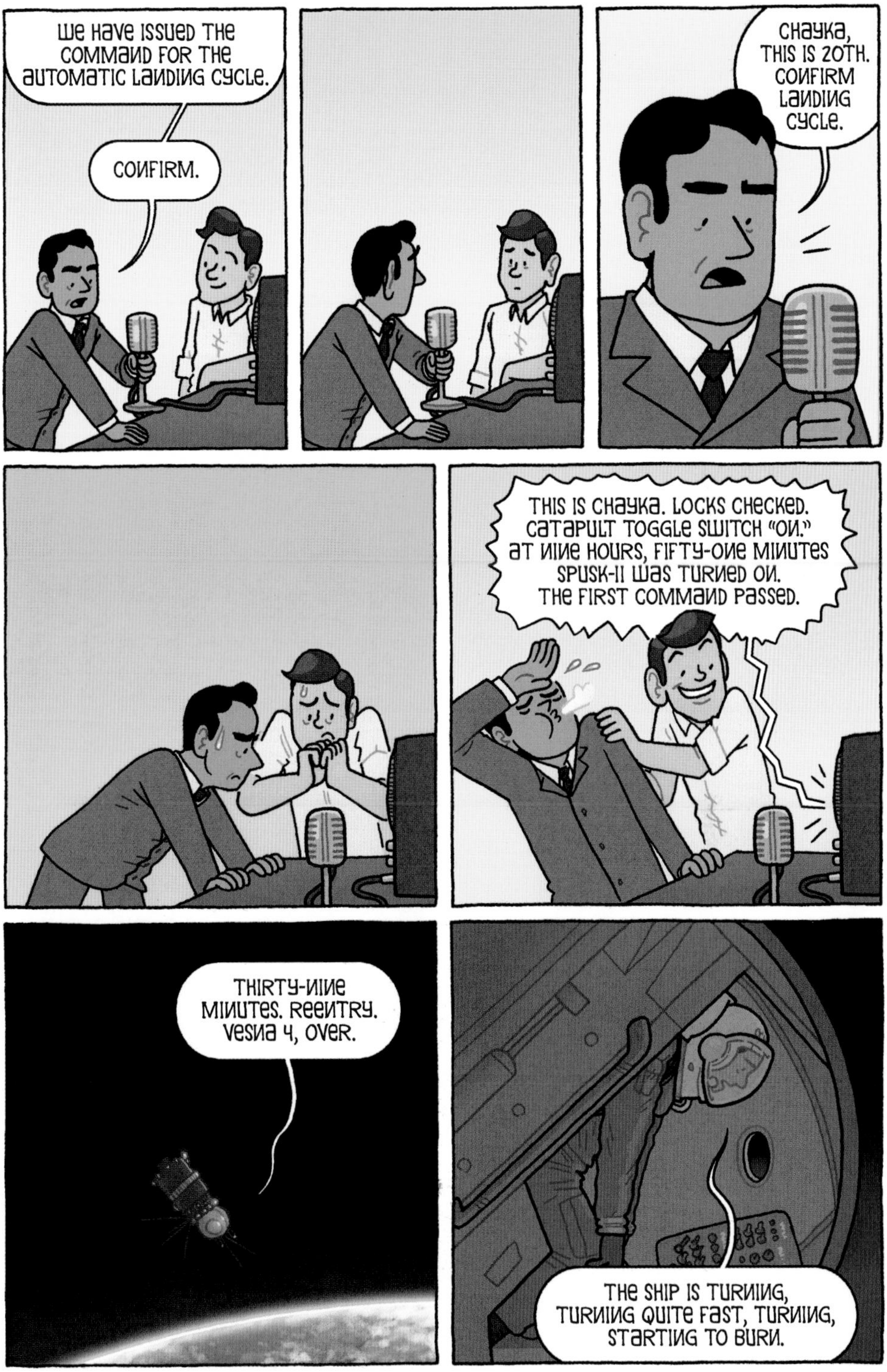
WE HAVE ISSUED THE COMMAND FOR THE AUTOMATIC LANDING CYCLE.
CONFIRM.
CHAYKA, THIS IS 20TH. CONFIRM LANDING CYCLE.
THIS IS CHAYKA. LOCKS CHECKED. CATAPULT TOGGLE SWITCH "ON." AT NINE HOURS, FIFTY-ONE MINUTES SPUSK-II WAS TURNED ON. THE FIRST COMMAND PASSED.
THIRTY-NINE MINUTES. REENTRY. VESNA 4, OVER.
THE SHIP IS TURNING, TURNING QUITE FAST, TURNING, STARTING TO BURN.

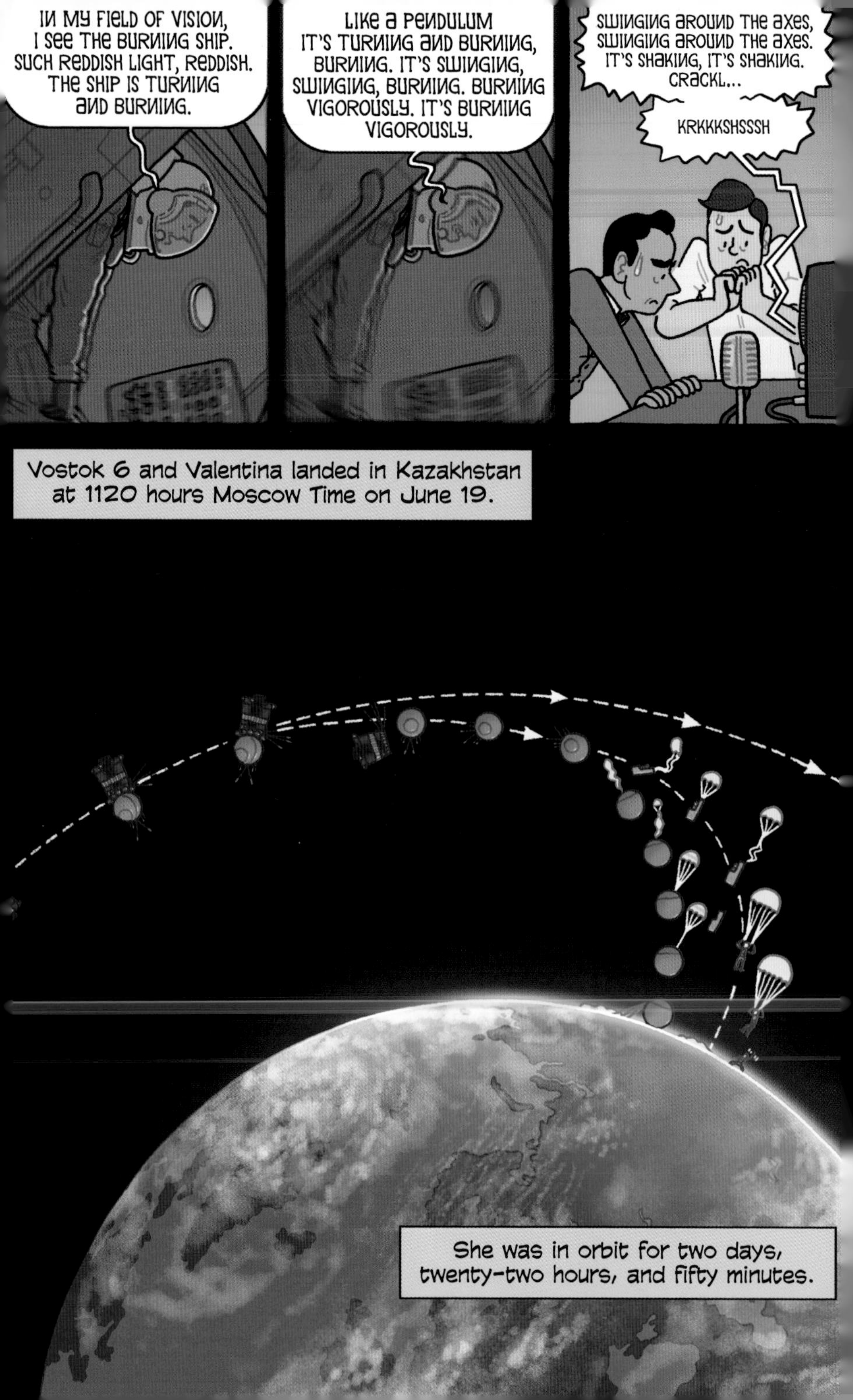

IN MY FIELD OF VISION, I SEE THE BURNING SHIP. SUCH REDDISH LIGHT, REDDISH. THE SHIP IS TURNING AND BURNING.

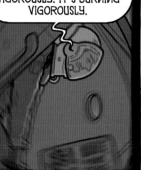

LIKE A PENDULUM IT'S TURNING AND BURNING, BURNING. IT'S SWINGING, SWINGING, BURNING. BURNING VIGOROUSLY. IT'S BURNING VIGOROUSLY.

SWINGING AROUND THE AXES, SWINGING AROUND THE AXES. IT'S SHAKING, IT'S SHAKING. CRACKL...

KRKKKSHSSSH

Vostok 6 and Valentina landed in Kazakhstan at 1120 hours Moscow Time on June 19.

She was in orbit for two days, twenty-two hours, and fifty minutes.

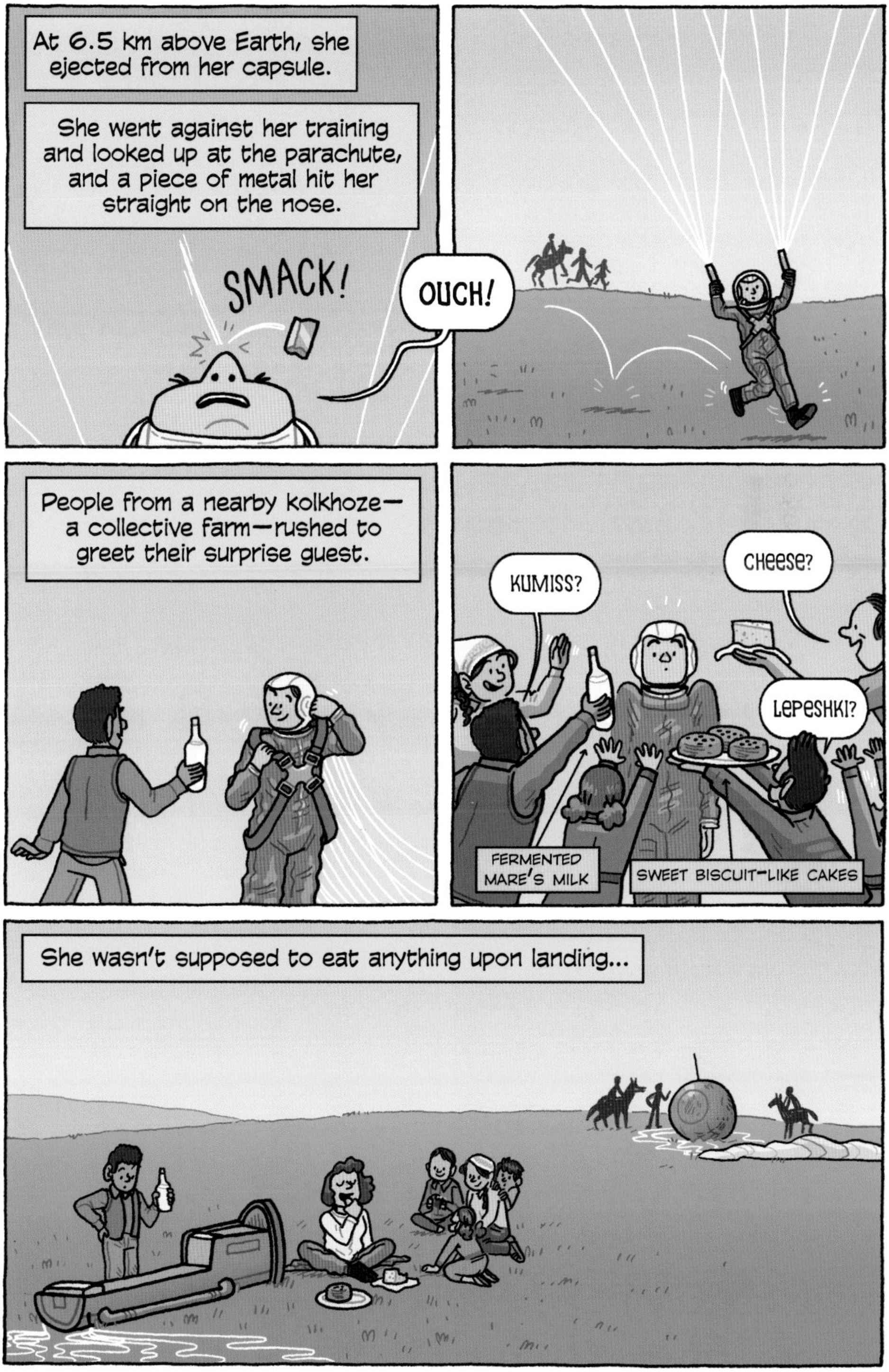
At 6.5 km above Earth, she ejected from her capsule.
She went against her training and looked up at the parachute, and a piece of metal hit her straight on the nose.
SMACK!
OUCH!
People from a nearby kolkhoze—a collective farm—rushed to greet their surprise guest.
KUMISS?
CHEESE?
LEPESHKI?
FERMENTED MARE'S MILK
SWEET BISCUIT-LIKE CAKES
She wasn't supposed to eat anything upon landing...

And she was also supposed to keep her leftover tubes of food so the doctors could better assess her...

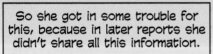
...well, her input and output while in space.

I COME FROM A FARMING COMMUNITY.

IT IS BASIC COURTESY TO EXCHANGE GIFTS OF FOOD.

TSK TSK

So she got in some trouble for this, because in later reports she didn't share all this information.

VALYA, YOU COMPLAINED ABOUT THE FOOD WHILE IN ORBIT, BUT IT WAS ALL GONE WHEN WE PICKED UP THE CAPSULE.

YES, THE BREAD WAS LIKE RUBBER AND THE MEAT WAS VERY TOUGH.

BUT YOU ATE IT ALL?

WELL... NO. NOT ALL, NO.

I DO NOT REMEMBER HOW MUCH. THERE WERE THE FARMERS.

AND I COULDN'T WRITE ANYTHING DOWN WITHOUT PENCILS, SO...

SO WE DON'T HAVE GOOD DATA FOR FUTURE FLIGHTS.

DISAPPOINTING, VALYA. QUITE DISAPPOINTING.

I'M. I'M VERY SORRY, CHIEF DESIGNER.

WELL?

THEY'RE NOT HAPPY WITH ME. HE'S NOT HAPPY WITH ME.

WELL, I UNDERSTAND KEEPING THINGS FROM THE MEDICS. FLIGHT DOCTORS CAN TAKE YOU OFF FLIGHT STATUS FOR ANY MINOR INFRACTION. BUT THE CHIEF DESIGNER IS DIFFERENT.

BUT DON'T WORRY! YOU AND I AREN'T GOING TO FLY AGAIN ANYWAY. WE'RE HEROES.

SYMBOLS.

WOULD YOU MIND TELLING THAT TO MY MOTHER?

HAH. PARENTS. SORRY, I CAN'T HELP YOU THERE. THEY ARE WORSE THAN FLIGHT DOCTORS!

Tereshkova's mom was furious with her.

Valentina's last letter, telling her what she was really doing, was delayed, so she only found out what her daughter was up to after she was in orbit.

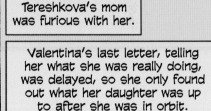

WHAT DO YOU MEAN SHE IS ON THE TELEVISION?

I HAVE A LETTER FROM HER RIGHT HERE, SAYING SHE'LL BE BACK FROM THE LAST STAGES OF HER PARACHUTE TRAINING IN A FEW DAYS.

ELENA, IT IS HER.

COME SEE.

49

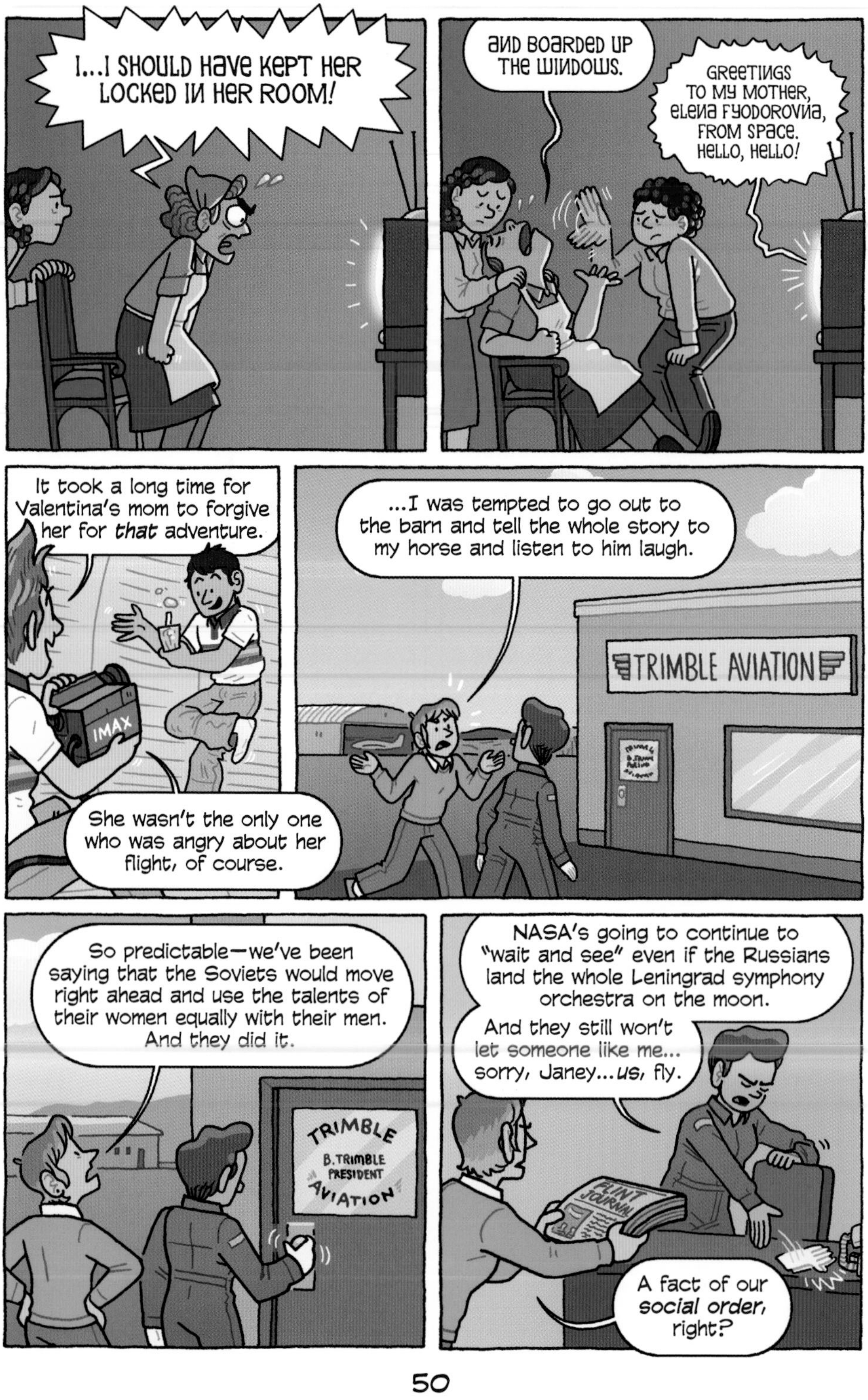

I...I SHOULD HAVE KEPT HER LOCKED IN HER ROOM!
AND BOARDED UP THE WINDOWS.
GREETINGS TO MY MOTHER, ELENA FYODOROVNA, FROM SPACE. HELLO, HELLO!
It took a long time for Valentina's mom to forgive her for *that* adventure.
IMAX
She wasn't the only one who was angry about her flight, of course.
...I was tempted to go out to the barn and tell the whole story to my horse and listen to him laugh.
TRIMBLE AVIATION
So predictable—we've been saying that the Soviets would move right ahead and use the talents of their women equally with their men. And they did it.
TRIMBLE
B. TRIMBLE
PRESIDENT
AVIATION
NASA's going to continue to "wait and see" even if the Russians land the whole Leningrad symphony orchestra on the moon.
And they still won't let someone like me... sorry, Janey...*us*, fly.
FLINT JOURNAL
A fact of our *social order*, right?

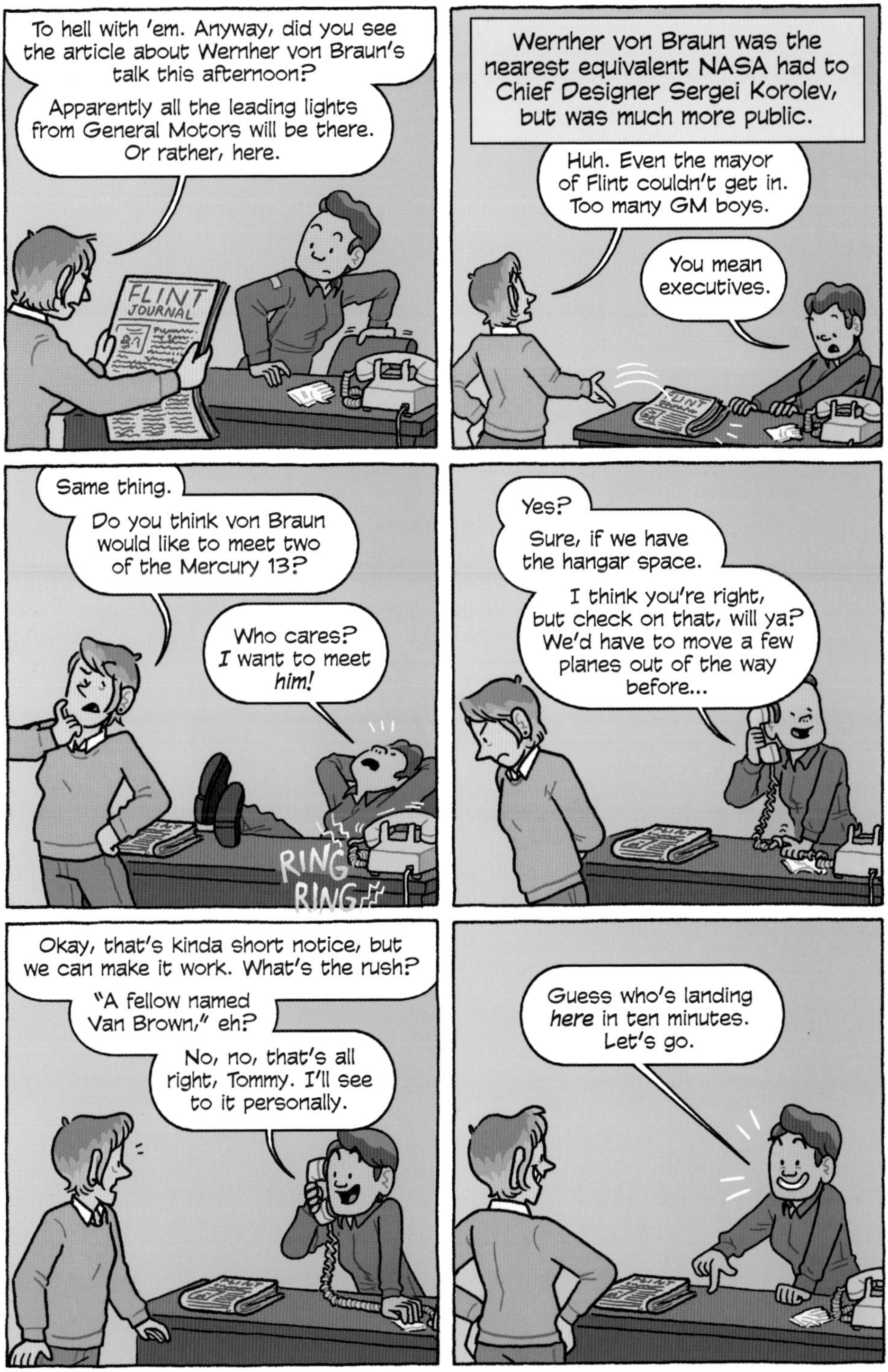
To hell with 'em. Anyway, did you see the article about Wernher von Braun's talk this afternoon?
Apparently all the leading lights from General Motors will be there. Or rather, here.
FLINT JOURNAL
Wernher von Braun was the nearest equivalent NASA had to Chief Designer Sergei Korolev, but was much more public.
Huh. Even the mayor of Flint couldn't get in. Too many GM boys.
You mean executives.
Same thing.
Do you think von Braun would like to meet two of the Mercury 13?
Who cares? *I* want to meet *him!*
RING RING
Yes?
Sure, if we have the hangar space.
I think you're right, but check on that, will ya? We'd have to move a few planes out of the way before...
Okay, that's kinda short notice, but we can make it work. What's the rush?
"A fellow named Van Brown," eh?
No, no, that's all right, Tommy. I'll see to it personally.
Guess who's landing *here* in ten minutes. Let's go.

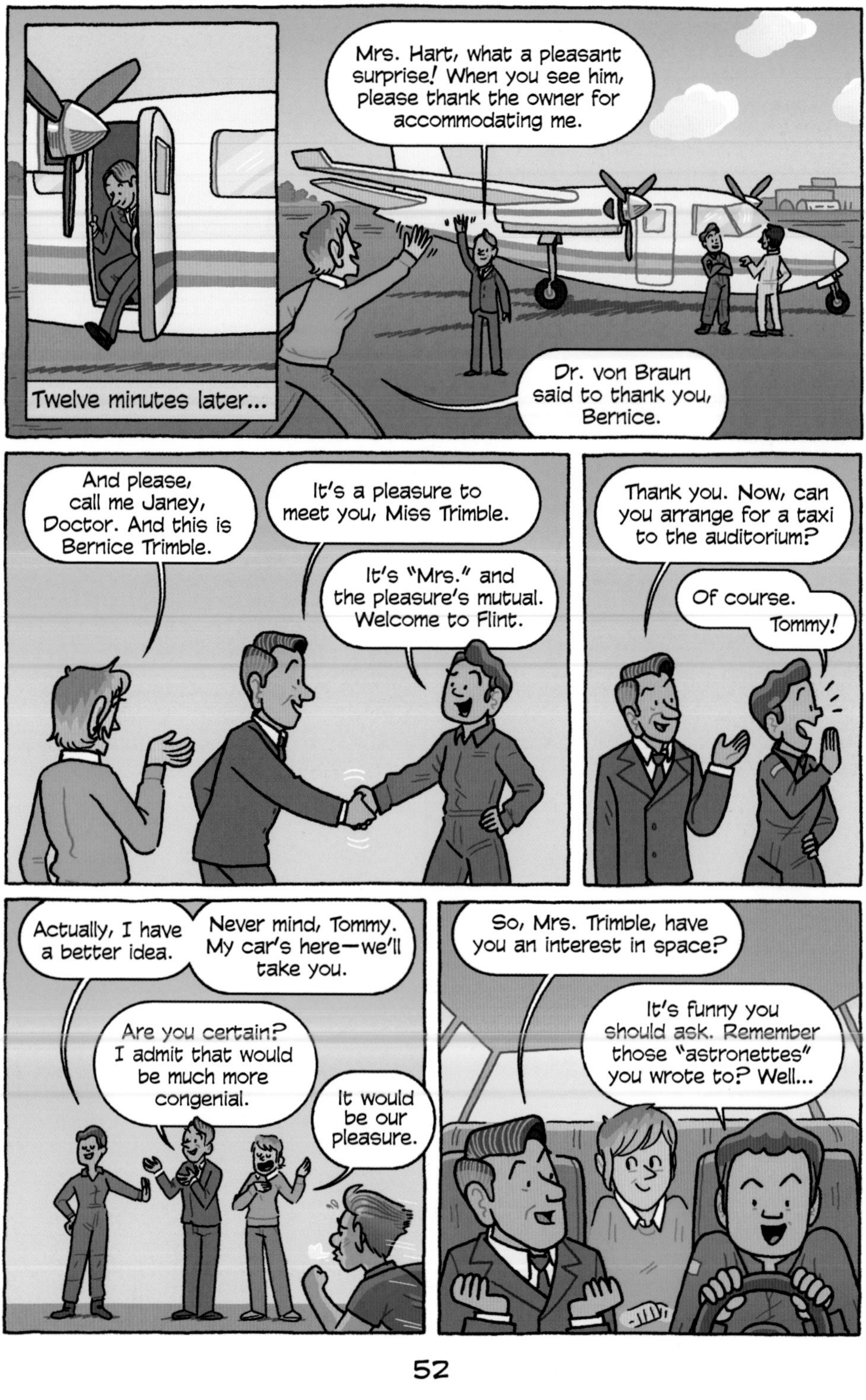
Twelve minutes later...
Mrs. Hart, what a pleasant surprise! When you see him, please thank the owner for accommodating me.
Dr. von Braun said to thank you, Bernice.
And please, call me Janey, Doctor. And this is Bernice Trimble.
It's a pleasure to meet you, Miss Trimble.
It's "Mrs." and the pleasure's mutual. Welcome to Flint.
Thank you. Now, can you arrange for a taxi to the auditorium?
Of course.
Tommy!
Actually, I have a better idea.
Never mind, Tommy. My car's here—we'll take you.
Are you certain? I admit that would be much more congenial.
It would be our pleasure.
So, Mrs. Trimble, have you an interest in space?
It's funny you should ask. Remember those "astronettes" you wrote to? Well...

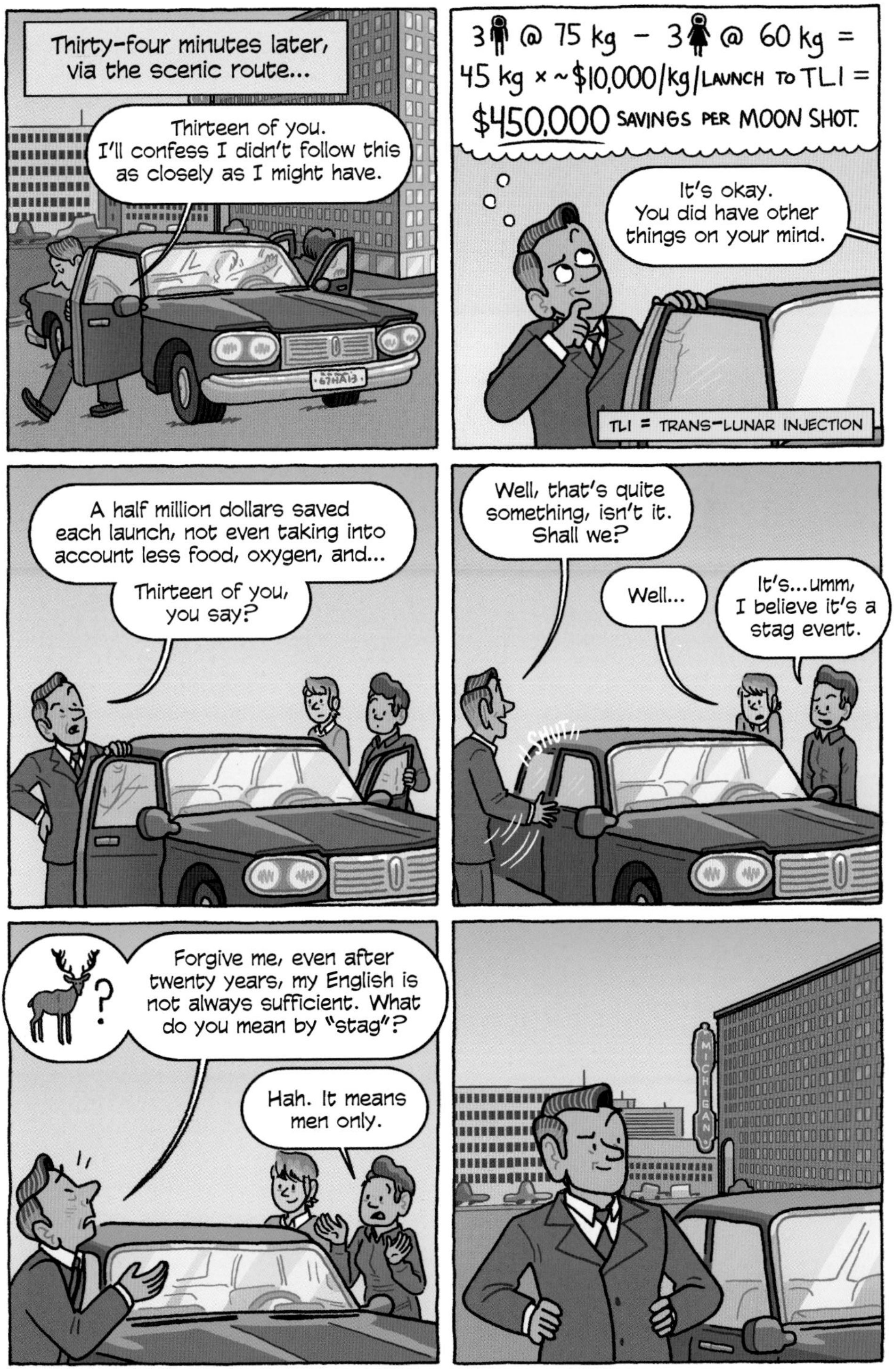
Thirty-four minutes later, via the scenic route...
Thirteen of you. I'll confess I didn't follow this as closely as I might have.
3 @ 75 kg − 3 @ 60 kg = 45 kg × ~$10,000/kg/LAUNCH TO TLI = $450,000 SAVINGS PER MOON SHOT.
It's okay. You did have other things on your mind.
TLI = TRANS-LUNAR INJECTION
A half million dollars saved each launch, not even taking into account less food, oxygen, and...
Thirteen of you, you say?
Well, that's quite something, isn't it. Shall we?
SHUT
Well...
It's...umm, I believe it's a stag event.
?
Forgive me, even after twenty years, my English is not always sufficient. What do you mean by "stag"?
Hah. It means men only.
MICHIGAN

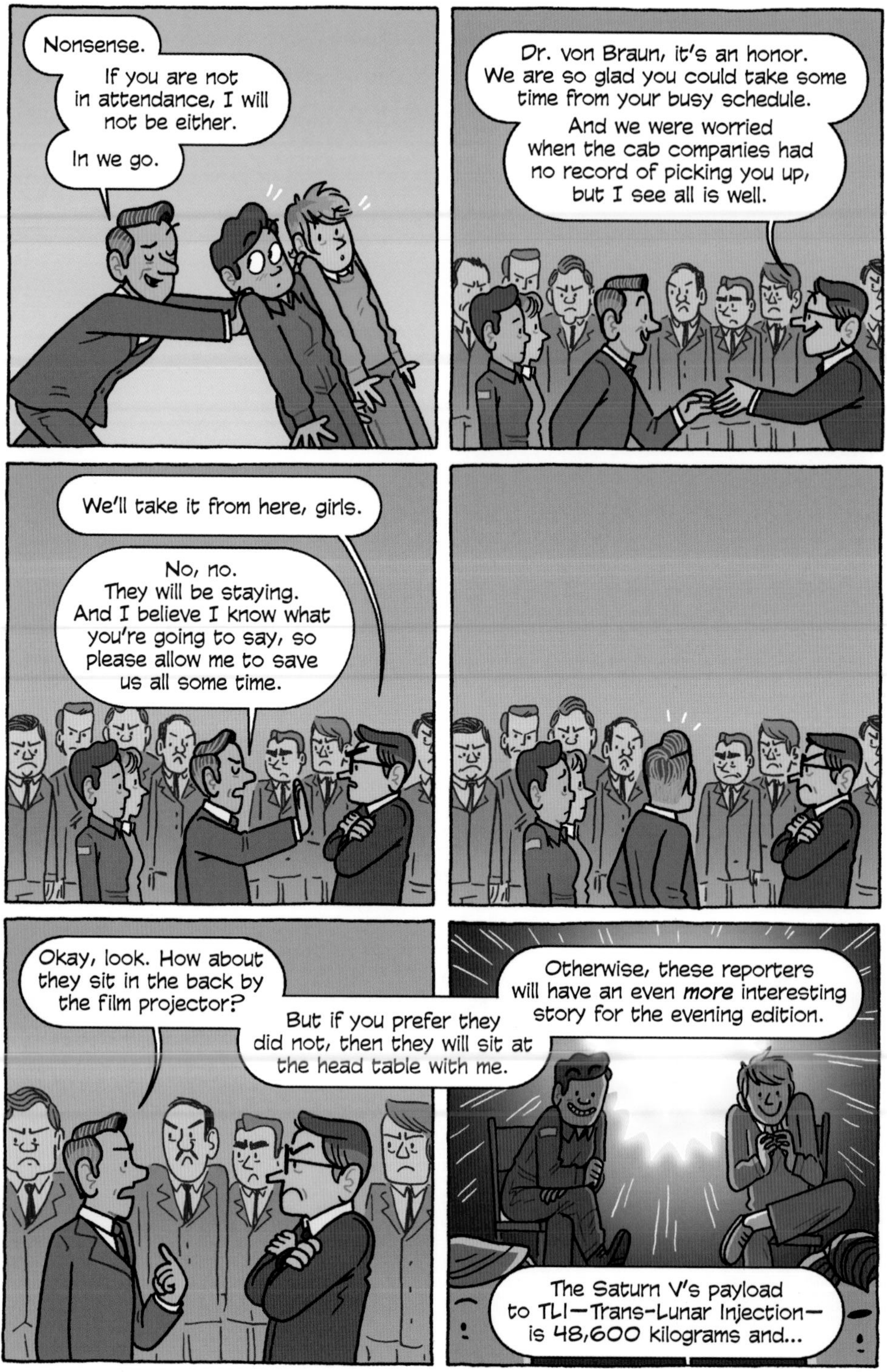
Nonsense.
If you are not in attendance, I will not be either.
In we go.
Dr. von Braun, it's an honor. We are so glad you could take some time from your busy schedule.
And we were worried when the cab companies had no record of picking you up, but I see all is well.
We'll take it from here, girls.
No, no. They will be staying. And I believe I know what you're going to say, so please allow me to save us all some time.
Okay, look. How about they sit in the back by the film projector?
But if you prefer they did not, then they will sit at the head table with me.
Otherwise, these reporters will have an even *more* interesting story for the evening edition.
The Saturn V's payload to TLI—Trans-Lunar Injection—is 48,600 kilograms and...

And here's where I come into the story. While Hart and Trimble crashed the stag party in Flint, I was in high school in New York. And didn't know much about the Mercury 13.

Not many did. They weren't front-page news for long.

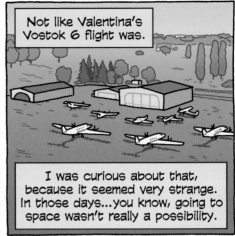

Not like Valentina's Vostok 6 flight was.

I was curious about that, because it seemed very strange. In those days...you know, going to space wasn't really a possibility.

I mean, reading about Valentina was sorta like...

Ooh, that's interesting.

First Woman in Space

It would be neat to fly a spaceship, wouldn't it, Walt?

Sure, but you're working on a license for things with wings right now, so let's do the preflight and get us up there.

So, what's first?

Cabin. Control Wheel Lock— remove it.

Correct. And then?

Ignition switch: Off.

Master switch: On.

I started flying when I was fourteen because I was a strange little kid that kept playing with model airplanes and...anyway, my parents were great.

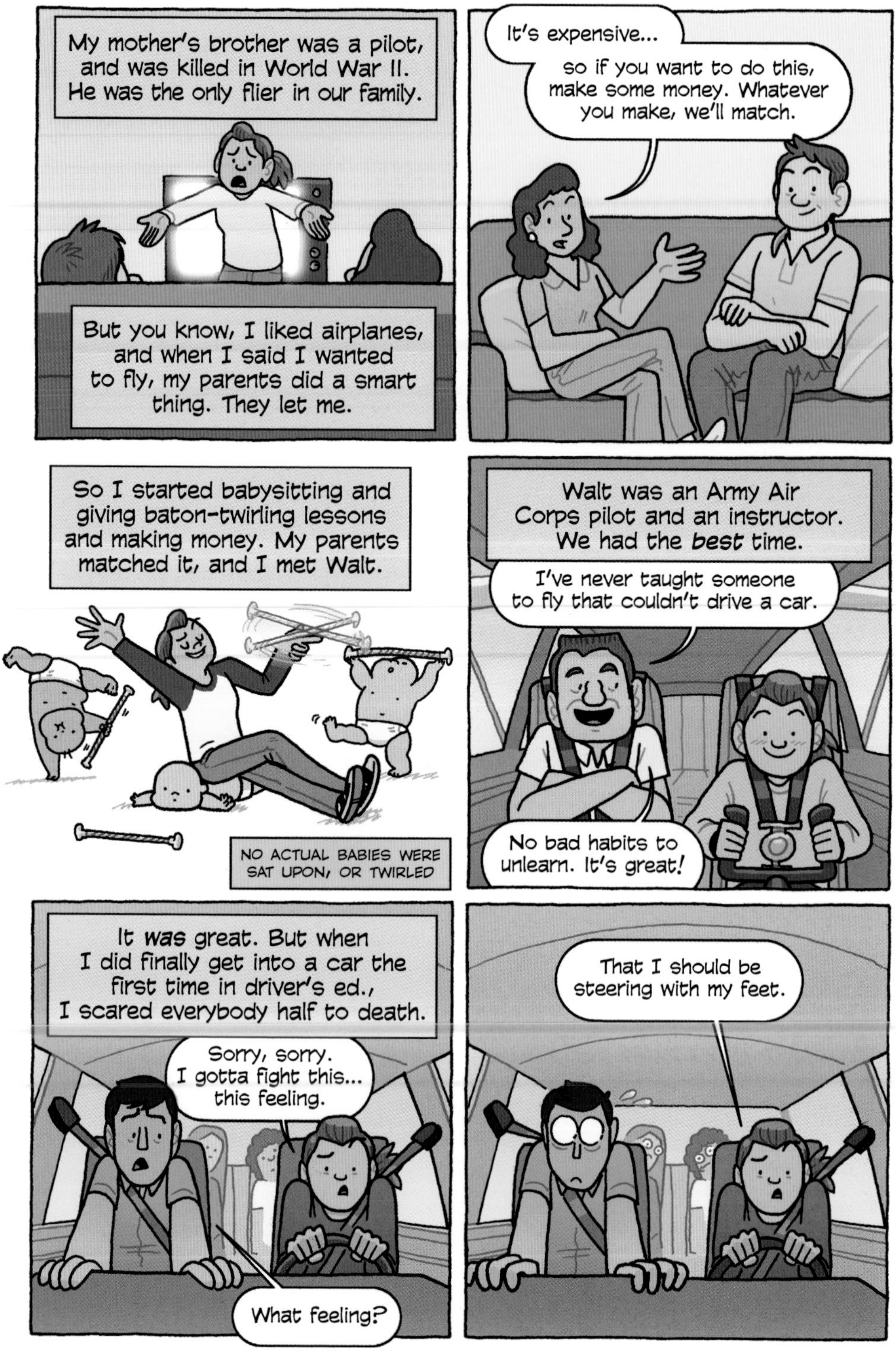

My mother's brother was a pilot, and was killed in World War II. He was the only flier in our family.
But you know, I liked airplanes, and when I said I wanted to fly, my parents did a smart thing. They let me.
It's expensive...
so if you want to do this, make some money. Whatever you make, we'll match.
So I started babysitting and giving baton-twirling lessons and making money. My parents matched it, and I met Walt.
NO ACTUAL BABIES WERE SAT UPON, OR TWIRLED
Walt was an Army Air Corps pilot and an instructor. We had the *best* time.
I've never taught someone to fly that couldn't drive a car.
No bad habits to unlearn. It's great!
It *was* great. But when I did finally get into a car the first time in driver's ed., I scared everybody half to death.
Sorry, sorry. I gotta fight this... this feeling.
What feeling?
That I should be steering with my feet.

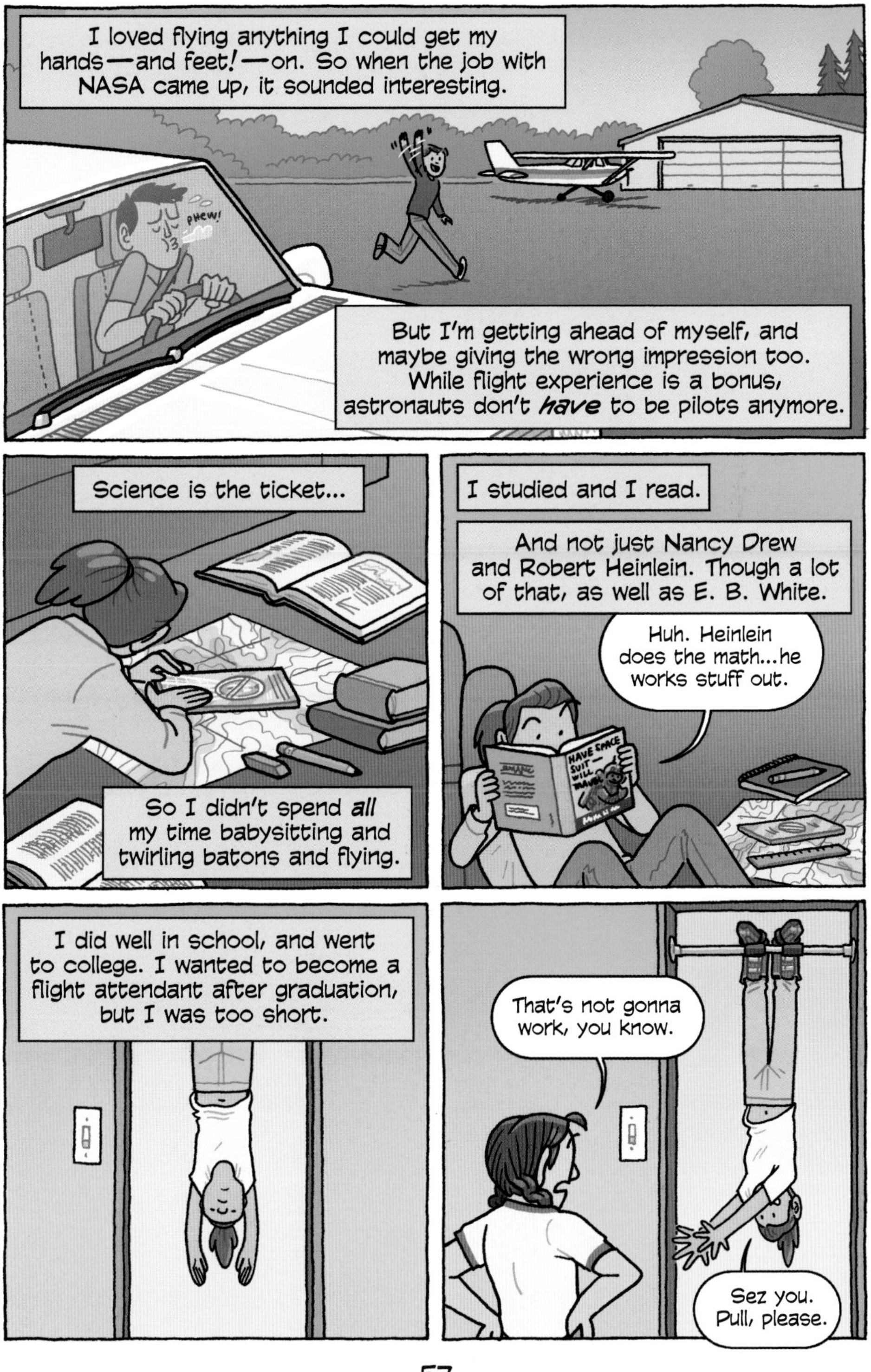

I loved flying anything I could get my hands—and feet!—on. So when the job with NASA came up, it sounded interesting.
PHEW!
But I'm getting ahead of myself, and maybe giving the wrong impression too. While flight experience is a bonus, astronauts don't *have* to be pilots anymore.
Science is the ticket...
So I didn't spend *all* my time babysitting and twirling batons and flying.
I studied and I read.
And not just Nancy Drew and Robert Heinlein. Though a lot of that, as well as E. B. White.
Huh. Heinlein does the math...he works stuff out.
HAVE SPACE SUIT—WILL TRAVEL
I did well in school, and went to college. I wanted to become a flight attendant after graduation, but I was too short.
That's not gonna work, you know.
Sez you. Pull, please.

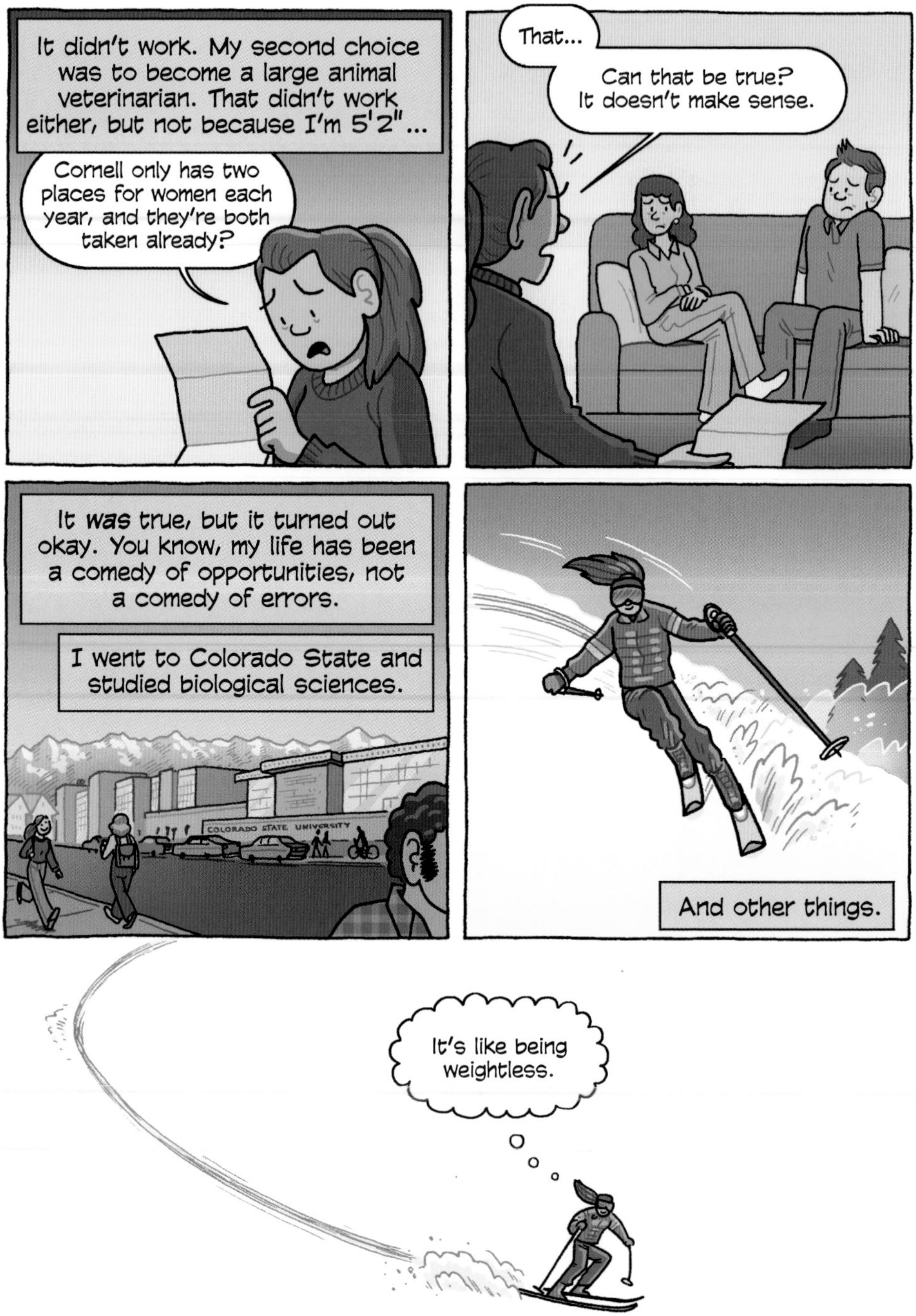
It didn't work. My second choice was to become a large animal veterinarian. That didn't work either, but not because I'm 5'2"...
Cornell only has two places for women each year, and they're both taken already?
That...
Can that be true? It doesn't make sense.
It *was* true, but it turned out okay. You know, my life has been a comedy of opportunities, not a comedy of errors.
I went to Colorado State and studied biological sciences.
COLORADO STATE UNIVERSITY
And other things.
It's like being weightless.

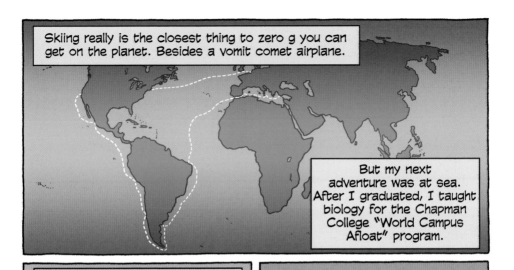

Skiing really is the closest thing to zero g you can get on the planet. Besides a vomit comet airplane.

But my next adventure was at sea. After I graduated, I taught biology for the Chapman College "World Campus Afloat" program.

I got interested in water quality and algae on that trip, and decided to go back to school.

I'm going to get my master's degree in microbial ecology.

Gonna be a phycologist.

Thanks.

Wait, how do psychology and algae...?

Hah! They don't... and I don't have a lisp!

It's *phycology*. Green slime.

Because water and algae are what make the world go round, you know?

I followed up my master's with fieldwork for the Utah Water Research Lab.

I worked up in the cold desert for them, studying the cryptogrammic crust.

That's the black stuff you see out there.

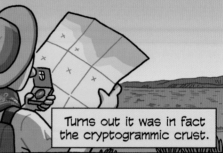

We were trying to figure out where all the carbon dioxide emitted by nearby cities was going. It was getting sucked up by plants, but we didn't know which ones, or where.

Turns out it was in fact the cryptogrammic crust.

This stuff is mostly dormant, but if it rains it's up and chugging full speed in twenty minutes. I mean, it's really amazing.

We set up these little research instruments all over, and protected them with a piece of plywood.

Every time!

HISSSSSSSSssss..

RATTLE
RATTTTLE

HISSSSssr

I actually carried a six-gun filled with snake shot on my hip when I was doing that work.

So that was really fun.

HUFF
HUFF

RATTLE
RATTLE

RATTLE
RATTLE

RATTLE

RATTLE

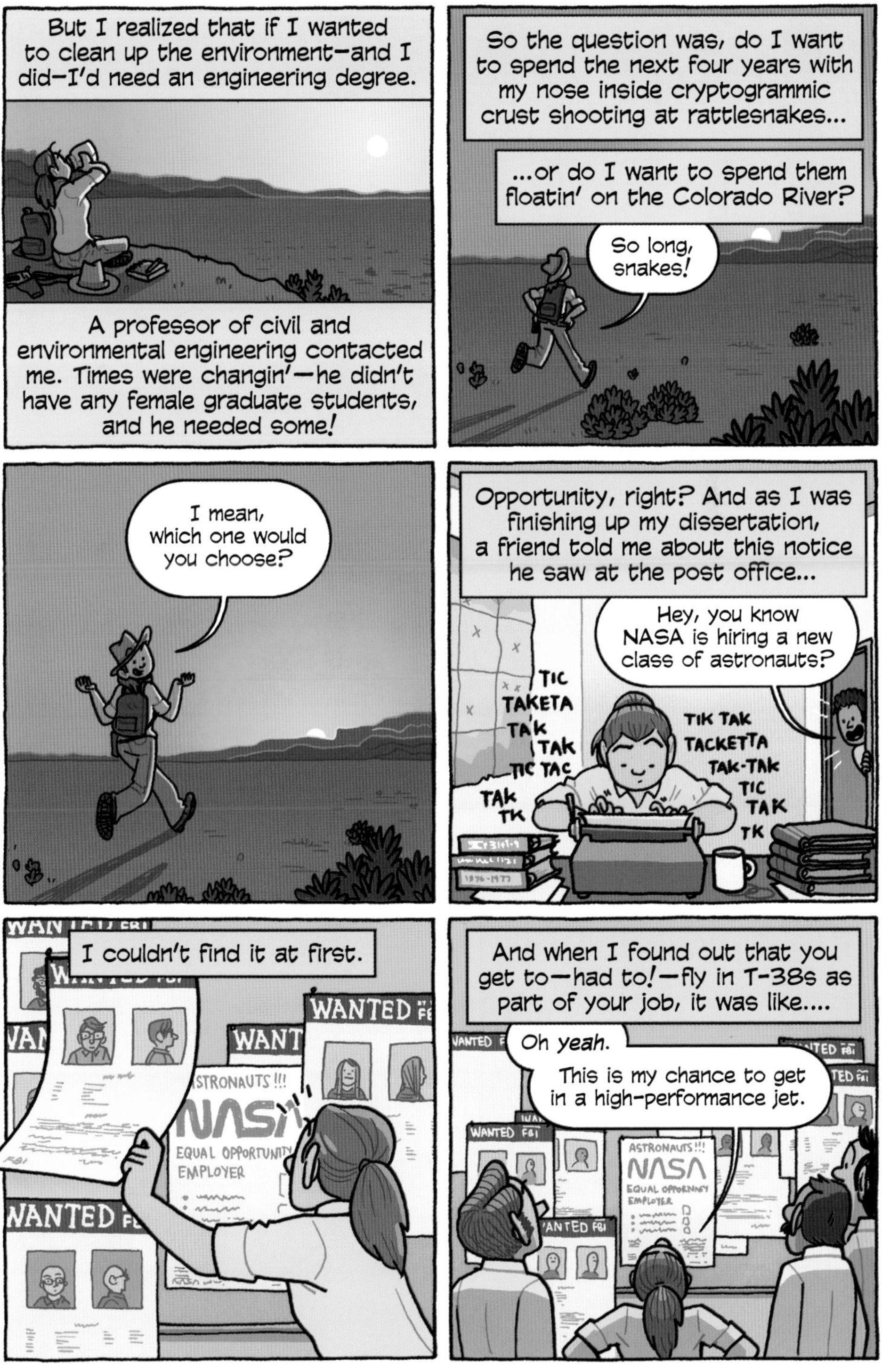
But I realized that if I wanted to clean up the environment—and I did—I'd need an engineering degree.
A professor of civil and environmental engineering contacted me. Times were changin'—he didn't have any female graduate students, and he needed some!
So the question was, do I want to spend the next four years with my nose inside cryptogrammic crust shooting at rattlesnakes...
...or do I want to spend them floatin' on the Colorado River?
So long, snakes!
I mean, which one would you choose?
Opportunity, right? And as I was finishing up my dissertation, a friend told me about this notice he saw at the post office...
Hey, you know NASA is hiring a new class of astronauts?
TIC TAKETA TAK TAK TIC TAC TAK TK
TIK TAK TACKETTA TAK-TAK TIC TAK TK
I couldn't find it at first.
WANTED FBI
ASTRONAUTS!!!
NASA
EQUAL OPPORTUNITY EMPLOYER
And when I found out that you get to—had to!—fly in T-38s as part of your job, it was like....
Oh *yeah.*
This is my chance to get in a high-performance jet.

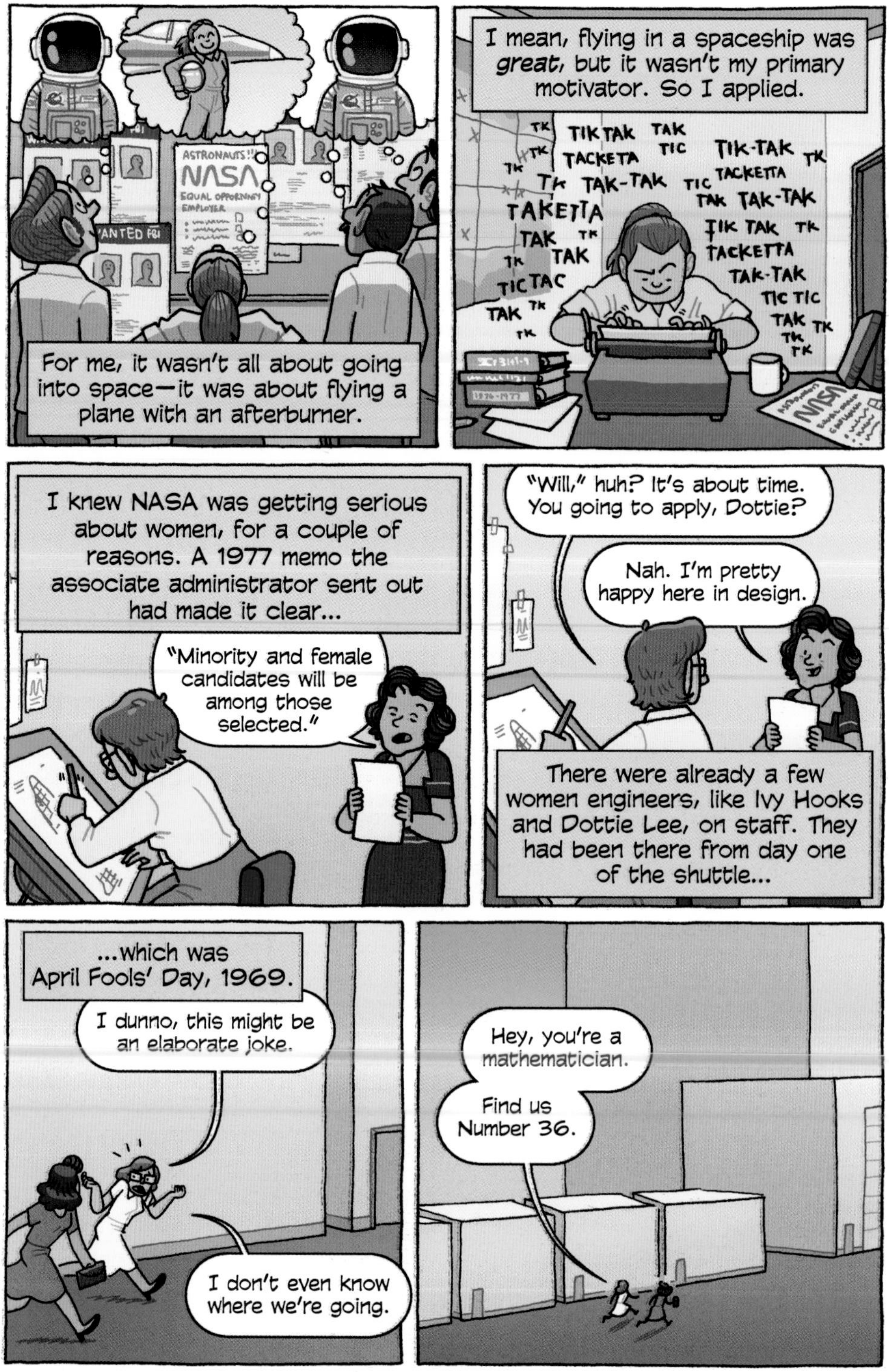
ASTRONAUTS!!
NASA
EQUAL OPPORTUNITY EMPLOYER
WANTED FBI
For me, it wasn't all about going into space—it was about flying a plane with an afterburner.
I mean, flying in a spaceship was *great*, but it wasn't my primary motivator. So I applied.
TK TIK TAK TAK TK TACKETA TIC TIK-TAK TK TK TK TAK-TAK TIC TACKETTA TAKETTA TAK TAK-TAK TAK TK TIK TAK TK TK TAK TACKETTA TK TIC TAC TAK-TAK TAK TK TIC TIC TK TAK TK TK TK TK
1976-1977
NASA
I knew NASA was getting serious about women, for a couple of reasons. A 1977 memo the associate administrator sent out had made it clear...
"Minority and female candidates will be among those selected."
"Will," huh? It's about time. You going to apply, Dottie?
Nah. I'm pretty happy here in design.
There were already a few women engineers, like Ivy Hooks and Dottie Lee, on staff. They had been there from day one of the shuttle...
...which was April Fools' Day, 1969.
I dunno, this might be an elaborate joke.
I don't even know where we're going.
Hey, you're a mathematician.
Find us Number 36.

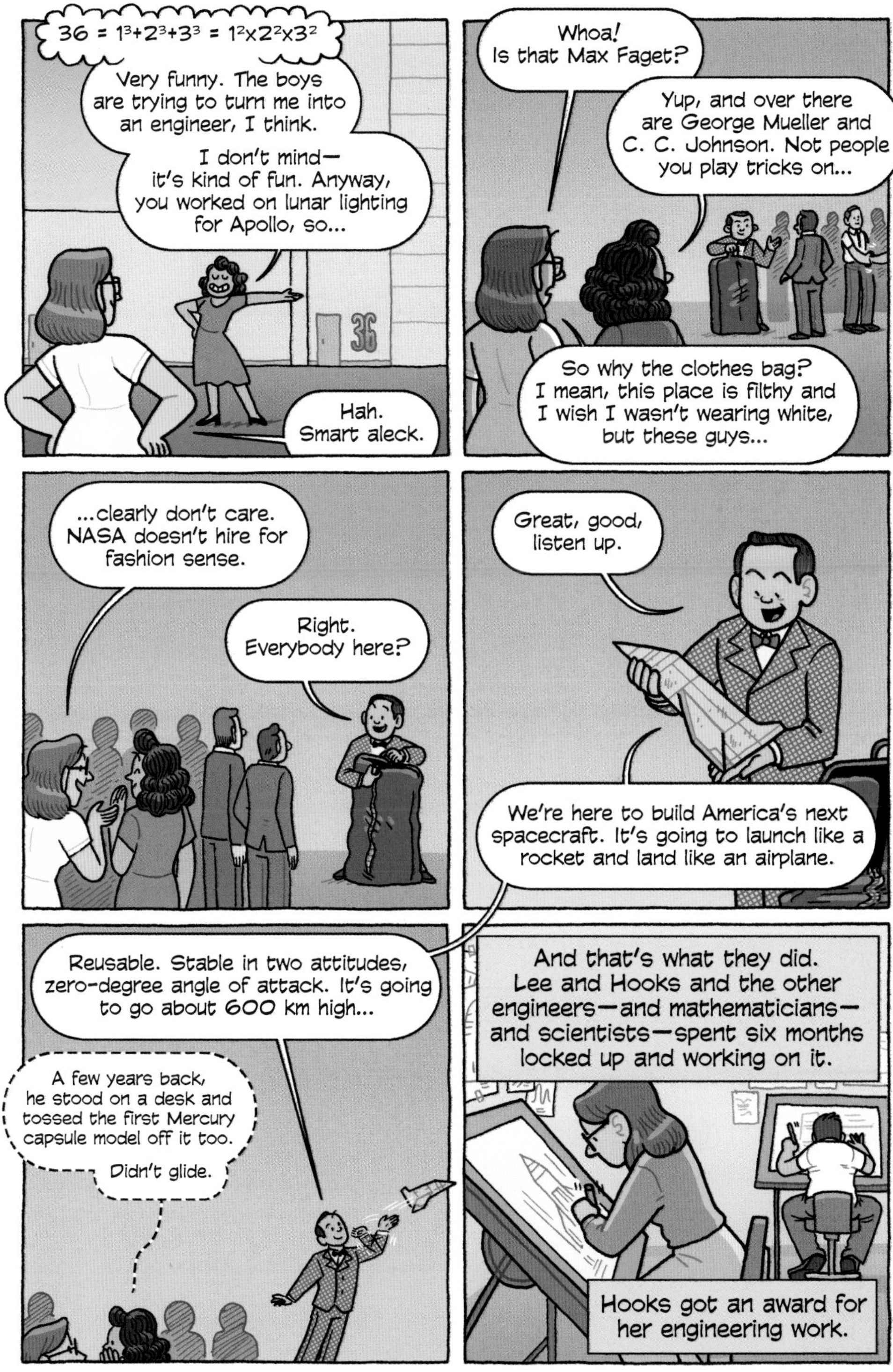
36 = 1³+2³+3³ = 1²x2²x3²
Very funny. The boys are trying to turn me into an engineer, I think.
I don't mind— it's kind of fun. Anyway, you worked on lunar lighting for Apollo, so...
Hah. Smart aleck.
Whoa! Is that Max Faget?
Yup, and over there are George Mueller and C. C. Johnson. Not people you play tricks on...
So why the clothes bag? I mean, this place is filthy and I wish I wasn't wearing white, but these guys...
...clearly don't care. NASA doesn't hire for fashion sense.
Right. Everybody here?
Great, good, listen up.
We're here to build America's next spacecraft. It's going to launch like a rocket and land like an airplane.
Reusable. Stable in two attitudes, zero-degree angle of attack. It's going to go about 600 km high...
A few years back, he stood on a desk and tossed the first Mercury capsule model off it too.
Didn't glide.
And that's what they did. Lee and Hooks and the other engineers—and mathematicians—and scientists—spent six months locked up and working on it.
Hooks got an award for her engineering work.

Lee redesigned the nose—the pointy one on the original model wasn't going to work for reentry.

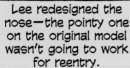

Are you sure?

Yup. I did the math and made an engineering judgment.

...okay, then.

So the shuttle ended up with what everybody called "Dottie's Nose."

The team spent six months in one room, with one telephone, one secretary, and no windows.

Anyone need a lift to the moon landing celebration?

That six months took them past Apollo 11 and the first moon landing.

Busy.

Busy.

Busy.

No thanks.

Maybe later.

Busy.

Busy.

Well, we landed.

That's wonderful. We'll celebrate when they make it back.

They didn't make it to the splashdown party either. Still busy.

There were other parties. We landed on the moon five more times, Apollo-Soyuz was a great joint mission with the Russians, Skylab went up—and came back down—and we made progress.

64

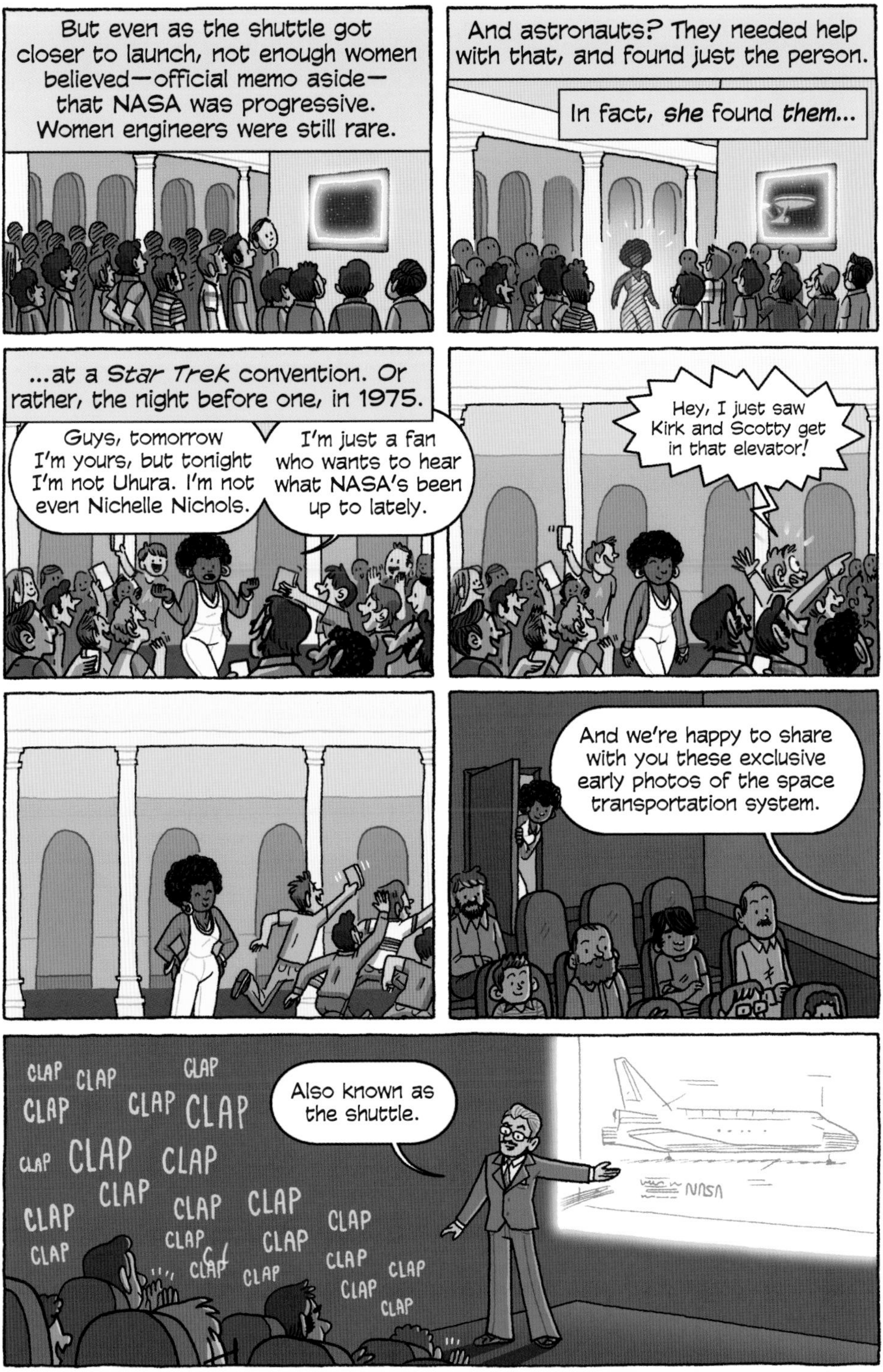
But even as the shuttle got closer to launch, not enough women believed—official memo aside—that NASA was progressive. Women engineers were still rare.
And astronauts? They needed help with that, and found just the person.
In fact, *she* found *them*...
...at a *Star Trek* convention. Or rather, the night before one, in 1975.
Guys, tomorrow I'm yours, but tonight I'm not Uhura. I'm not even Nichelle Nichols.
I'm just a fan who wants to hear what NASA's been up to lately.
Hey, I just saw Kirk and Scotty get in that elevator!
And we're happy to share with you these exclusive early photos of the space transportation system.
Also known as the shuttle.
CLAP CLAP CLAP CLAP CLAP CLAP CLAP CLAP CLAP CLAP CLAP CLAP CLAP CLAP CLAP CLAP CLAP CLAP CLAP CLAP CLAP CLAP CLAP
NASA

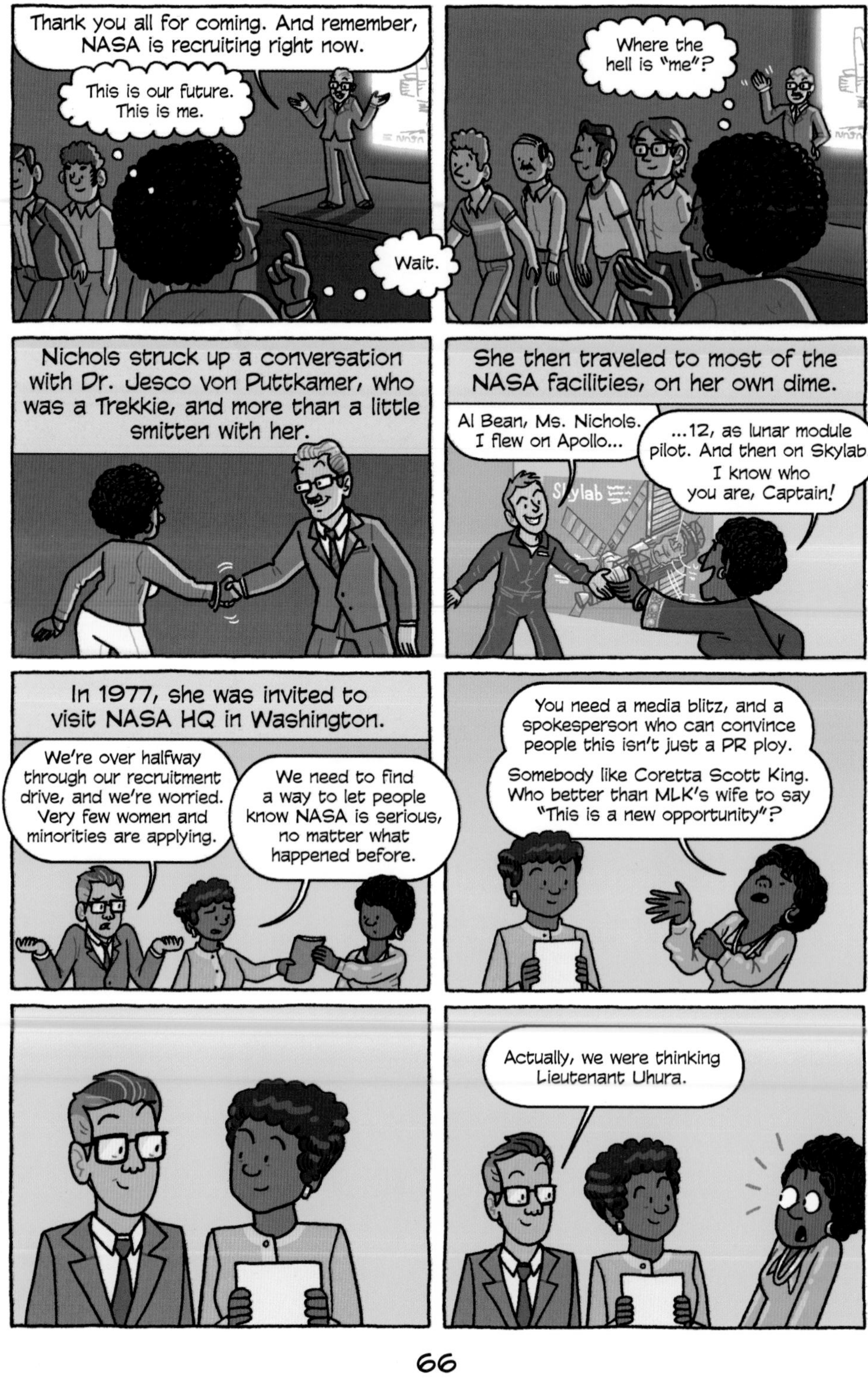
Thank you all for coming. And remember, NASA is recruiting right now.
This is our future. This is me.
Wait.
Where the hell is "me"?
Nichols struck up a conversation with Dr. Jesco von Puttkamer, who was a Trekkie, and more than a little smitten with her.
She then traveled to most of the NASA facilities, on her own dime.
Al Bean, Ms. Nichols. I flew on Apollo...
...12, as lunar module pilot. And then on Skylab. I know who you are, Captain!
Skylab
In 1977, she was invited to visit NASA HQ in Washington.
We're over halfway through our recruitment drive, and we're worried. Very few women and minorities are applying.
We need to find a way to let people know NASA is serious, no matter what happened before.
You need a media blitz, and a spokesperson who can convince people this isn't just a PR ploy.
Somebody like Coretta Scott King. Who better than MLK's wife to say "This is a new opportunity"?
Actually, we were thinking Lieutenant Uhura.

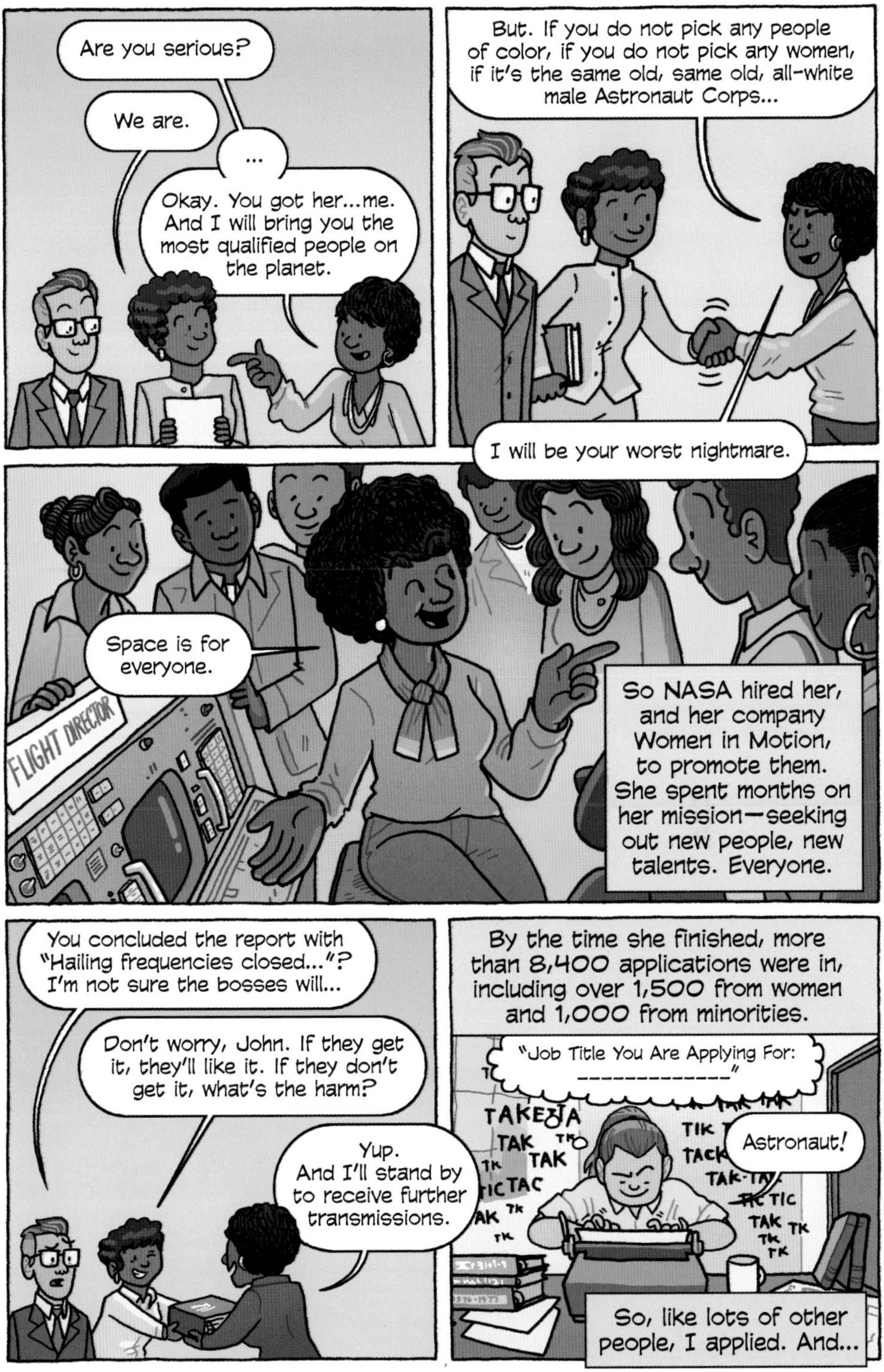
Are you serious?
We are.
...
Okay. You got her...me. And I will bring you the most qualified people on the planet.
But. If you do not pick any people of color, if you do not pick any women, if it's the same old, same old, all-white male Astronaut Corps...
I will be your worst nightmare.
Space is for everyone.
FLIGHT DIRECTOR
So NASA hired her, and her company Women in Motion, to promote them. She spent months on her mission—seeking out new people, new talents. Everyone.
You concluded the report with "Hailing frequencies closed..."? I'm not sure the bosses will...
Don't worry, John. If they get it, they'll like it. If they don't get it, what's the harm?
Yup. And I'll stand by to receive further transmissions.
By the time she finished, more than 8,400 applications were in, including over 1,500 from women and 1,000 from minorities.
"Job Title You Are Applying For: ____________"
TAKETA TAK TK TAK TICTAC TK TIK TACK TAK-TAK TIC TAK TK TK
Astronaut!
So, like lots of other people, I applied. And...

...I didn't make the cut.

Maybe it's because I haven't finished my degree.

RADO SPRINGS, COLORADO

All right. Okay. Pretty soon I'll be "Dr. Cleave"...

It really was okay. I mean, that was the astronaut class that included Sally Ride, Judy Resnik, Ron McNair, Guy Bluford, and Ellison Onizuka.

GUION S. BLUFORD

ANNA L. FISHER

NASA

SPACE SHUTTLE

RONALD E. McNAIR

SHANNON W. LUCID

ELLISON S. ONIZUKA

JUDITH A. RESNIK

SALLY K. RIDE

M. RHEA SEDDON

KATHRYN D. SULLIVAN

NASA

And thirty others. Twenty-six white guys and nine...well...people who were not. Pretty diverse, for NASA.

Pilots, engineers, medical doctors... men and women. Not as diverse as we'd expect today, but yeah.

Impressive group. And they get to fly T-38 jets.

So I applied again. And...

TAK-TAK
TK
TAK TAK TK TAK-TAK TIC TACKETTA TIC TAK
TAK TAK-TAK TAK-TAK
TAKETTA TIK TAK TK
TIC TAC TAK TK TACKETTA TAK-TAK
TK TK TAK TAK-TAK TIC TAK
TIC TAC TIC TIC TA
TAK TK TAK TK
TIC TIC TK
TAK TK TK
TK

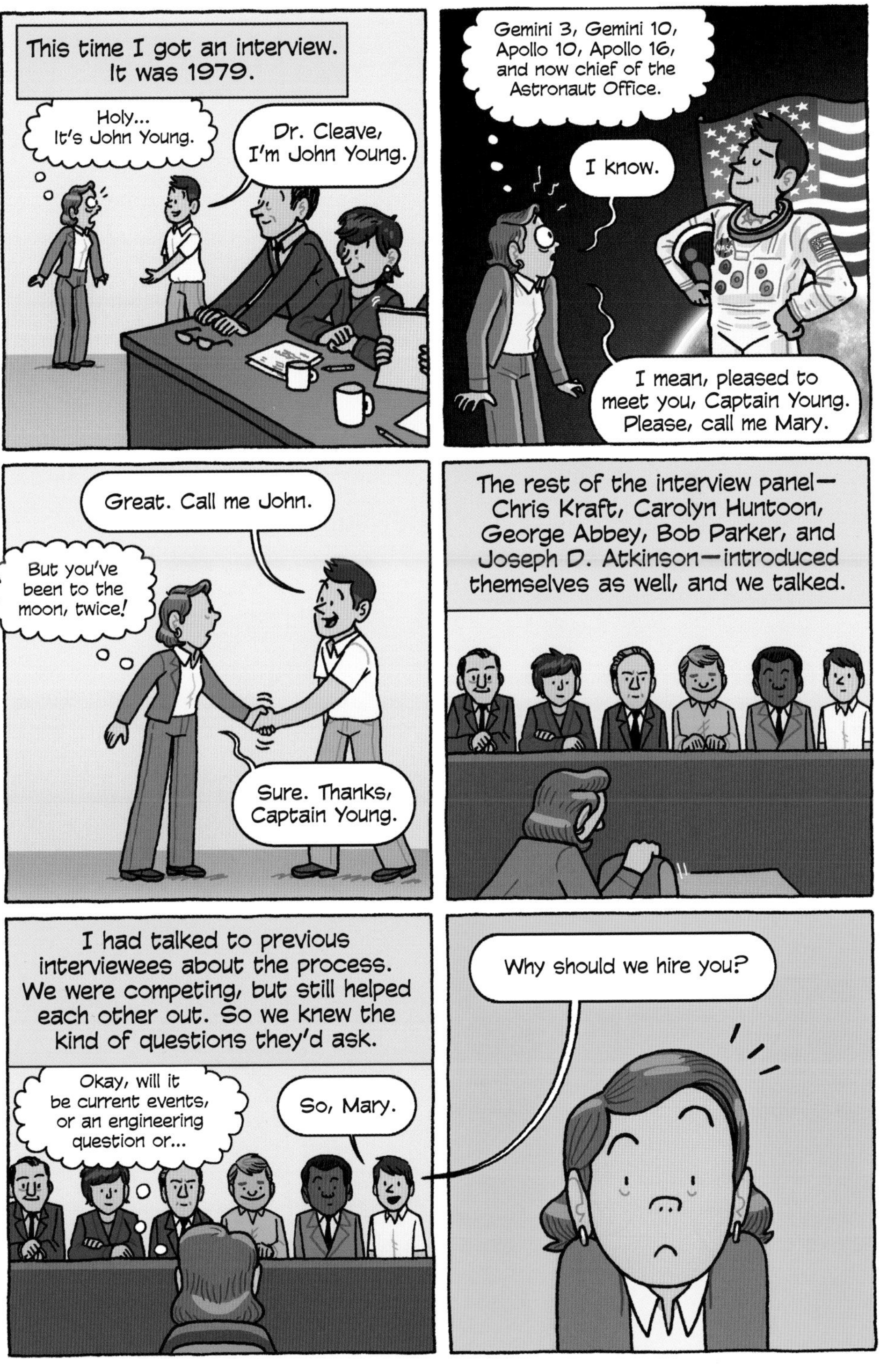

This time I got an interview. It was 1979.
Holy... It's John Young.
Dr. Cleave, I'm John Young.
Gemini 3, Gemini 10, Apollo 10, Apollo 16, and now chief of the Astronaut Office.
I know.
I mean, pleased to meet you, Captain Young. Please, call me Mary.
Great. Call me John.
But you've been to the moon, twice!
Sure. Thanks, Captain Young.
The rest of the interview panel—Chris Kraft, Carolyn Huntoon, George Abbey, Bob Parker, and Joseph D. Atkinson—introduced themselves as well, and we talked.
I had talked to previous interviewees about the process. We were competing, but still helped each other out. So we knew the kind of questions they'd ask.
Okay, will it be current events, or an engineering question or...
So, Mary.
Why should we hire you?

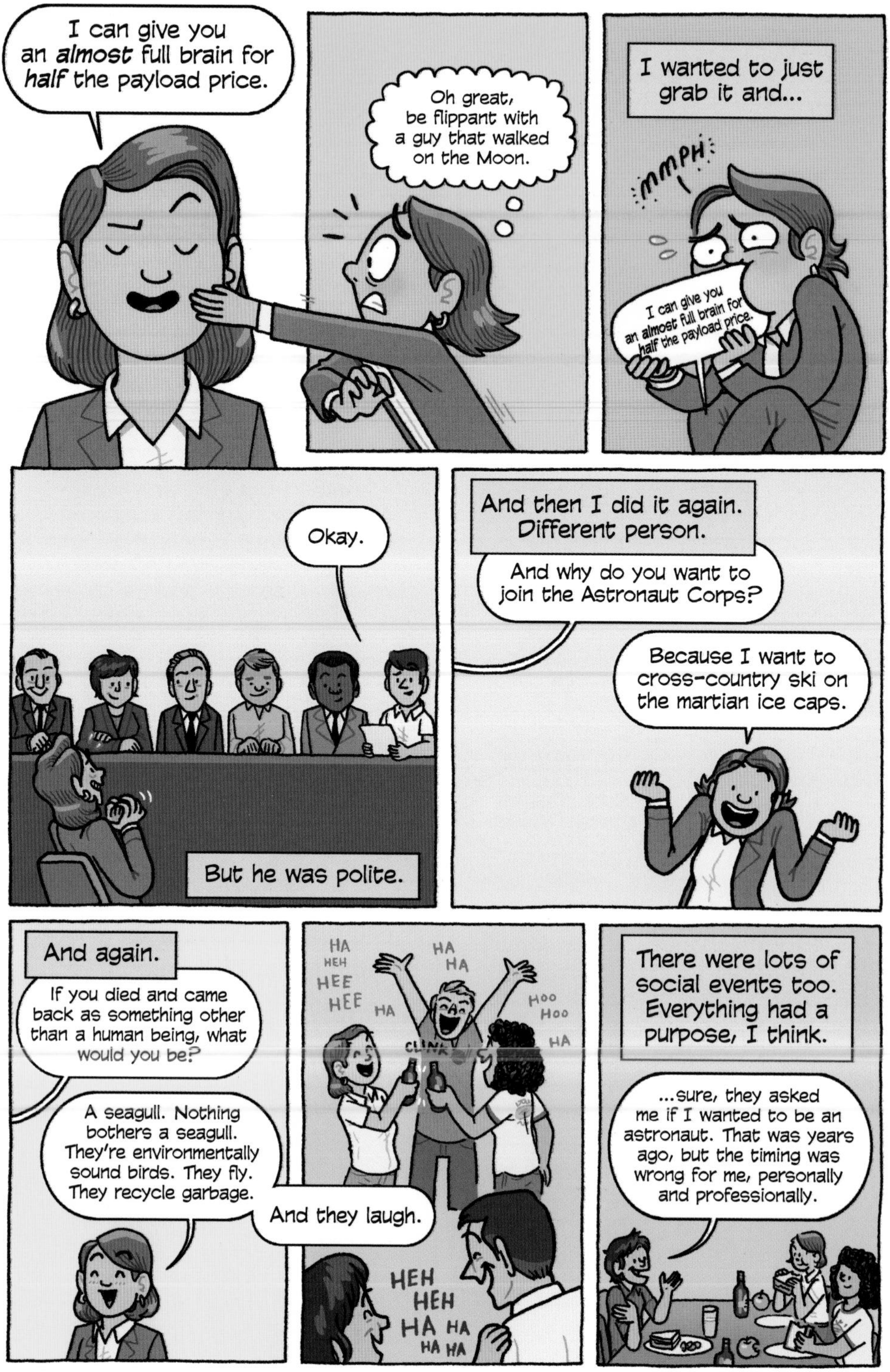
I can give you an *almost* full brain for *half* the payload price.
Oh great, be flippant with a guy that walked on the Moon.
I wanted to just grab it and...
MMPH
I can give you an almost full brain for half the payload price.
Okay.
But he was polite.
And then I did it again. Different person.
And why do you want to join the Astronaut Corps?
Because I want to cross-country ski on the martian ice caps.
And again.
If you died and came back as something other than a human being, what would you be?
A seagull. Nothing bothers a seagull. They're environmentally sound birds. They fly. They recycle garbage.
And they laugh.
HA HEH HEE HEE HA
HA HA
HOO HOO HA
CLINK
HEH HEH HA HA HA HA
There were lots of social events too. Everything had a purpose, I think.
...sure, they asked me if I wanted to be an astronaut. That was years ago, but the timing was wrong for me, personally and professionally.

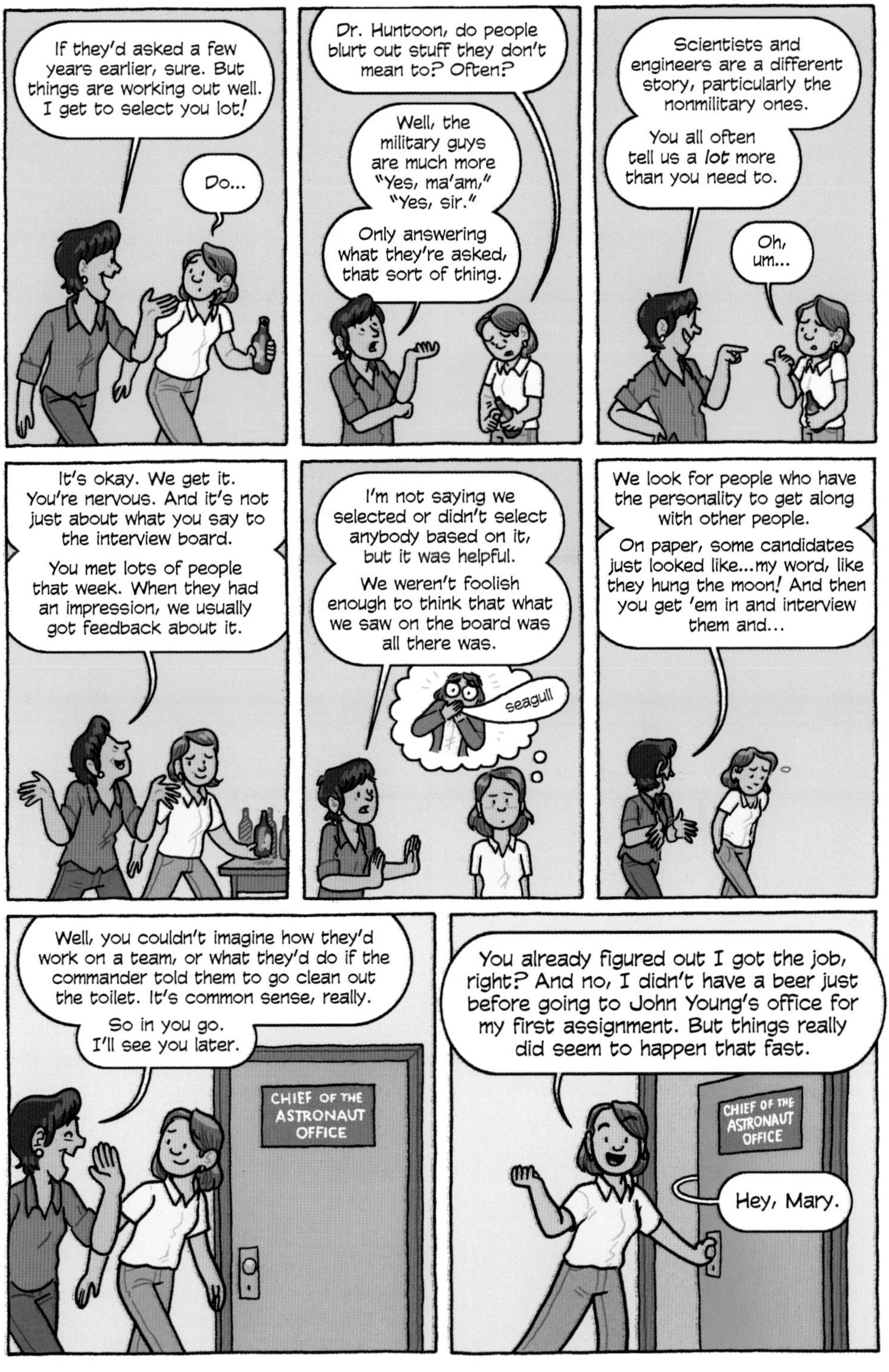

If they'd asked a few years earlier, sure. But things are working out well. I get to select you lot!
Do...
Dr. Huntoon, do people blurt out stuff they don't mean to? Often?
Well, the military guys are much more "Yes, ma'am," "Yes, sir."
Only answering what they're asked, that sort of thing.
Scientists and engineers are a different story, particularly the nonmilitary ones.
You all often tell us a *lot* more than you need to.
Oh, um...
It's okay. We get it. You're nervous. And it's not just about what you say to the interview board.
You met lots of people that week. When they had an impression, we usually got feedback about it.
I'm not saying we selected or didn't select anybody based on it, but it was helpful.
We weren't foolish enough to think that what we saw on the board was all there was.
seagull
We look for people who have the personality to get along with other people.
On paper, some candidates just looked like...my word, like they hung the moon! And then you get 'em in and interview them and...
Well, you couldn't imagine how they'd work on a team, or what they'd do if the commander told them to go clean out the toilet. It's common sense, really.
So in you go. I'll see you later.
CHIEF OF THE ASTRONAUT OFFICE
You already figured out I got the job, right? And no, I didn't have a beer just before going to John Young's office for my first assignment. But things really did seem to happen that fast.
CHIEF OF THE ASTRONAUT OFFICE
Hey, Mary.

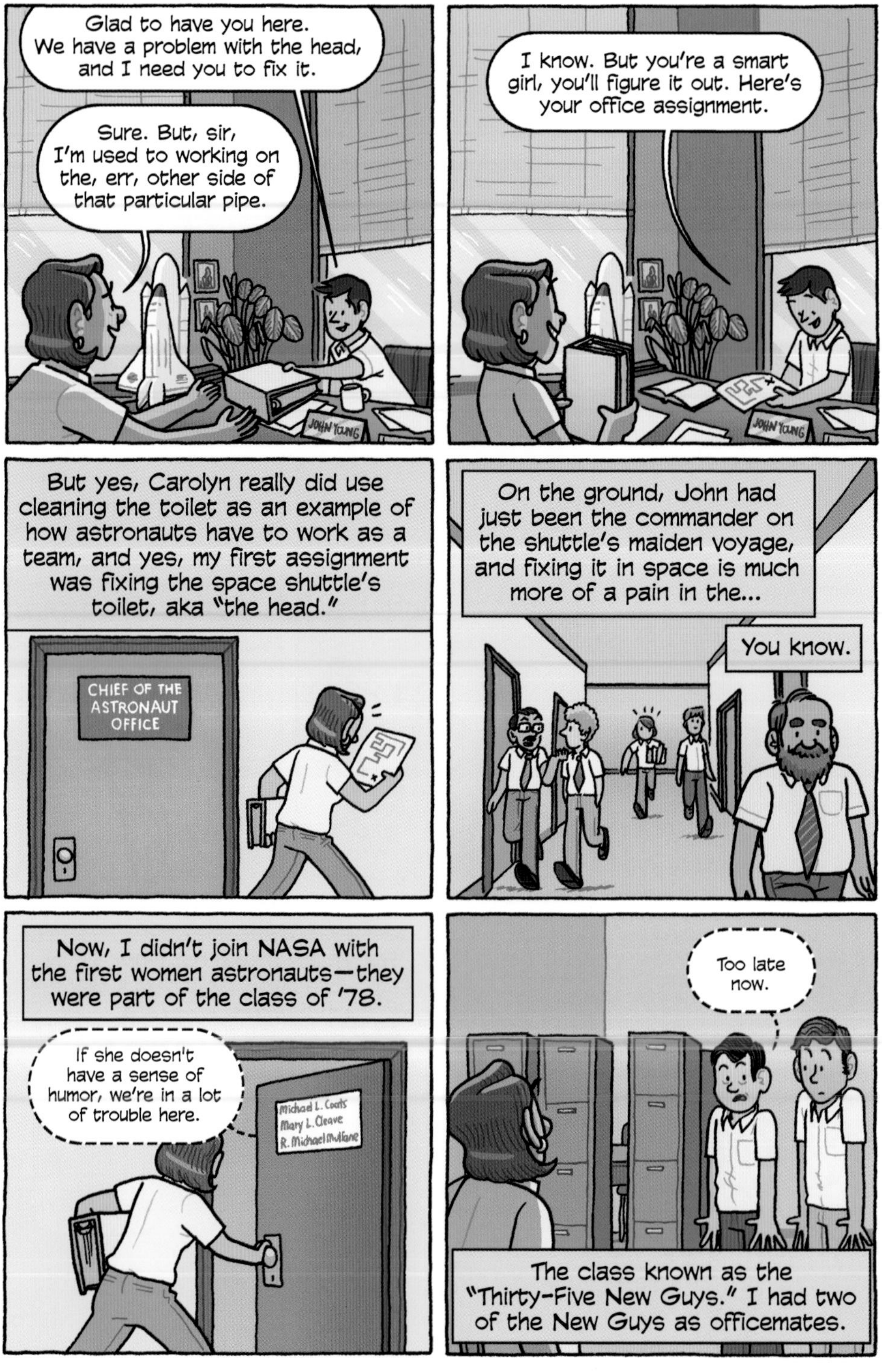

Glad to have you here. We have a problem with the head, and I need you to fix it.
Sure. But, sir, I'm used to working on the, err, other side of that particular pipe.
JOHN YOUNG
I know. But you're a smart girl, you'll figure it out. Here's your office assignment.
JOHN YOUNG
But yes, Carolyn really did use cleaning the toilet as an example of how astronauts have to work as a team, and yes, my first assignment was fixing the space shuttle's toilet, aka "the head."
CHIEF OF THE ASTRONAUT OFFICE
On the ground, John had just been the commander on the shuttle's maiden voyage, and fixing it in space is much more of a pain in the...
You know.
Now, I didn't join NASA with the first women astronauts—they were part of the class of '78.
If she doesn't have a sense of humor, we're in a lot of trouble here.
Michael L. Coats
Mary L. Cleave
R. Michael Mullane
Too late now.
The class known as the "Thirty-Five New Guys." I had two of the New Guys as officemates.

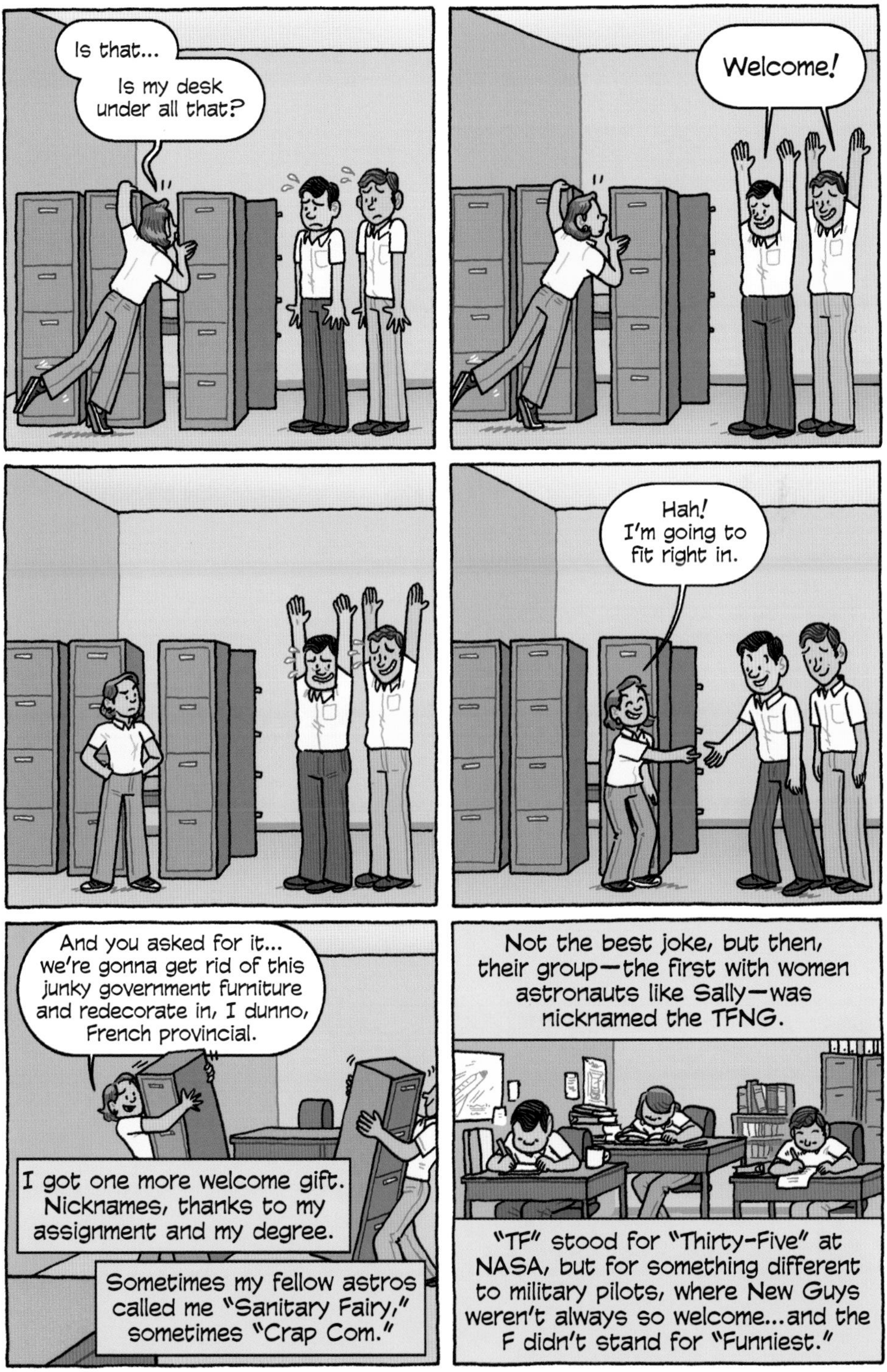

Is that...
Is my desk under all that?
Welcome!
Hah! I'm going to fit right in.
And you asked for it... we're gonna get rid of this junky government furniture and redecorate in, I dunno, French provincial.
I got one more welcome gift. Nicknames, thanks to my assignment and my degree.
Sometimes my fellow astros called me "Sanitary Fairy," sometimes "Crap Com."
Not the best joke, but then, their group—the first with women astronauts like Sally—was nicknamed the TFNG.
"TF" stood for "Thirty-Five" at NASA, but for something different to military pilots, where New Guys weren't always so welcome...and the F didn't stand for "Funniest."

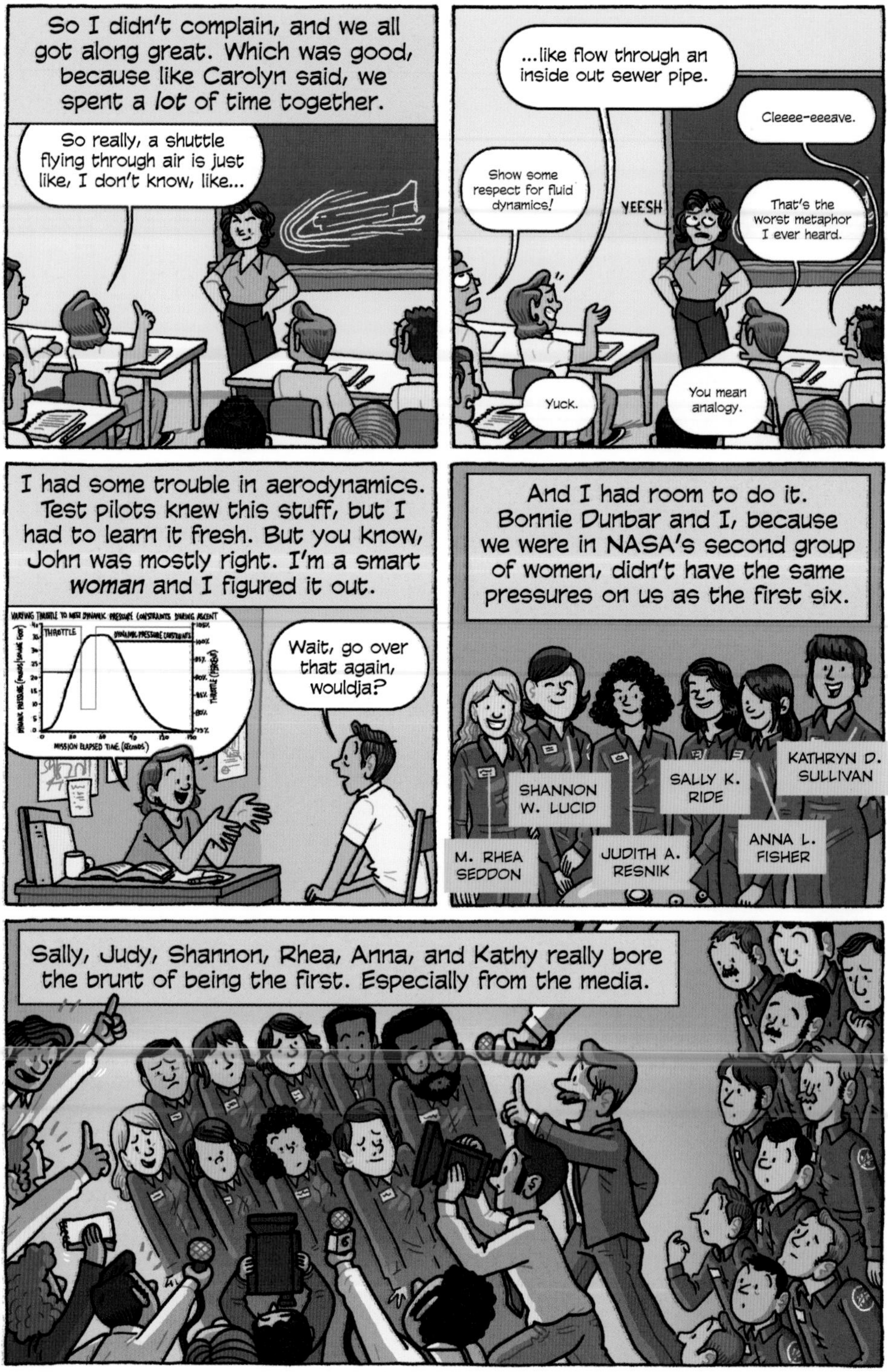
So I didn't complain, and we all got along great. Which was good, because like Carolyn said, we spent a *lot* of time together.
So really, a shuttle flying through air is just like, I don't know, like...
...like flow through an inside out sewer pipe.
Cleeee-eeeave.
Show some respect for fluid dynamics!
YEESH
That's the worst metaphor I ever heard.
Yuck.
You mean analogy.
I had some trouble in aerodynamics. Test pilots knew this stuff, but I had to learn it fresh. But you know, John was mostly right. I'm a smart *woman* and I figured it out.
VARYING THROTTLE TO MEET DYNAMIC PRESSURE CONSTRAINTS DURING ASCENT
THROTTLE
DYNAMIC PRESSURE CONSTRAINTS
MISSION ELAPSED TIME (SECONDS)
Wait, go over that again, wouldja?
And I had room to do it. Bonnie Dunbar and I, because we were in NASA's second group of women, didn't have the same pressures on us as the first six.
KATHRYN D. SULLIVAN
SALLY K. RIDE
SHANNON W. LUCID
ANNA L. FISHER
M. RHEA SEDDON
JUDITH A. RESNIK
Sally, Judy, Shannon, Rhea, Anna, and Kathy really bore the brunt of being the first. Especially from the media.

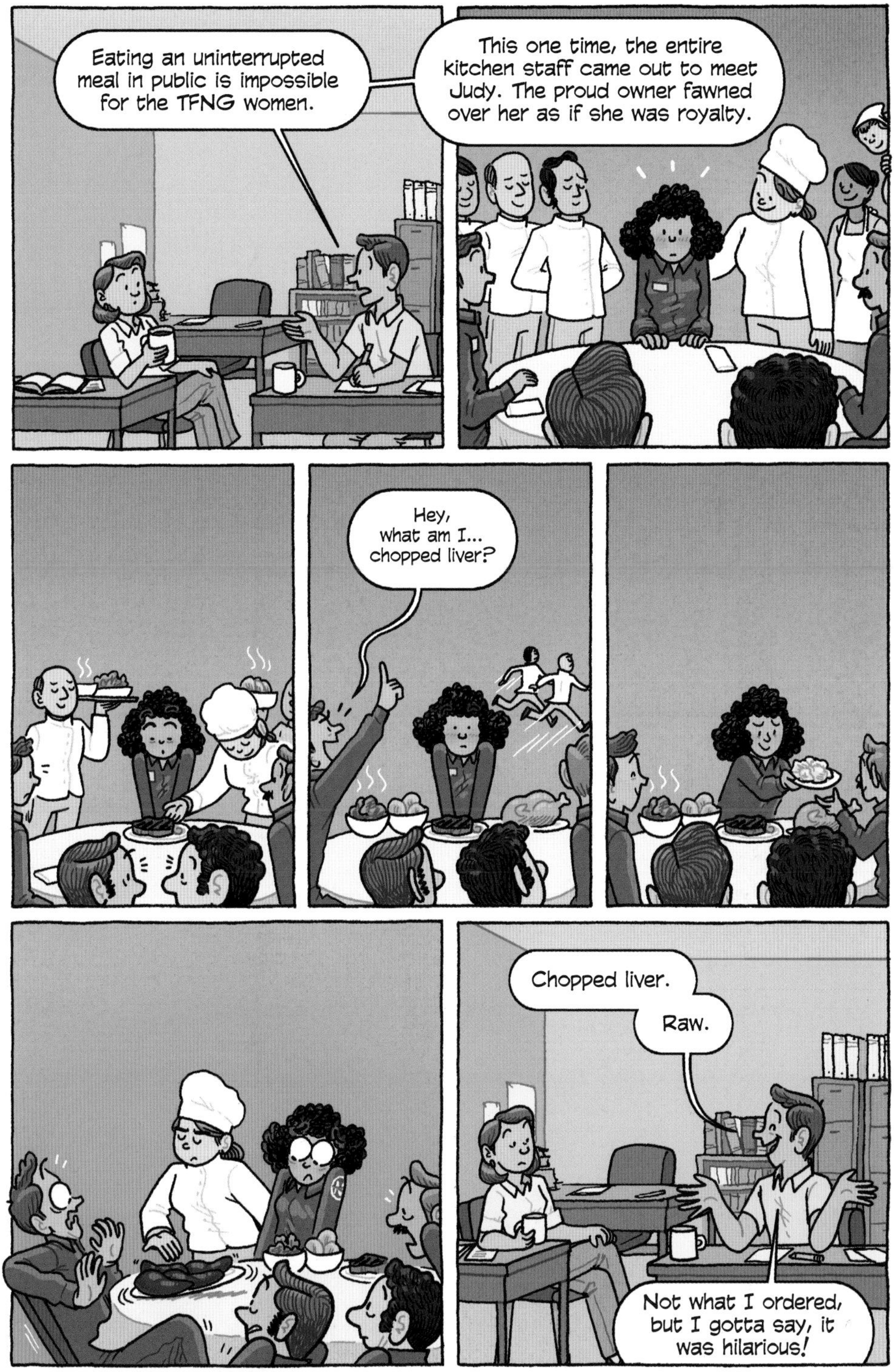
Eating an uninterrupted meal in public is impossible for the TFNG women.
This one time, the entire kitchen staff came out to meet Judy. The proud owner fawned over her as if she was royalty.
Hey, what am I... chopped liver?
Chopped liver.
Raw.
Not what I ordered, but I gotta say, it was hilarious!

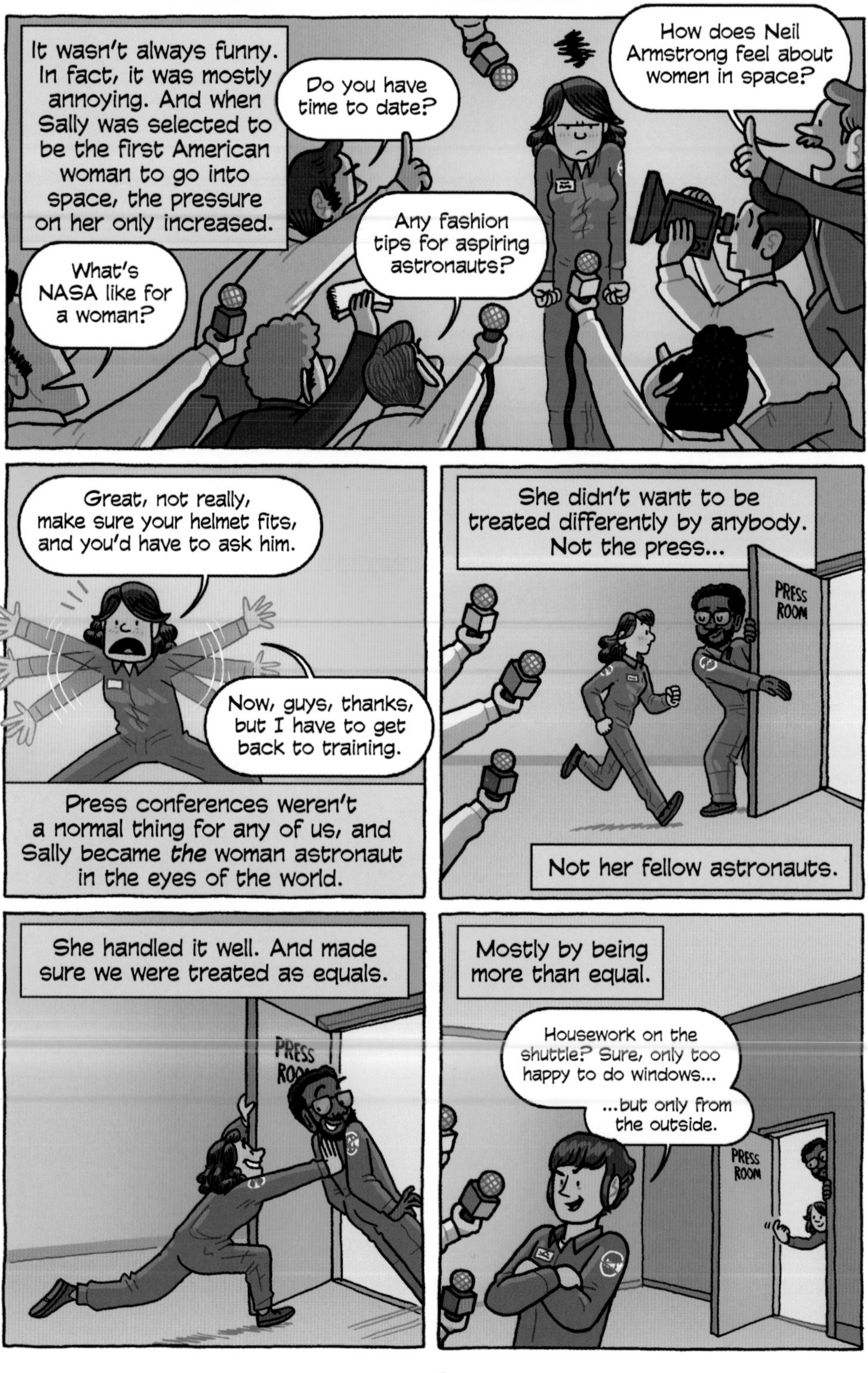
It wasn't always funny. In fact, it was mostly annoying. And when Sally was selected to be the first American woman to go into space, the pressure on her only increased.
Do you have time to date?
How does Neil Armstrong feel about women in space?
Any fashion tips for aspiring astronauts?
What's NASA like for a woman?
Great, not really, make sure your helmet fits, and you'd have to ask him.
Now, guys, thanks, but I have to get back to training.
Press conferences weren't a normal thing for any of us, and Sally became *the* woman astronaut in the eyes of the world.
She didn't want to be treated differently by anybody. Not the press...
PRESS ROOM
Not her fellow astronauts.
She handled it well. And made sure we were treated as equals.
PRESS RO
Mostly by being more than equal.
Housework on the shuttle? Sure, only too happy to do windows...
...but only from the outside.
PRESS ROOM

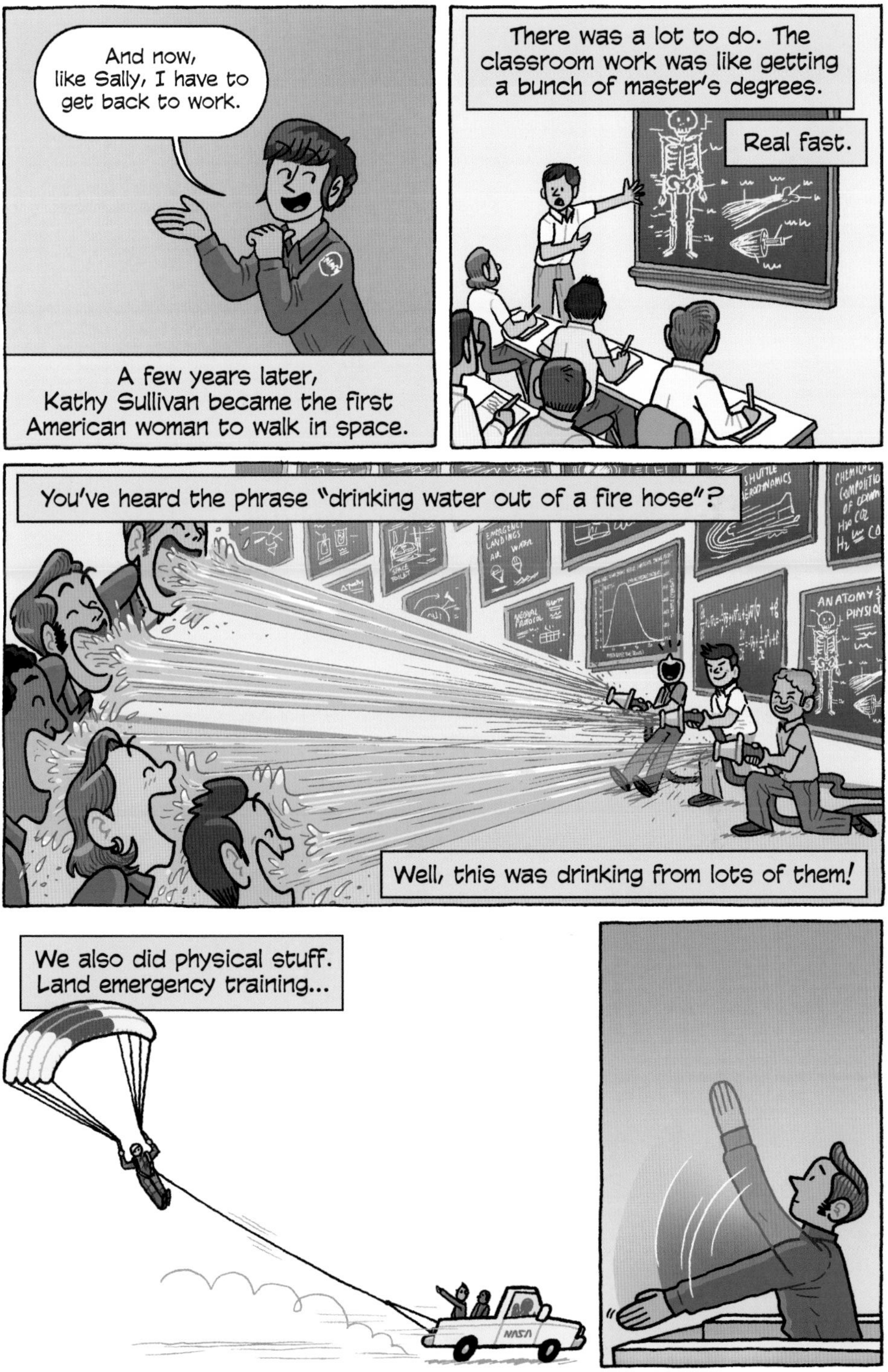
And now, like Sally, I have to get back to work.
A few years later, Kathy Sullivan became the first American woman to walk in space.
There was a lot to do. The classroom work was like getting a bunch of master's degrees.
Real fast.
You've heard the phrase "drinking water out of a fire hose"?
Well, this was drinking from lots of them!
We also did physical stuff. Land emergency training...
NASA

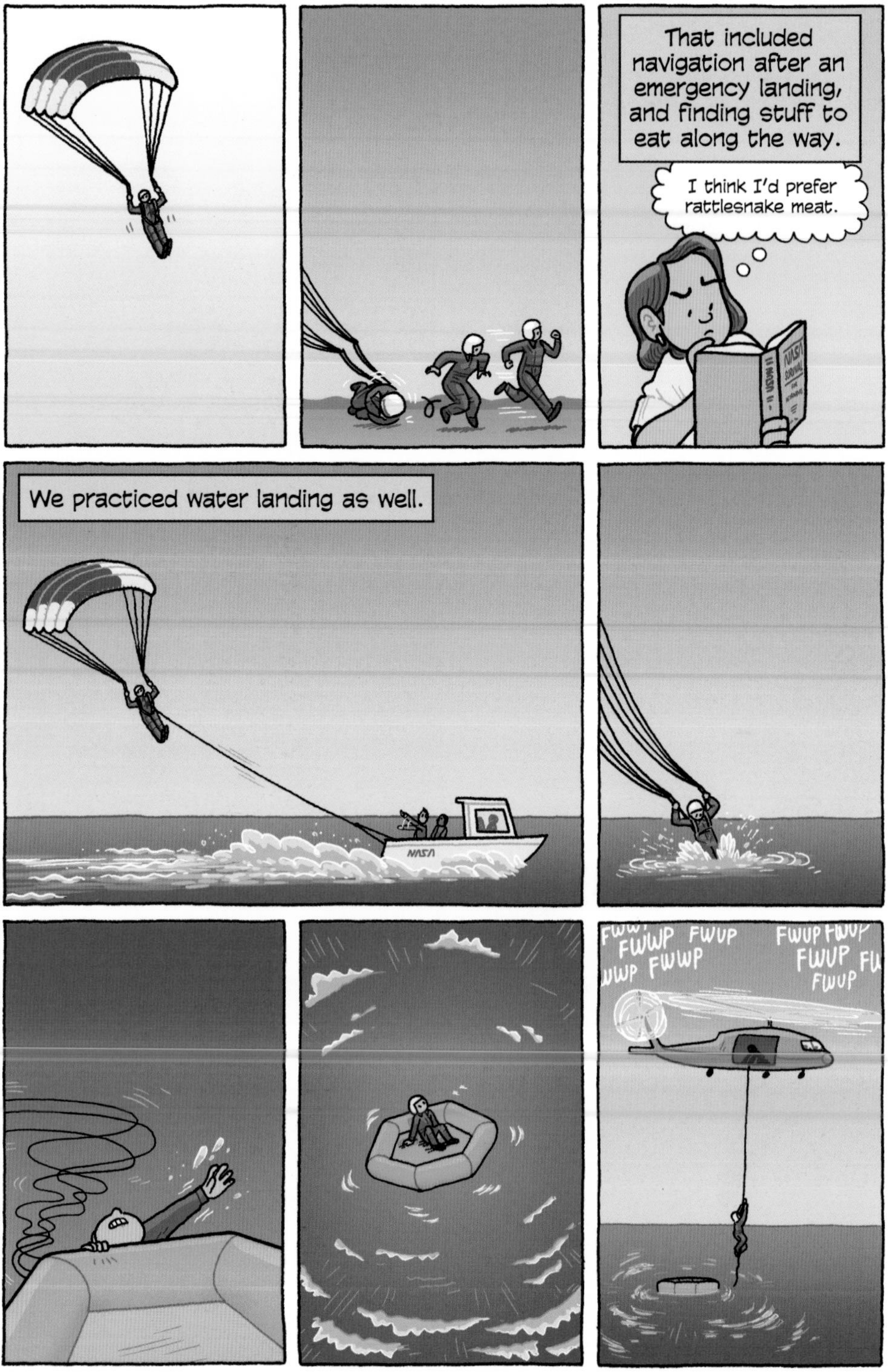

That included navigation after an emergency landing, and finding stuff to eat along the way.
I think I'd prefer rattlesnake meat.
NASA SURVIVAL
We practiced water landing as well.
NASA
FWUP
FWUP
FWUP
FWUP
FWUP
FWUP
FWUP

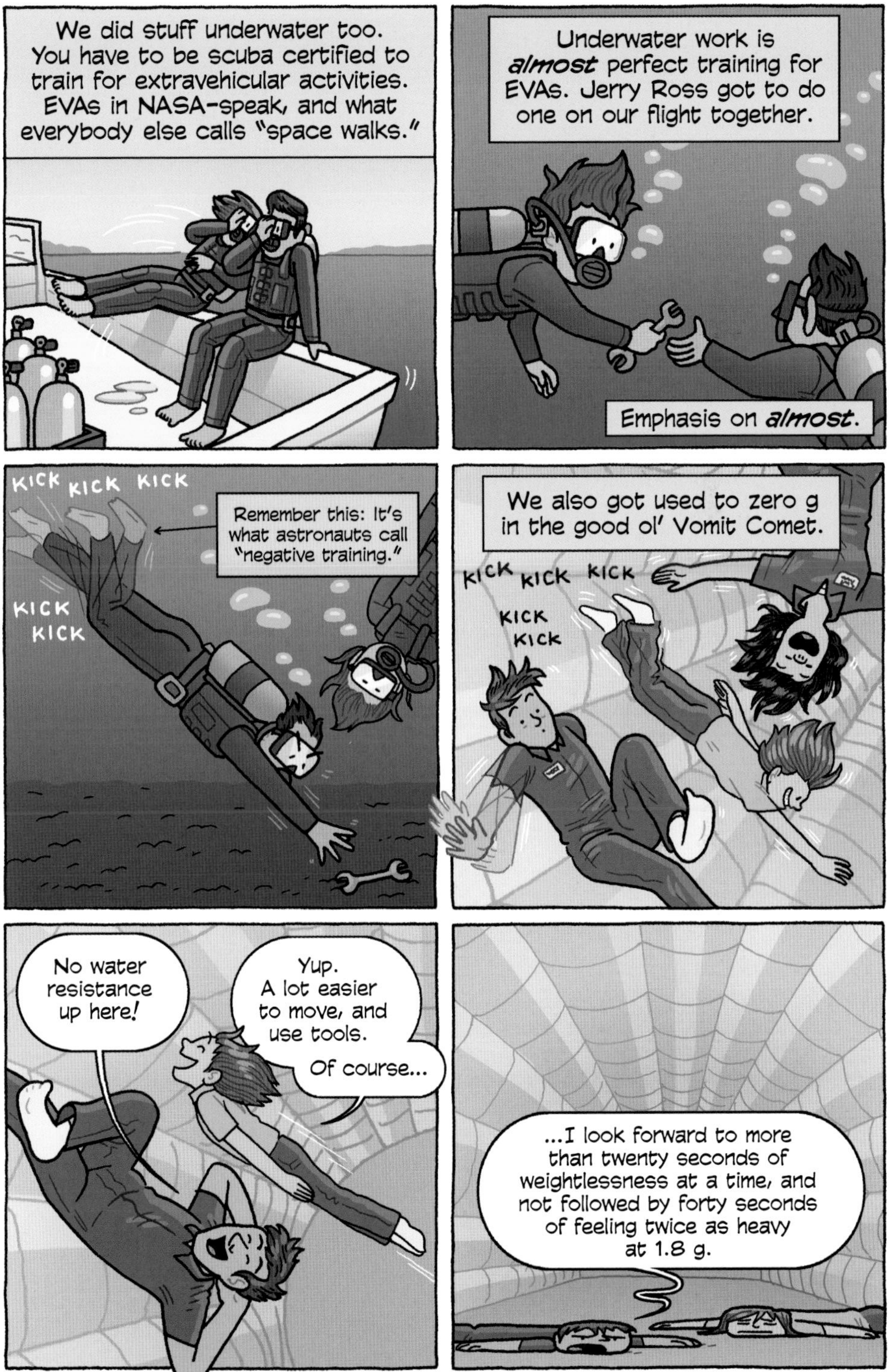
We did stuff underwater too. You have to be scuba certified to train for extravehicular activities. EVAs in NASA-speak, and what everybody else calls "space walks."
Underwater work is *almost* perfect training for EVAs. Jerry Ross got to do one on our flight together.
Emphasis on *almost*.
KICK KICK KICK
KICK KICK
Remember this: It's what astronauts call "negative training."
We also got used to zero g in the good ol' Vomit Comet.
KICK KICK KICK
KICK KICK
No water resistance up here!
Yup. A lot easier to move, and use tools.
Of course...
...I look forward to more than twenty seconds of weightlessness at a time, and not followed by forty seconds of feeling twice as heavy at 1.8 g.

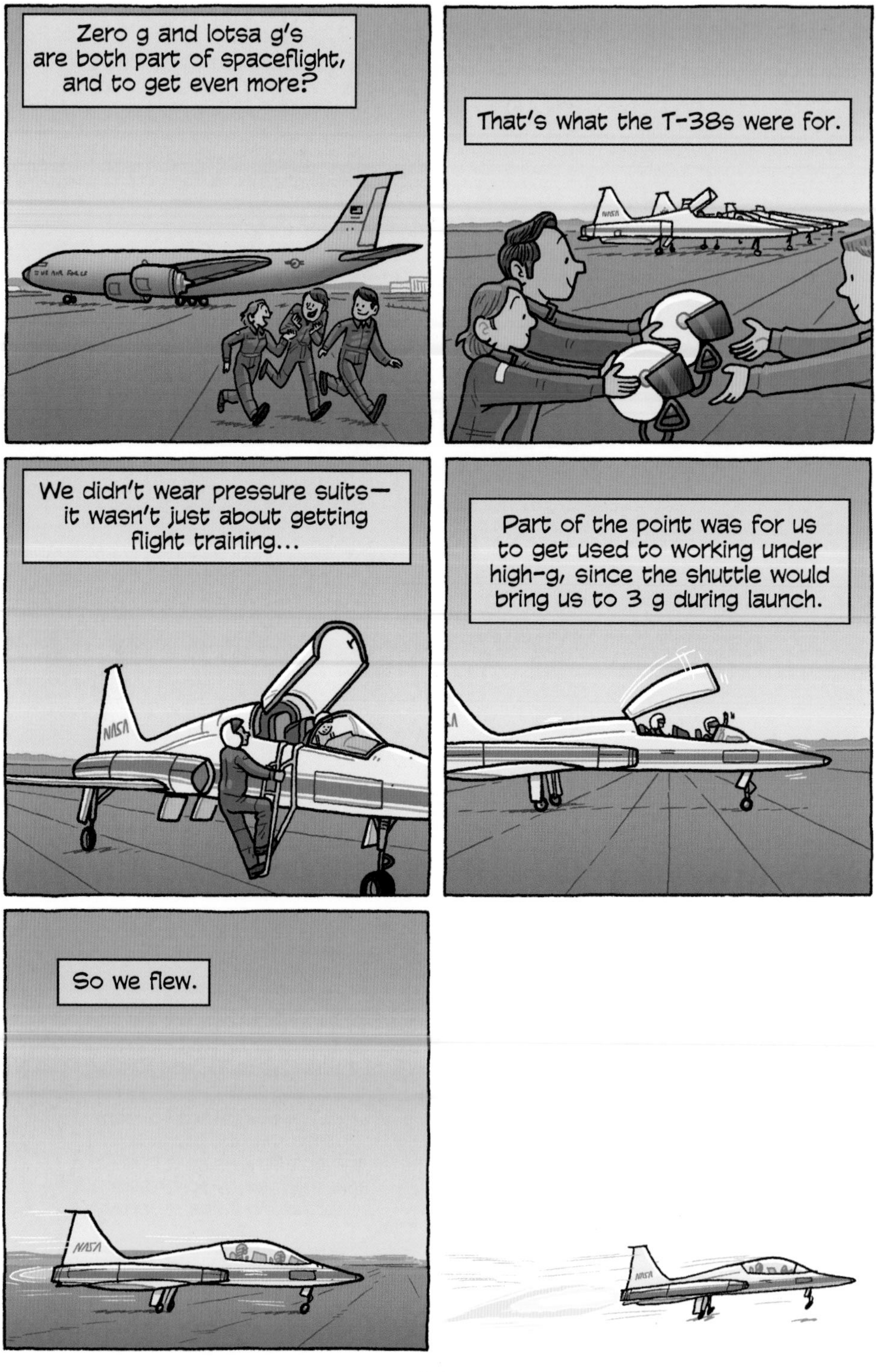
Zero g and lotsa g's
are both part of spaceflight,
and to get even more?
That's what the T-38s were for.
We didn't wear pressure suits—
it wasn't just about getting
flight training...
Part of the point was for us
to get used to working under
high-g, since the shuttle would
bring us to 3 g during launch.
So we flew.

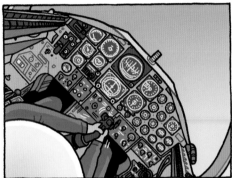

Mach zero-point-six—
g force probably around
two-point-oh.

Air traffic control
has cleared us into
the safe zone.

I'm going to take
the stick and bring us
down to 250 feet.

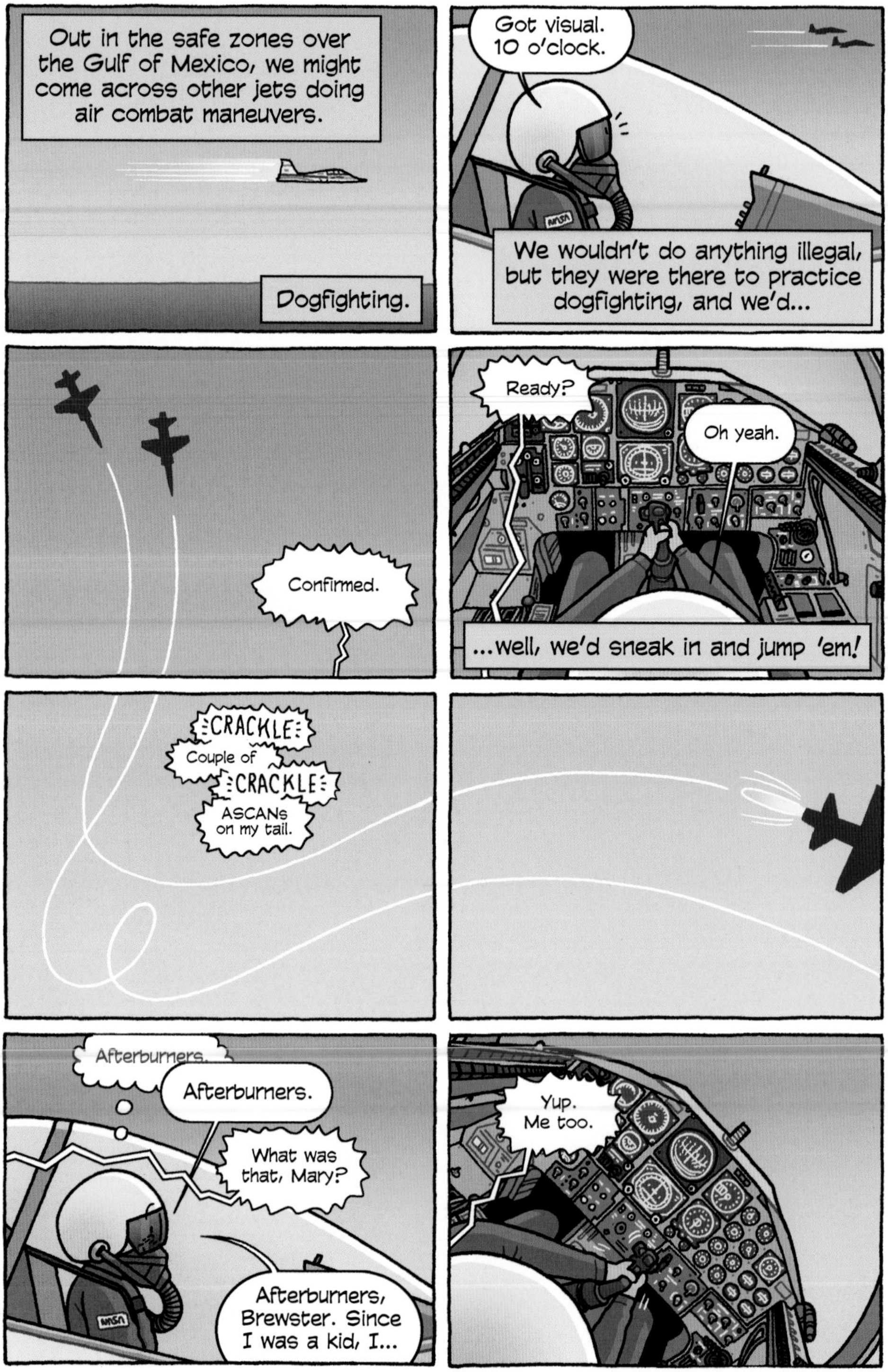
Out in the safe zones over the Gulf of Mexico, we might come across other jets doing air combat maneuvers.
Dogfighting.
Got visual. 10 o'clock.
We wouldn't do anything illegal, but they were there to practice dogfighting, and we'd...
Confirmed.
Ready?
Oh yeah.
...well, we'd sneak in and jump 'em!
CRACKLE
Couple of
CRACKLE
ASCANs on my tail.
Afterburners.
Afterburners.
What was that, Mary?
Afterburners, Brewster. Since I was a kid, I...
Yup. Me too.

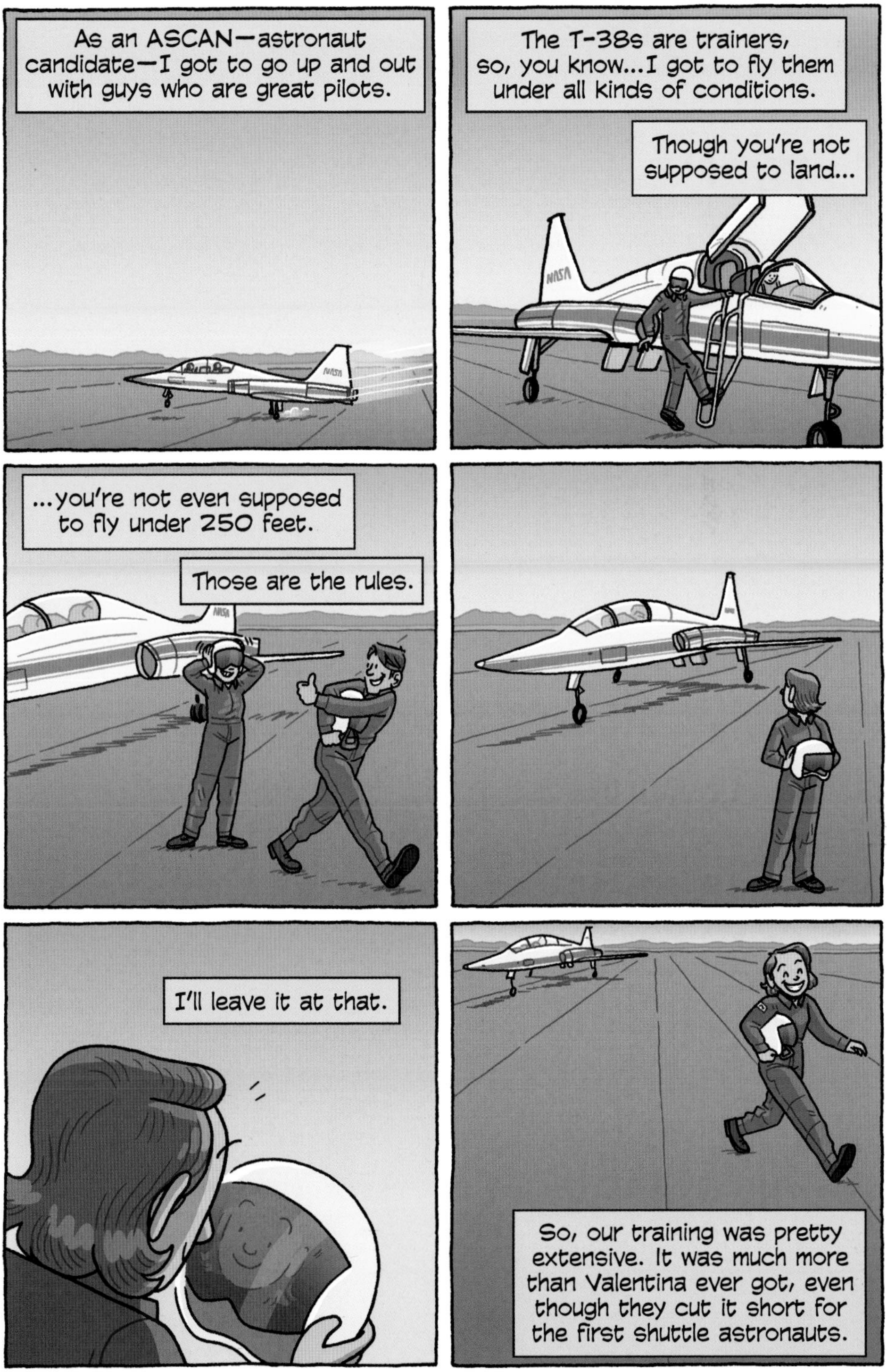
As an ASCAN—astronaut candidate—I got to go up and out with guys who are great pilots.
The T-38s are trainers, so, you know...I got to fly them under all kinds of conditions.
Though you're not supposed to land...
...you're not even supposed to fly under 250 feet.
Those are the rules.
I'll leave it at that.
So, our training was pretty extensive. It was much more than Valentina ever got, even though they cut it short for the first shuttle astronauts.

...cutting it short.

The plan was for two years of training, but there's a lot of work to do, and we need you all to get into the eighteen-month mission flow.

I'm flying the first shuttle, and launch is coming up fast. But mine is just a test flight.

APRIL 1981
STS-1
COMMANDER: YOUNG
PILOT: CRIPPEN

It's time for you all to start getting ready to go on the missions that follow.

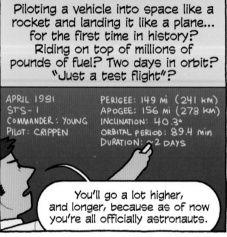

Piloting a vehicle into space like a rocket and landing it like a plane... for the first time in history? Riding on top of millions of pounds of fuel? Two days in orbit? "Just a test flight"?

APRIL 1981
STS-1
COMMANDER: YOUNG
PILOT: CRIPPEN

PERIGEE: 149 mi (241 km)
APOGEE: 156 mi (278 km)
INCLINATION: 40.3°
ORBITAL PERIOD: 89.4 min
DURATION: ~2 DAYS

You'll go a lot higher, and longer, because as of now you're all officially astronauts.

Congratulations.

John was a cool customer, that's for sure.

Your silver pins will be delivered to your offices.

Now get back to work!

He was a great boss too, and we ended up being good friends.

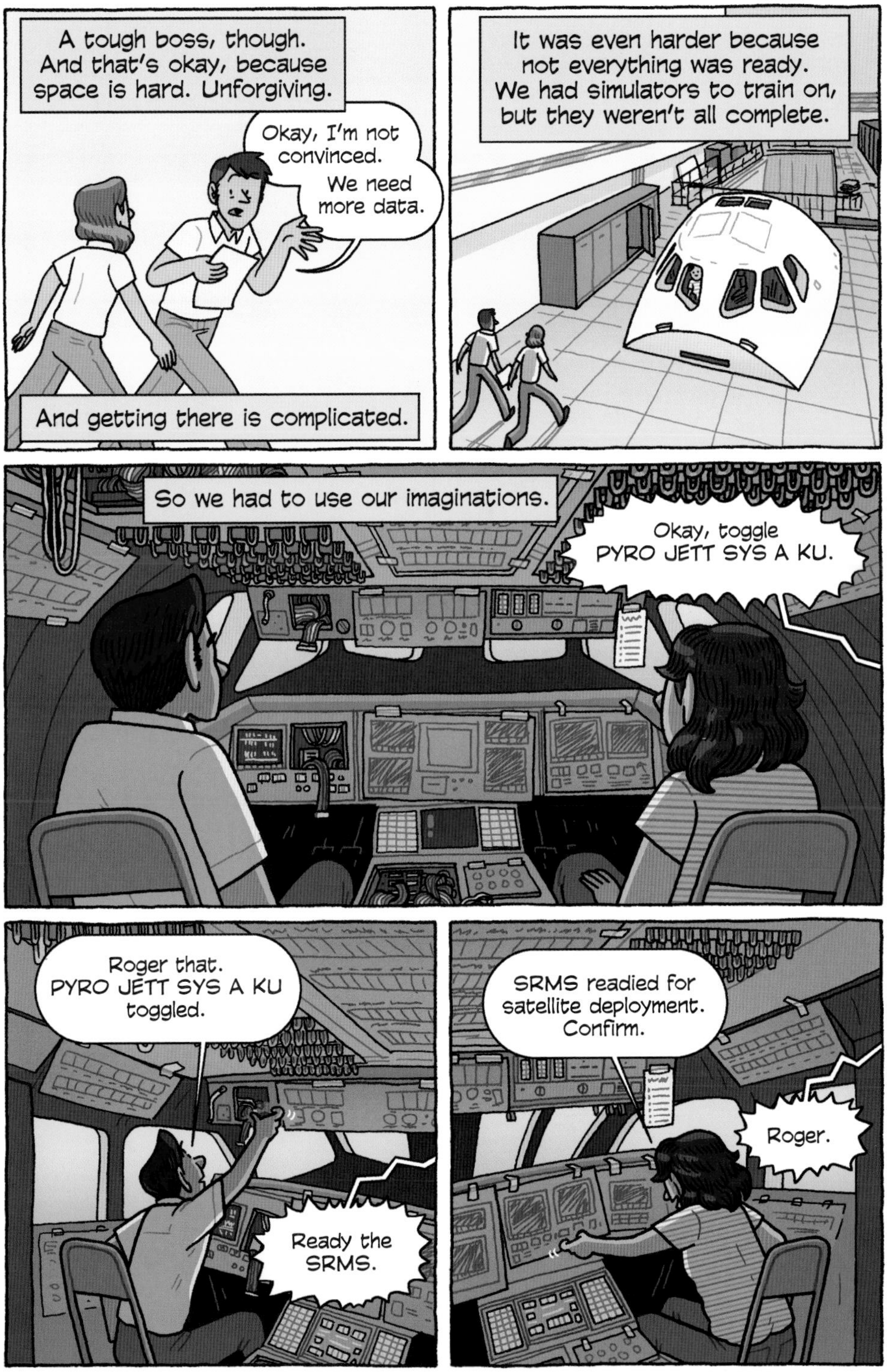
A tough boss, though. And that's okay, because space is hard. Unforgiving.
Okay, I'm not convinced.
We need more data.
And getting there is complicated.
It was even harder because not everything was ready. We had simulators to train on, but they weren't all complete.
So we had to use our imaginations.
Okay, toggle PYRO JETT SYS A KU.
Roger that. PYRO JETT SYS A KU toggled.
Ready the SRMS.
SRMS readied for satellite deployment. Confirm.
Roger.

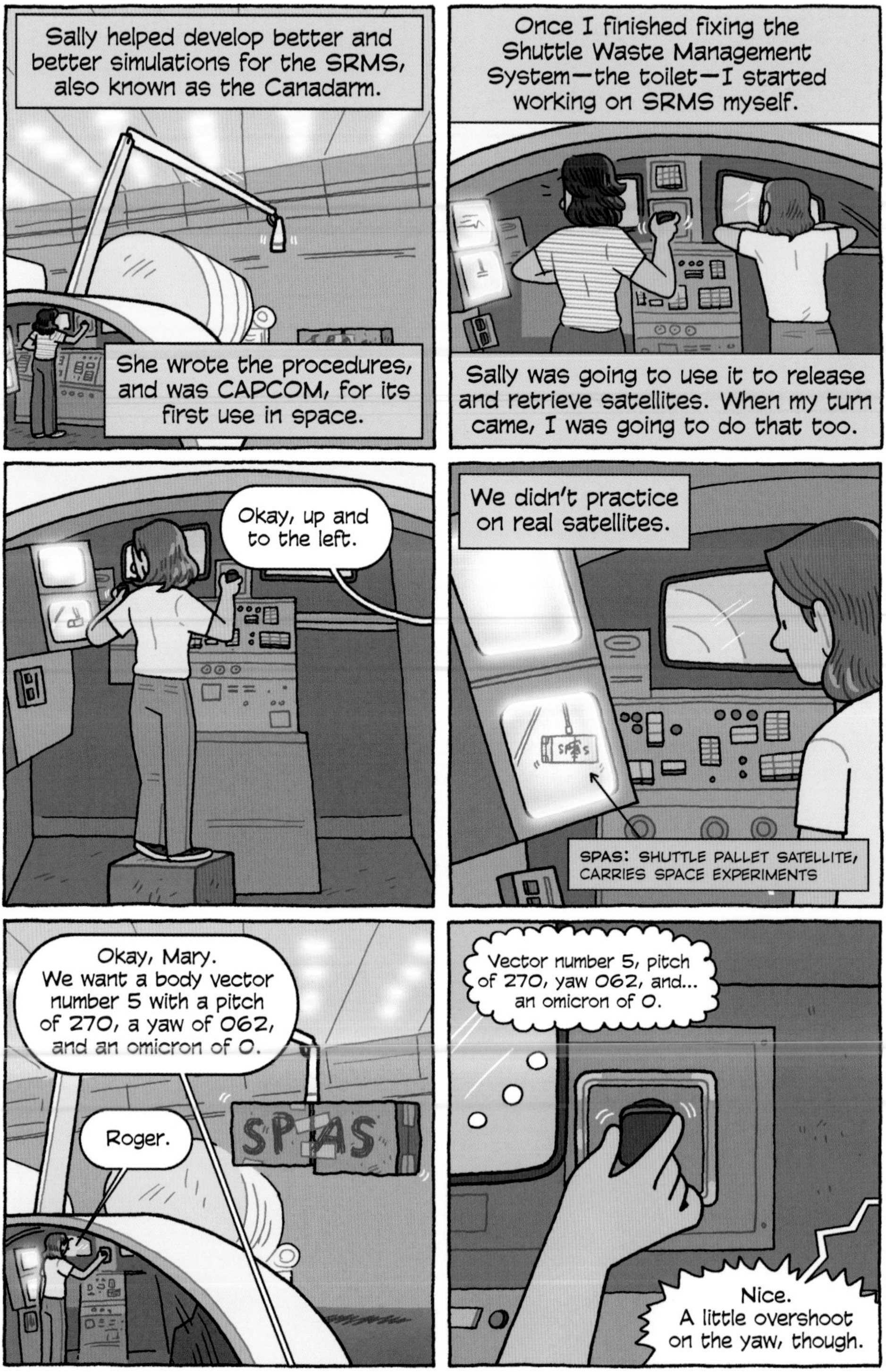
Sally helped develop better and better simulations for the SRMS, also known as the Canadarm.
She wrote the procedures, and was CAPCOM, for its first use in space.
Once I finished fixing the Shuttle Waste Management System—the toilet—I started working on SRMS myself.
Sally was going to use it to release and retrieve satellites. When my turn came, I was going to do that too.
Okay, up and to the left.
We didn't practice on real satellites.
SPAS
SPAS: SHUTTLE PALLET SATELLITE, CARRIES SPACE EXPERIMENTS
Okay, Mary. We want a body vector number 5 with a pitch of 270, a yaw of 062, and an omicron of 0.
SPAS
Roger.
Vector number 5, pitch of 270, yaw 062, and... an omicron of 0.
Nice. A little overshoot on the yaw, though.

Dang it. Let me run that again.

CLONK

SPA

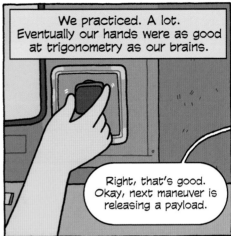

We practiced. A lot. Eventually our hands were as good at trigonometry as our brains.

Right, that's good. Okay, next maneuver is releasing a payload.

Like I said, not everything was ready.

PALAPA: INDONESIAN COMMUNICATIONS SATELLITE

SPAS

PALAPA

Okay, returning to rest position.

Whenever you're ready, Sally.

Not everyone was ready either. At least not right away.

Fellas, this is Alan Bean. Apollo 12, Skylab 3.

PALAPA

The TFNG and my class, Group 9, were fine. Sure, there's always somebody who's gonna have a problem with somebody else, who pushes someone's buttons, who gets on somebody's nerves.

PALAPA

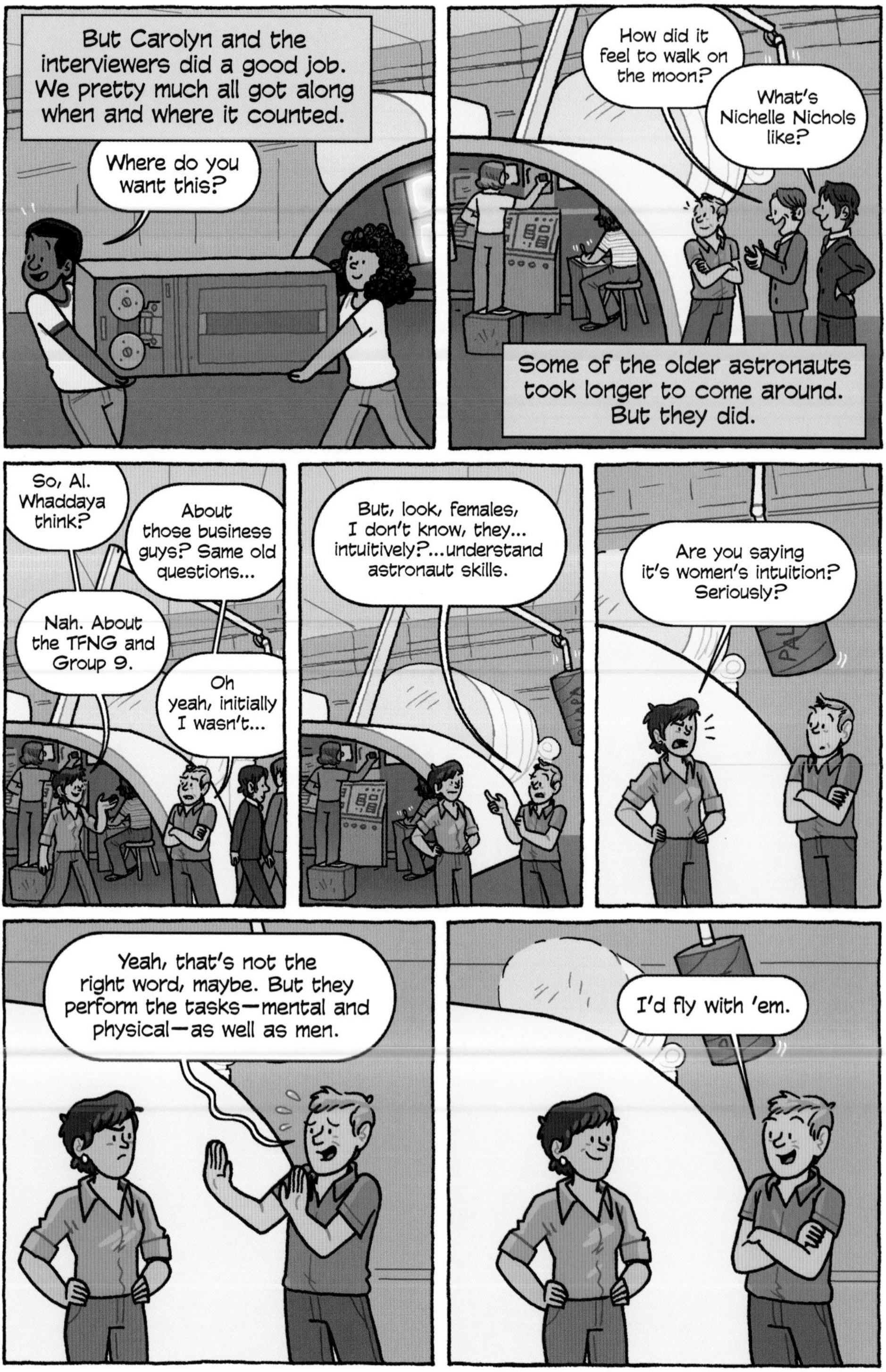
But Carolyn and the interviewers did a good job. We pretty much all got along when and where it counted.
Where do you want this?
How did it feel to walk on the moon?
What's Nichelle Nichols like?
Some of the older astronauts took longer to come around. But they did.
So, Al. Whaddaya think?
About those business guys? Same old questions...
Nah. About the TFNG and Group 9.
Oh yeah, initially I wasn't...
But, look, females, I don't know, they... intuitively?...understand astronaut skills.
Are you saying it's women's intuition? Seriously?
Yeah, that's not the right word, maybe. But they perform the tasks—mental and physical—as well as men.
I'd fly with 'em.

We were a team. And as crew assignments came down, smaller teams formed within the big one as well.

We all brought something to the program. Even the old guys and military pilots saw this.

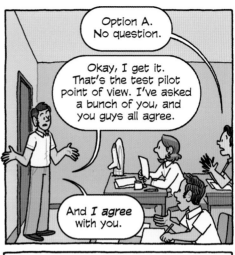

Option A. No question.

Okay, I get it. That's the test pilot point of view. I've asked a bunch of you, and you guys all agree.

And *I agree* with you.

And maybe it's because we're right. But maybe it's because we're all ex-military. Or test pilots.

Thing is, we're flying a *spaceship* now, not a capsule shoved into space from behind by a rocket.

And the point isn't just to fly this thing. Shuttle missions are going to be longer, we're going to have mission specialists on 'em doing lab experiments, building stuff.

Yeah, I get it.

Gender and race? Not important. Different backgrounds? Mission critical.

So fifteen test pilots all coming up with the same answer is not a good thing. Complicated missions need...

...diversity of thinking.

I don't know much about the biology here. Heck, I didn't even know how to dress myself until coming to NASA.

So, is this even going to work?

Actually, Rhea can answer that better than me. She's the medical doc—I'm just a PhD.

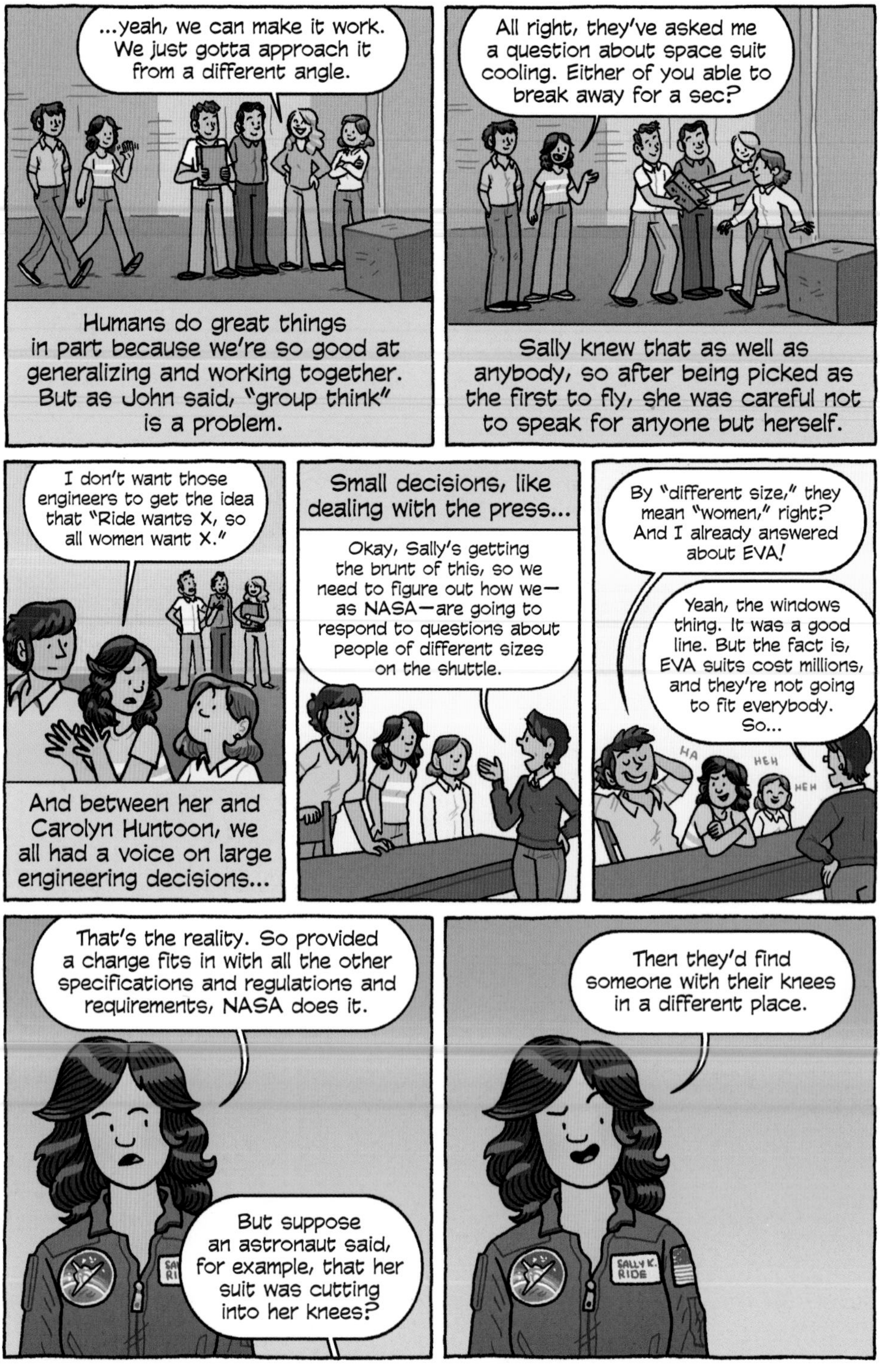
...yeah, we can make it work. We just gotta approach it from a different angle.
Humans do great things in part because we're so good at generalizing and working together. But as John said, "group think" is a problem.
All right, they've asked me a question about space suit cooling. Either of you able to break away for a sec?
Sally knew that as well as anybody, so after being picked as the first to fly, she was careful not to speak for anyone but herself.
I don't want those engineers to get the idea that "Ride wants X, so all women want X."
And between her and Carolyn Huntoon, we all had a voice on large engineering decisions...
Small decisions, like dealing with the press...
Okay, Sally's getting the brunt of this, so we need to figure out how we—as NASA—are going to respond to questions about people of different sizes on the shuttle.
By "different size," they mean "women," right? And I already answered about EVA!
Yeah, the windows thing. It was a good line. But the fact is, EVA suits cost millions, and they're not going to fit everybody. So...
HA
HEH
HEH
That's the reality. So provided a change fits in with all the other specifications and regulations and requirements, NASA does it.
But suppose an astronaut said, for example, that her suit was cutting into her knees?
Then they'd find someone with their knees in a different place.
SALLY K. RIDE

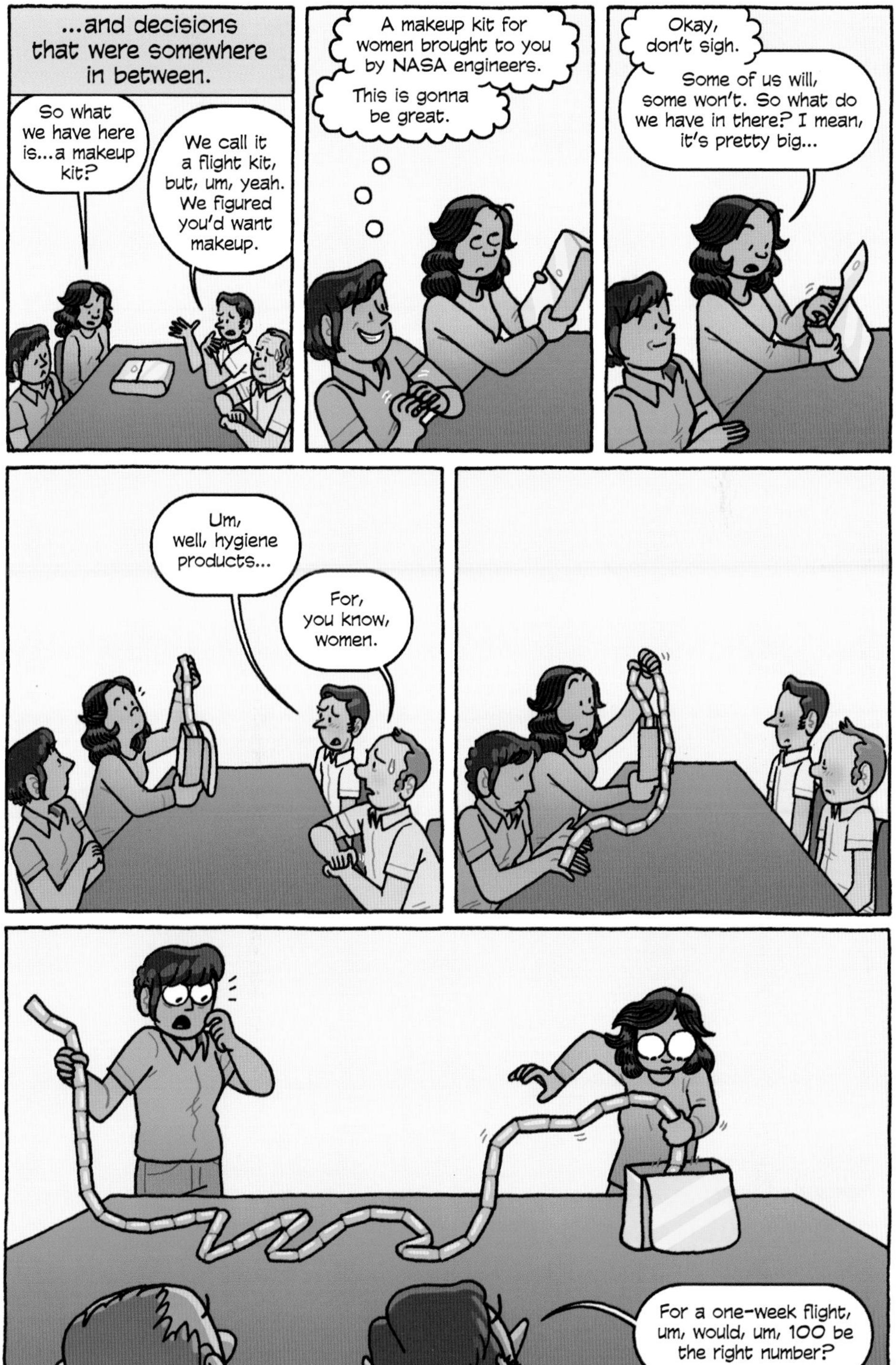
...and decisions that were somewhere in between.
So what we have here is...a makeup kit?
We call it a flight kit, but, um, yeah. We figured you'd want makeup.
A makeup kit for women brought to you by NASA engineers.
This is gonna be great.
Okay, don't sigh.
Some of us will, some won't. So what do we have in there? I mean, it's pretty big...
Um, well, hygiene products...
For, you know, women.
For a one-week flight, um, would, um, 100 be the right number?

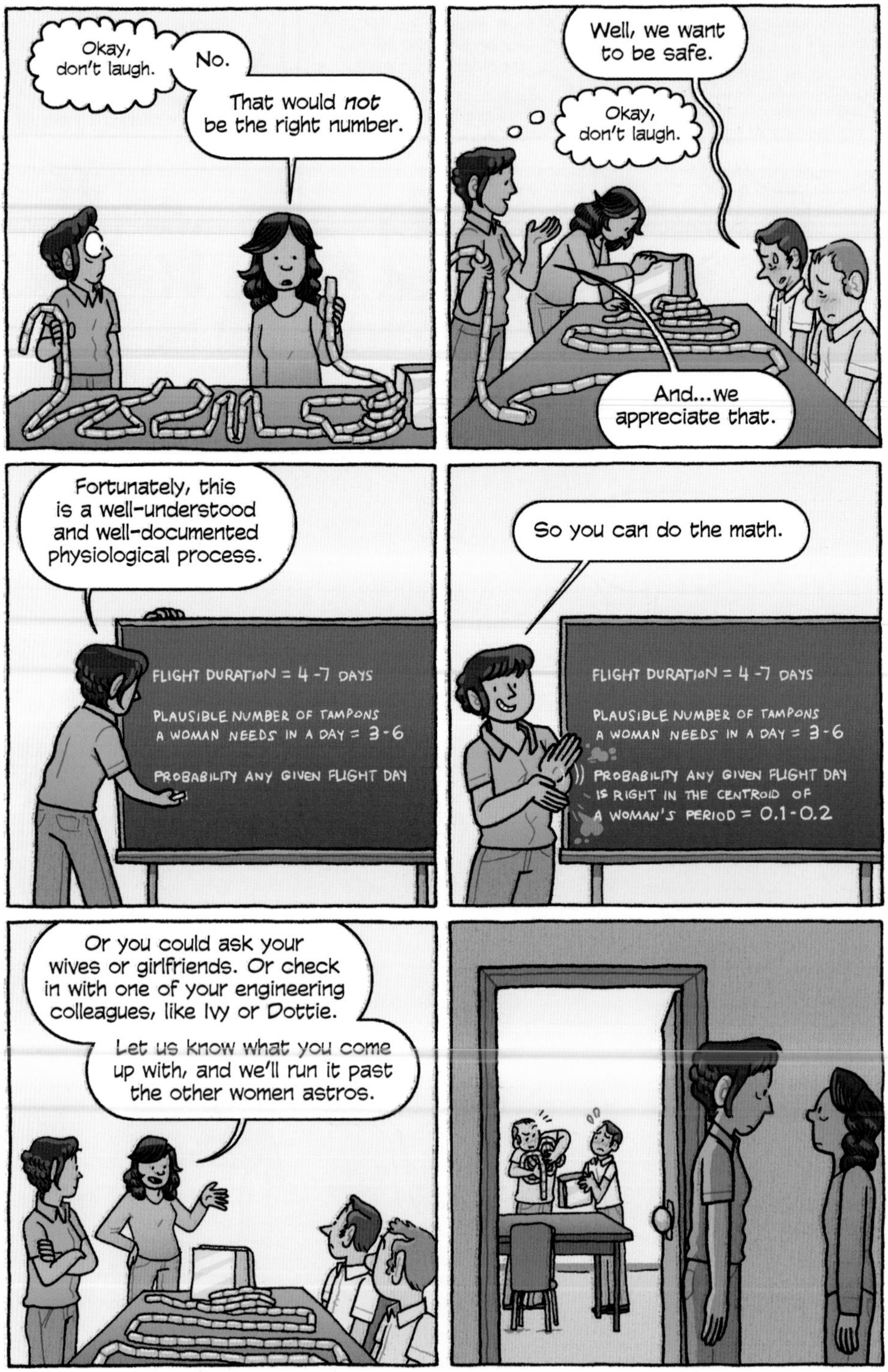
Okay, don't laugh.
No.
That would *not* be the right number.
Well, we want to be safe.
Okay, don't laugh.
And...we appreciate that.
Fortunately, this is a well-understood and well-documented physiological process.
FLIGHT DURATION = 4-7 DAYS
PLAUSIBLE NUMBER OF TAMPONS A WOMAN NEEDS IN A DAY = 3-6
PROBABILITY ANY GIVEN FLIGHT DAY
So you can do the math.
FLIGHT DURATION = 4-7 DAYS
PLAUSIBLE NUMBER OF TAMPONS A WOMAN NEEDS IN A DAY = 3-6
PROBABILITY ANY GIVEN FLIGHT DAY IS RIGHT IN THE CENTROID OF A WOMAN'S PERIOD = 0.1-0.2
Or you could ask your wives or girlfriends. Or check in with one of your engineering colleagues, like Ivy or Dottie.
Let us know what you come up with, and we'll run it past the other women astros.

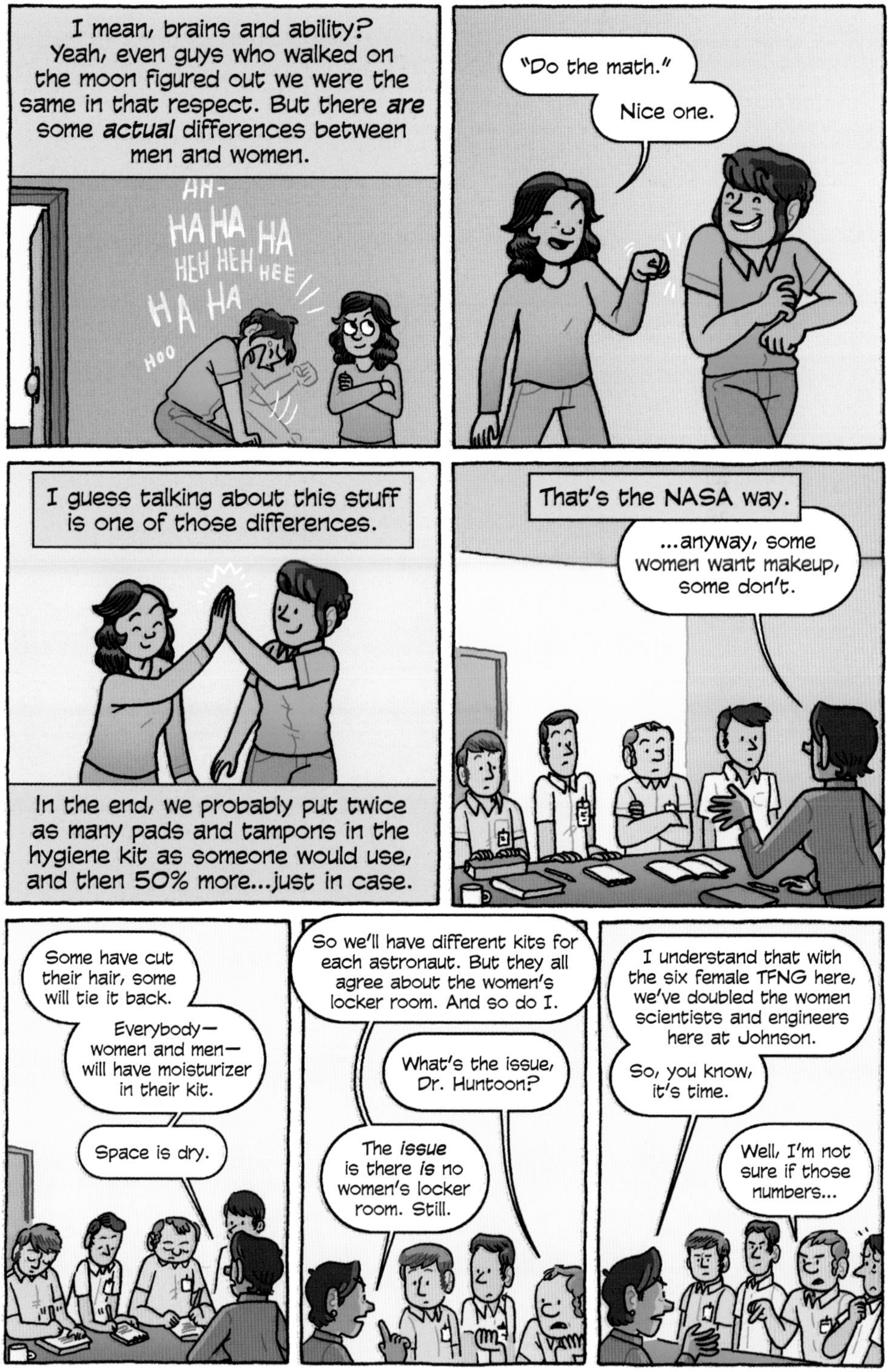
I mean, brains and ability? Yeah, even guys who walked on the moon figured out we were the same in that respect. But there *are* some *actual* differences between men and women.
AH-
HA HA HA
HEH HEH HEE
HA HA
HOO
"Do the math."
Nice one.
I guess talking about this stuff is one of those differences.
In the end, we probably put twice as many pads and tampons in the hygiene kit as someone would use, and then 50% more...just in case.
That's the NASA way.
...anyway, some women want makeup, some don't.
Some have cut their hair, some will tie it back.
Everybody—women and men—will have moisturizer in their kit.
Space is dry.
So we'll have different kits for each astronaut. But they all agree about the women's locker room. And so do I.
What's the issue, Dr. Huntoon?
The *issue* is there *is* no women's locker room. Still.
I understand that with the six female TFNG here, we've doubled the women scientists and engineers here at Johnson.
So, you know, it's time.
Well, I'm not sure if those numbers...

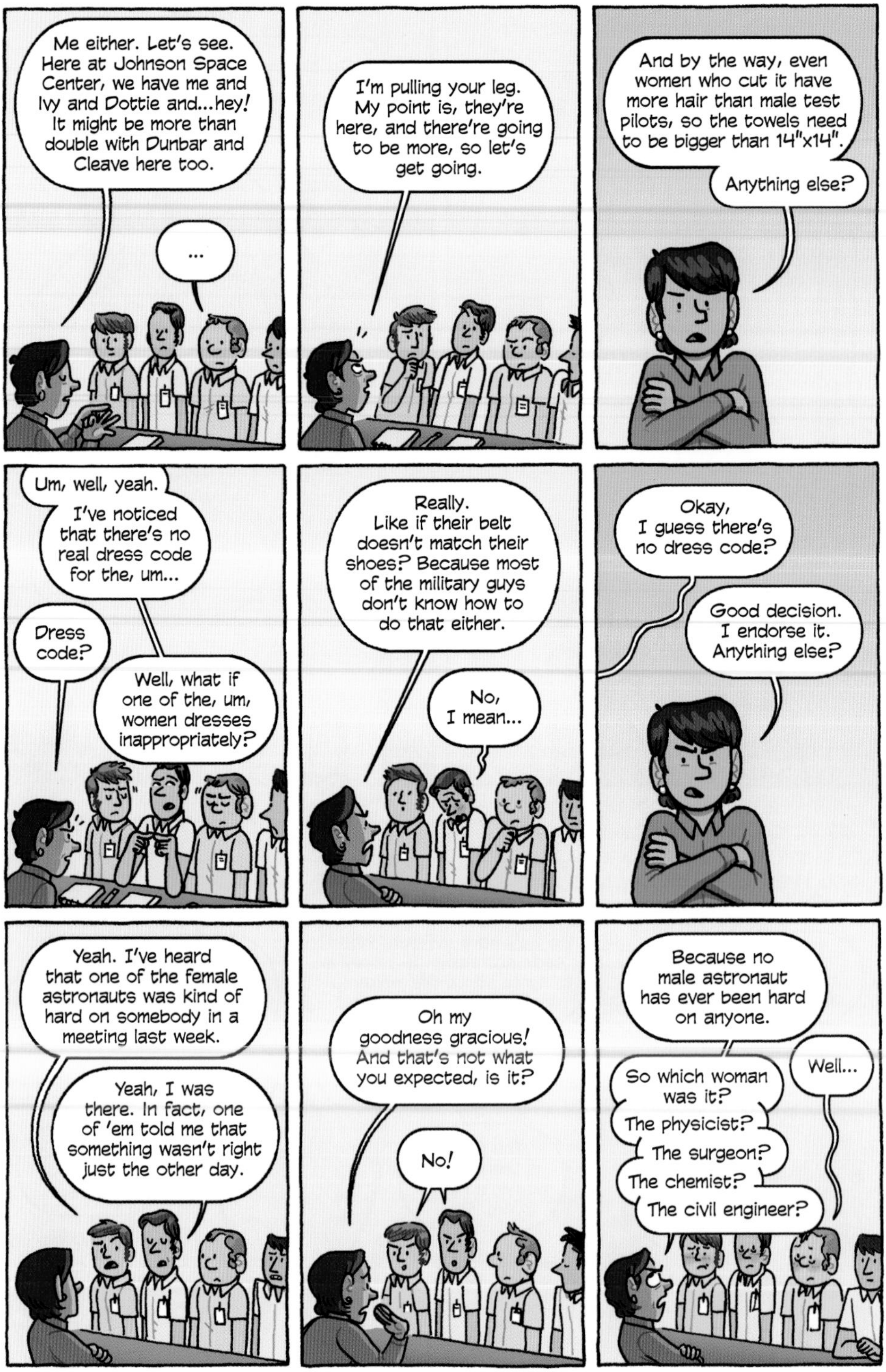
Me either. Let's see. Here at Johnson Space Center, we have me and Ivy and Dottie and...hey! It might be more than double with Dunbar and Cleave here too.
...
I'm pulling your leg. My point is, they're here, and there're going to be more, so let's get going.
And by the way, even women who cut it have more hair than male test pilots, so the towels need to be bigger than 14"x14".
Anything else?
Um, well, yeah.
I've noticed that there's no real dress code for the, um...
Dress code?
Well, what if one of the, um, women dresses inappropriately?
Really. Like if their belt doesn't match their shoes? Because most of the military guys don't know how to do that either.
No, I mean...
Okay, I guess there's no dress code?
Good decision. I endorse it. Anything else?
Yeah. I've heard that one of the female astronauts was kind of hard on somebody in a meeting last week.
Yeah, I was there. In fact, one of 'em told me that something wasn't right just the other day.
Oh my goodness gracious! And that's not what you expected, is it?
No!
Because no male astronaut has ever been hard on anyone.
So which woman was it?
The physicist?
The surgeon?
The chemist?
The civil engineer?
Well...

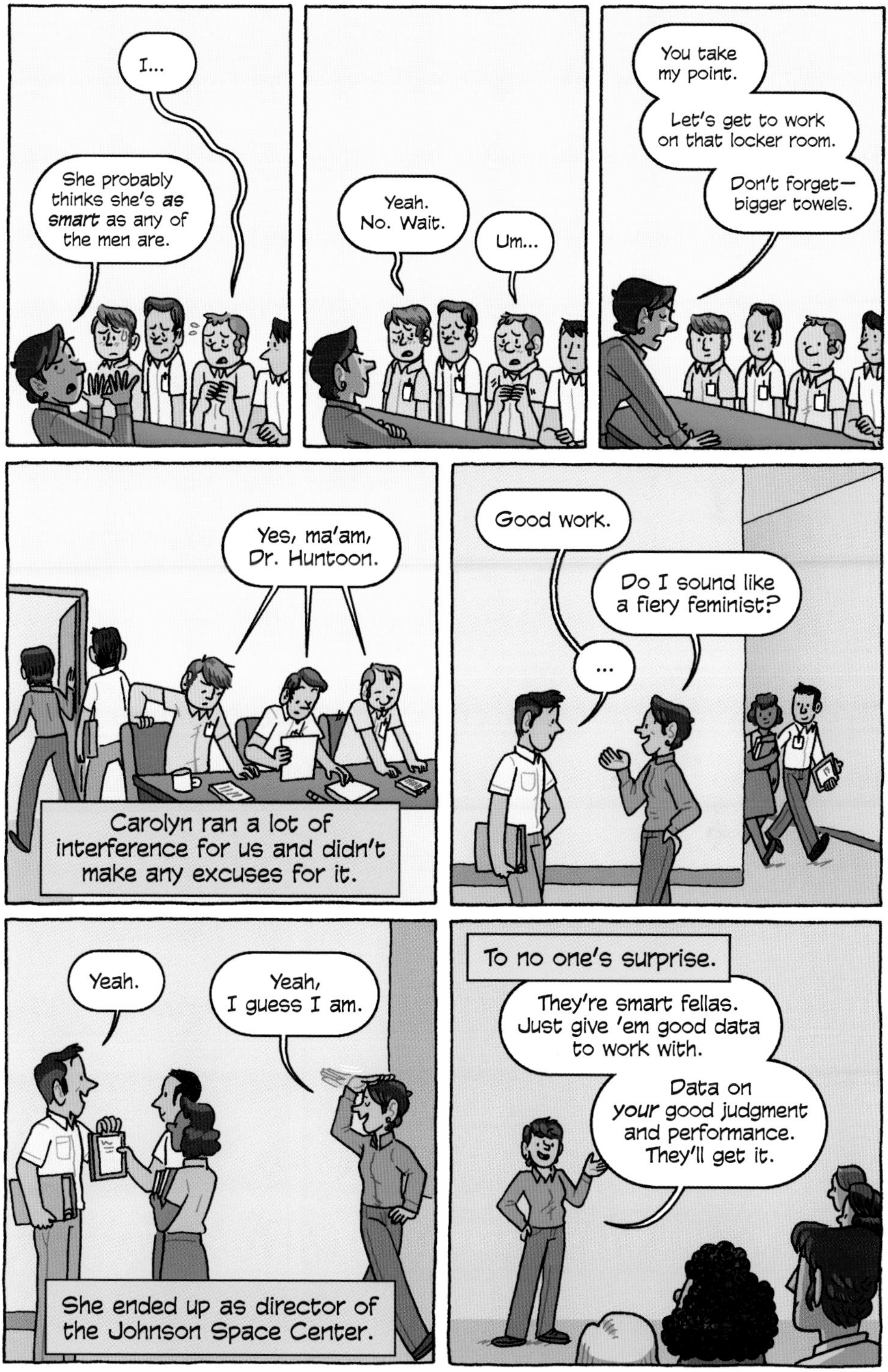
I...
She probably thinks she's ***as smart*** as any of the men are.
Yeah. No. Wait.
Um...
You take my point.
Let's get to work on that locker room.
Don't forget—bigger towels.
Yes, ma'am, Dr. Huntoon.
Carolyn ran a lot of interference for us and didn't make any excuses for it.
Good work.
Do I sound like a fiery feminist?
...
Yeah.
Yeah, I guess I am.
She ended up as director of the Johnson Space Center.
To no one's surprise.
They're smart fellas. Just give 'em good data to work with.
Data on *your* good judgment and performance. They'll get it.

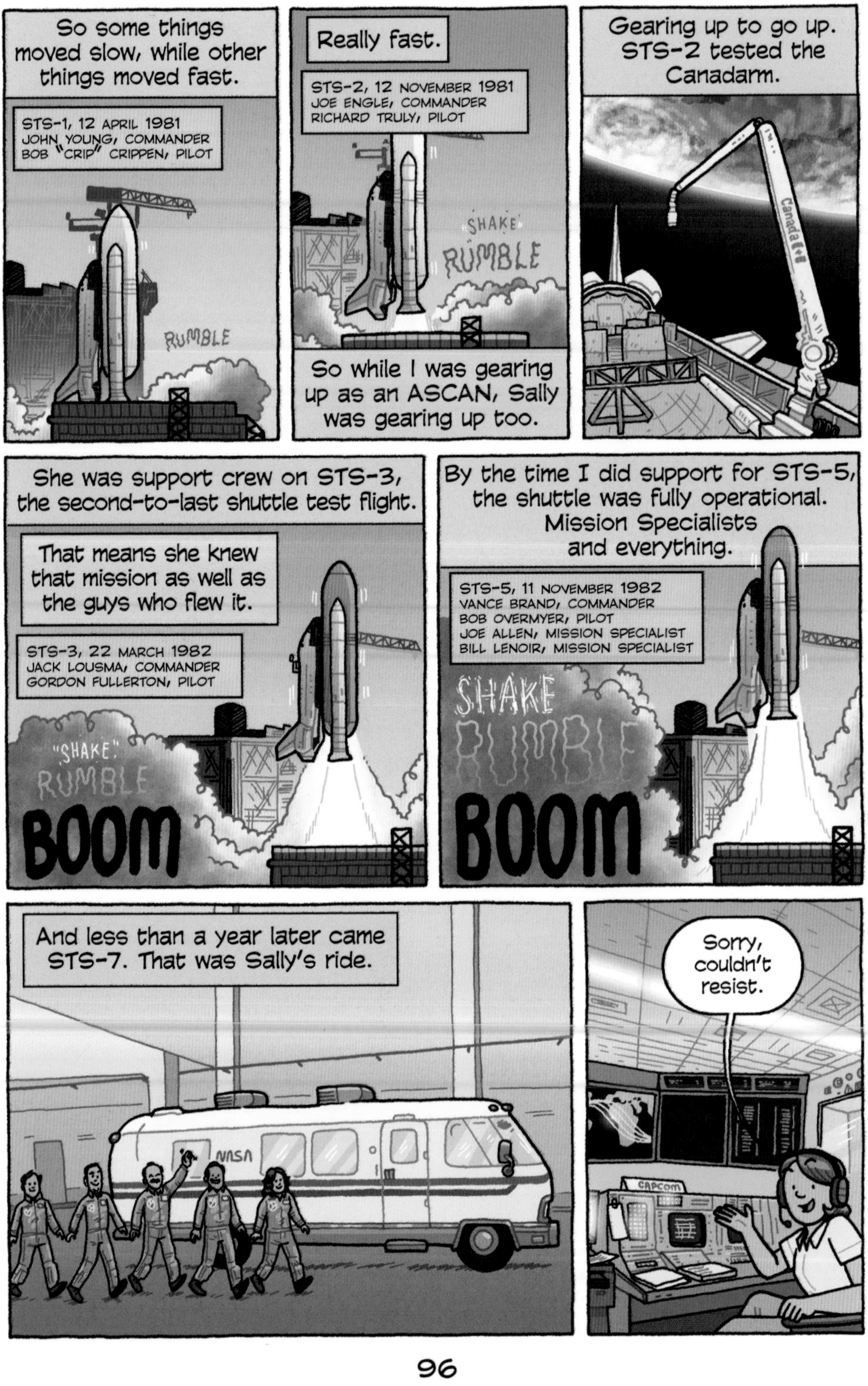
So some things moved slow, while other things moved fast.
STS-1, 12 APRIL 1981
JOHN YOUNG, COMMANDER
BOB "CRIP" CRIPPEN, PILOT
RUMBLE
Really fast.
STS-2, 12 NOVEMBER 1981
JOE ENGLE, COMMANDER
RICHARD TRULY, PILOT
SHAKE
RUMBLE
So while I was gearing up as an ASCAN, Sally was gearing up too.
Gearing up to go up. STS-2 tested the Canadarm.
Canada
She was support crew on STS-3, the second-to-last shuttle test flight.
That means she knew that mission as well as the guys who flew it.
STS-3, 22 MARCH 1982
JACK LOUSMA, COMMANDER
GORDON FULLERTON, PILOT
"SHAKE"
RUMBLE
BOOM
By the time I did support for STS-5, the shuttle was fully operational. Mission Specialists and everything.
STS-5, 11 NOVEMBER 1982
VANCE BRAND, COMMANDER
BOB OVERMYER, PILOT
JOE ALLEN, MISSION SPECIALIST
BILL LENOIR, MISSION SPECIALIST
SHAKE
RUMBLE
BOOM
And less than a year later came STS-7. That was Sally's ride.
NASA
Sorry, couldn't resist.
CAPCOM

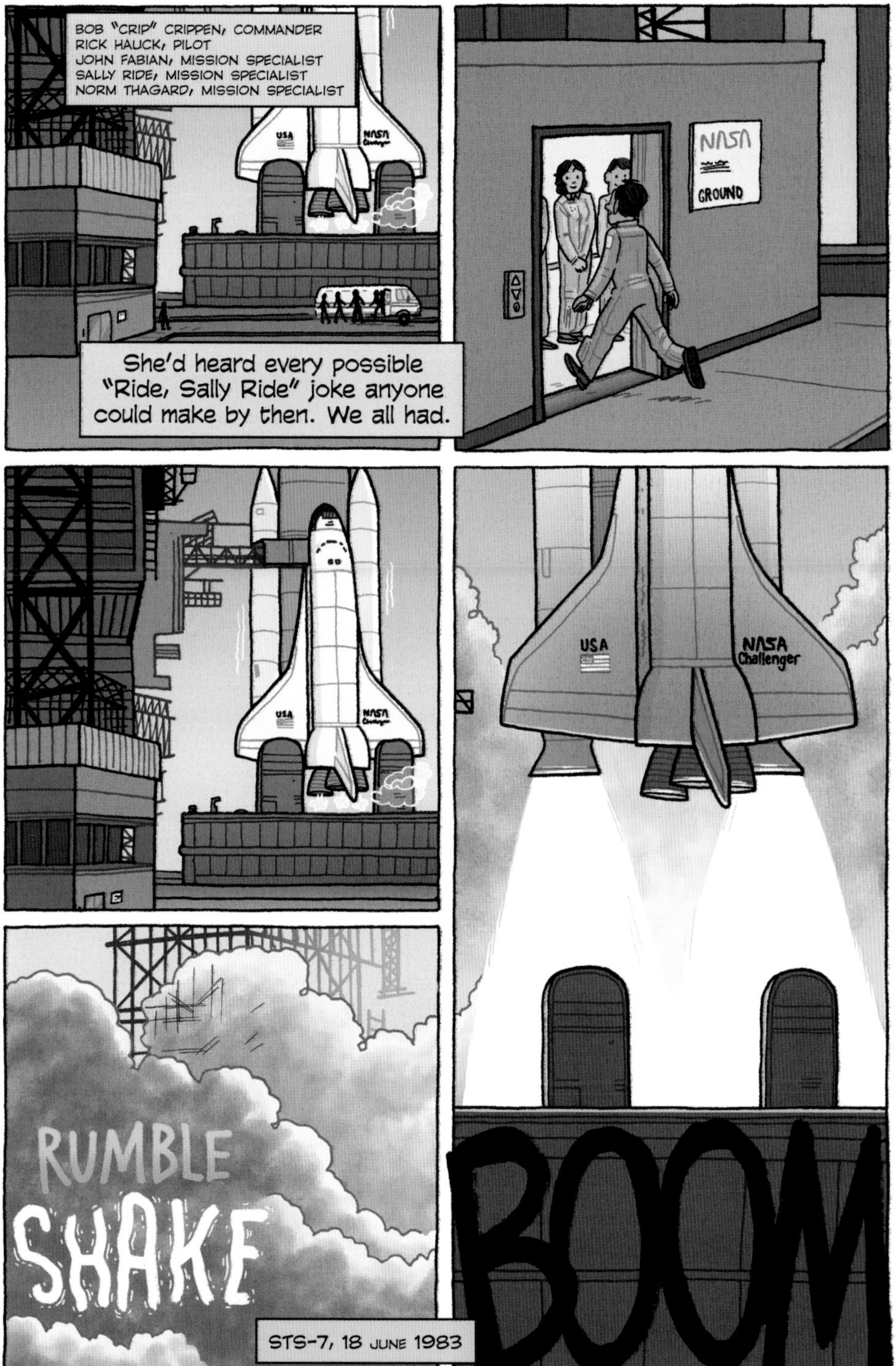
BOB "CRIP" CRIPPEN, COMMANDER
RICK HAUCK, PILOT
JOHN FABIAN, MISSION SPECIALIST
SALLY RIDE, MISSION SPECIALIST
NORM THAGARD, MISSION SPECIALIST
USA
NASA Challenger
She'd heard every possible "Ride, Sally Ride" joke anyone could make by then. We all had.
NASA
GROUND
USA
NASA Challenger
USA
NASA Challenger
RUMBLE
SHAKE
STS-7, 18 JUNE 1983
BOOM

I was a CAPCOM for Sally's flight.

CAPCOM stands for "capsule communicator," an abbreviation from back in the 1960s when spacecraft were capsules.

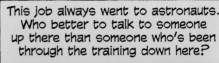

This job always went to astronauts. Who better to talk to someone up there than someone who's been through the training down here?

Double check that, would ya, please?

They had a long day, and I don't want to disturb their sleep period if we don't have to.

It turns out that not only was Sally the first U.S. woman in space, but with me on the other end of the comm link, it was the first time a woman talked to another woman up in orbit.

Okay.

Good evening, Sally. Sorry to wake you up.

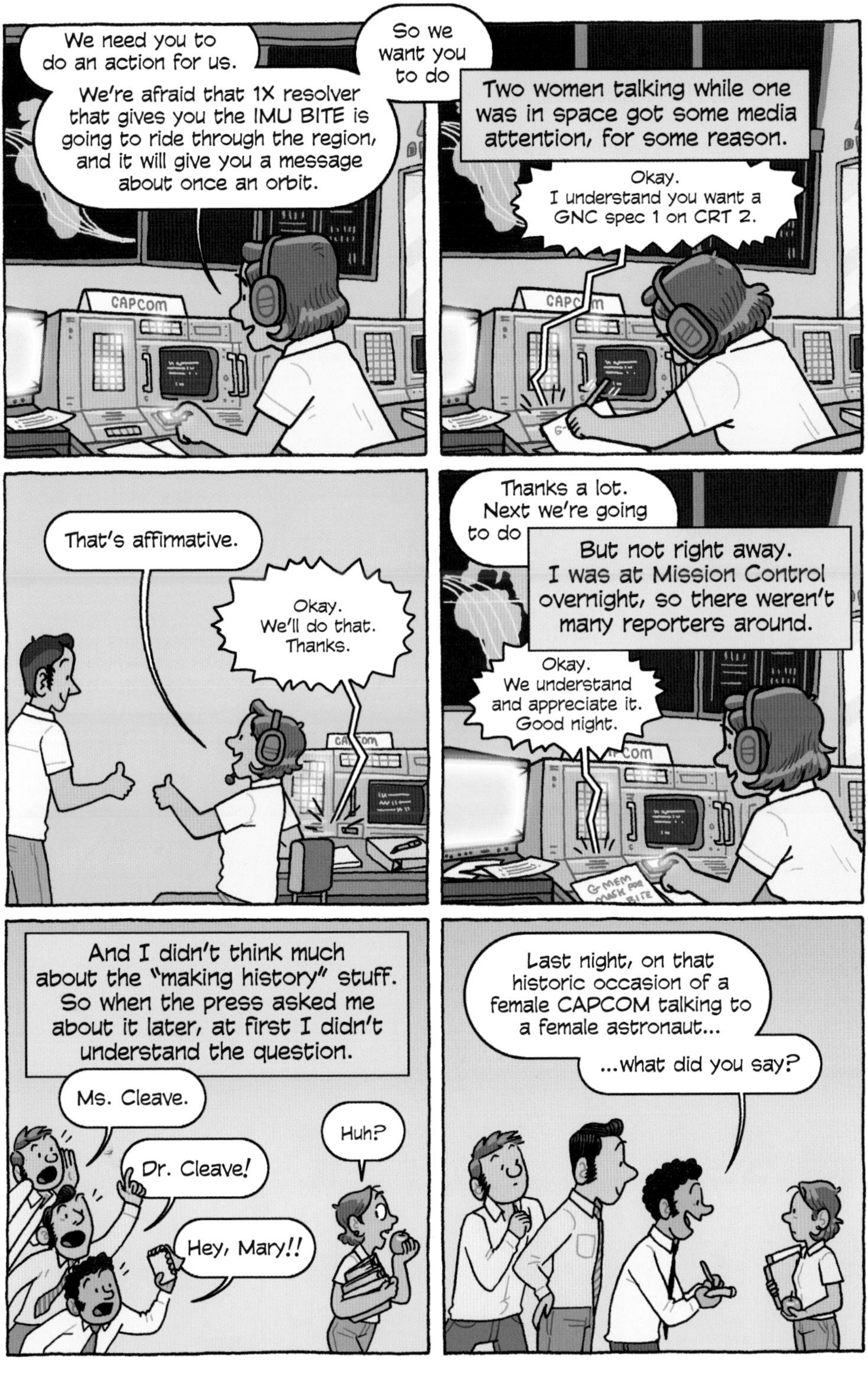
We need you to do an action for us.
We're afraid that 1X resolver that gives you the IMU BITE is going to ride through the region, and it will give you a message about once an orbit.
So we want you to do
Two women talking while one was in space got some media attention, for some reason.
Okay. I understand you want a GNC spec 1 on CRT 2.
CAPCOM
That's affirmative.
Okay. We'll do that. Thanks.
Thanks a lot. Next we're going to do
But not right away. I was at Mission Control overnight, so there weren't many reporters around.
Okay. We understand and appreciate it. Good night.
And I didn't think much about the "making history" stuff. So when the press asked me about it later, at first I didn't understand the question.
Ms. Cleave.
Dr. Cleave!
Hey, Mary!!
Huh?
Last night, on that historic occasion of a female CAPCOM talking to a female astronaut...
...what did you say?

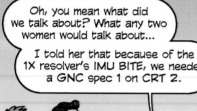

Oh, you mean what did we talk about? What any two women would talk about...

I told her that because of the 1X resolver's IMU BITE, we needed a GNC spec 1 on CRT 2.

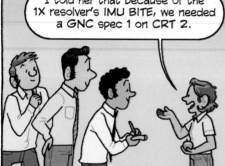

What kind of gizmo is a 1X resolver?

Wha—?

"Why say *that* on such a momentous occasion?" you might ask. And it's a good question.

Once the woman up there—Sally— did that, the woman down here—me—could G-MEM a mask for it.

Huh?

CRUNCH

So... you know. Girl talk.

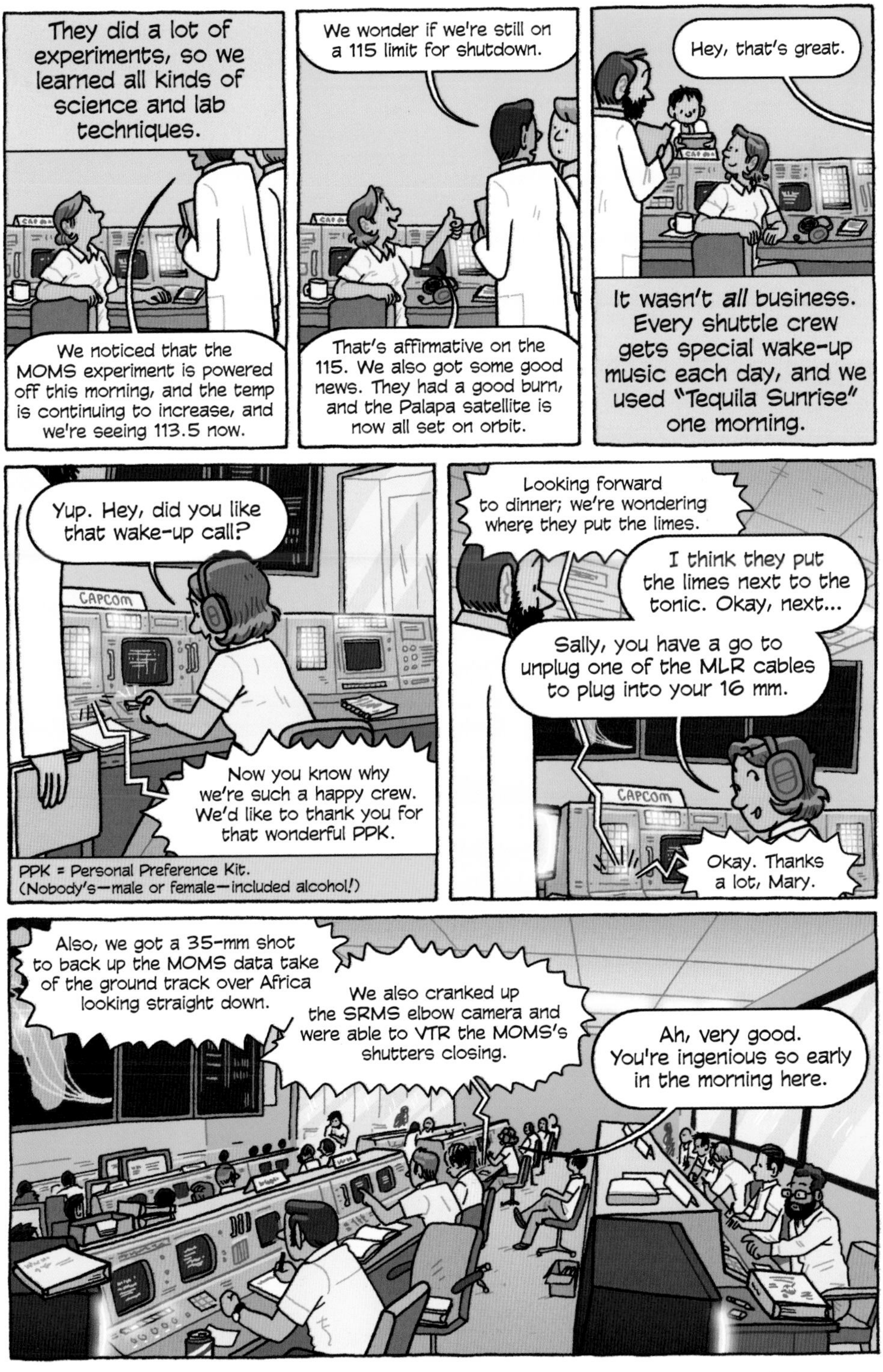
They did a lot of experiments, so we learned all kinds of science and lab techniques.
We noticed that the MOMS experiment is powered off this morning, and the temp is continuing to increase, and we're seeing 113.5 now.
We wonder if we're still on a 115 limit for shutdown.
That's affirmative on the 115. We also got some good news. They had a good burn, and the Palapa satellite is now all set on orbit.
Hey, that's great.
It wasn't *all* business. Every shuttle crew gets special wake-up music each day, and we used "Tequila Sunrise" one morning.
Yup. Hey, did you like that wake-up call?
CAPCOM
Now you know why we're such a happy crew. We'd like to thank you for that wonderful PPK.
PPK = Personal Preference Kit. (Nobody's—male or female—included alcohol!)
Looking forward to dinner; we're wondering where they put the limes.
I think they put the limes next to the tonic. Okay, next...
Sally, you have a go to unplug one of the MLR cables to plug into your 16 mm.
CAPCOM
Okay. Thanks a lot, Mary.
Also, we got a 35-mm shot to back up the MOMS data take of the ground track over Africa looking straight down.
We also cranked up the SRMS elbow camera and were able to VTR the MOMS's shutters closing.
Ah, very good. You're ingenious so early in the morning here.

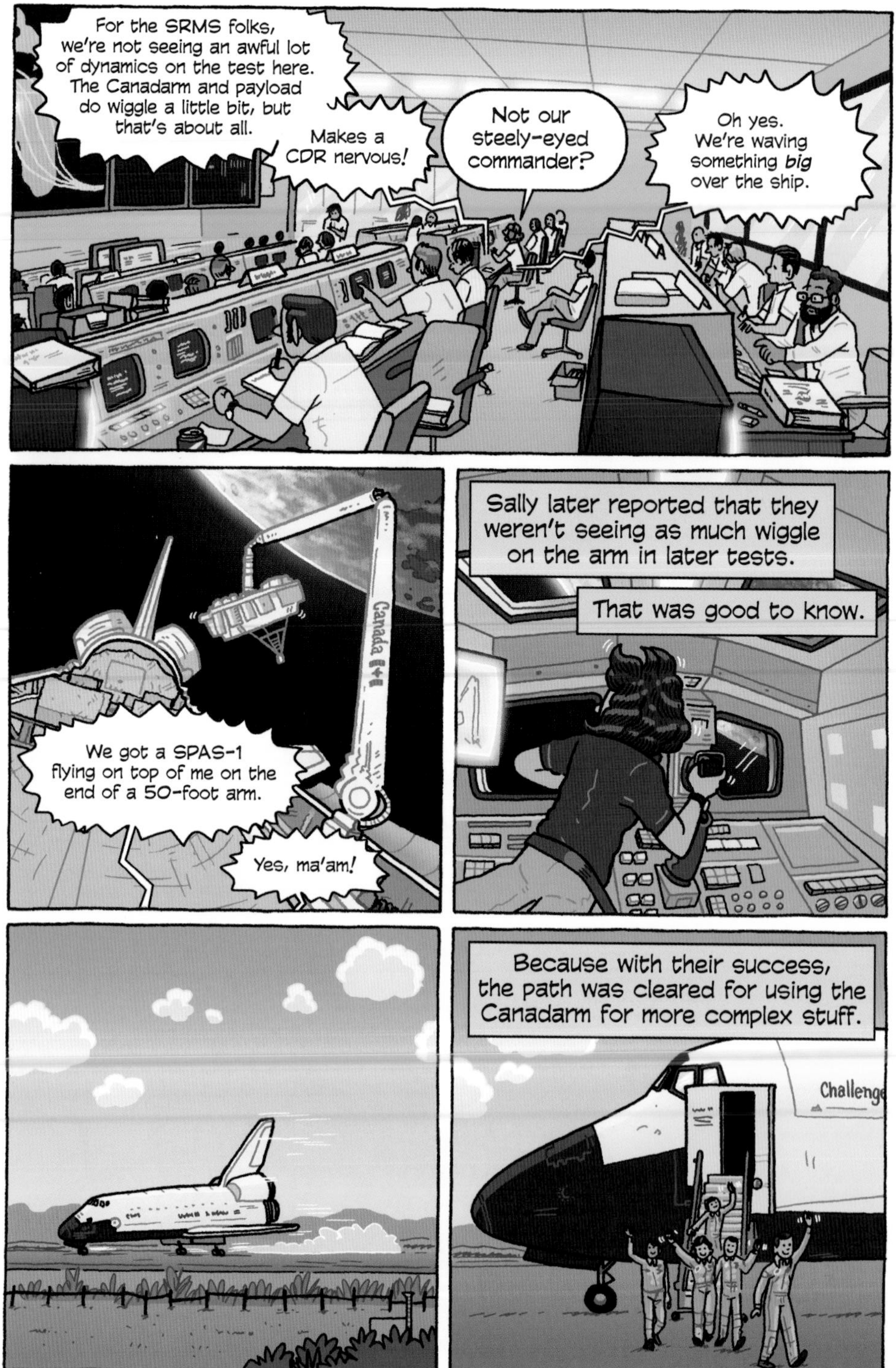
For the SRMS folks, we're not seeing an awful lot of dynamics on the test here. The Canadarm and payload do wiggle a little bit, but that's about all.
Makes a CDR nervous!
Not our steely-eyed commander?
Oh yes. We're waving something *big* over the ship.
Canada
We got a SPAS-1 flying on top of me on the end of a 50-foot arm.
Yes, ma'am!
Sally later reported that they weren't seeing as much wiggle on the arm in later tests.
That was good to know.
Because with their success, the path was cleared for using the Canadarm for more complex stuff.
Challenge

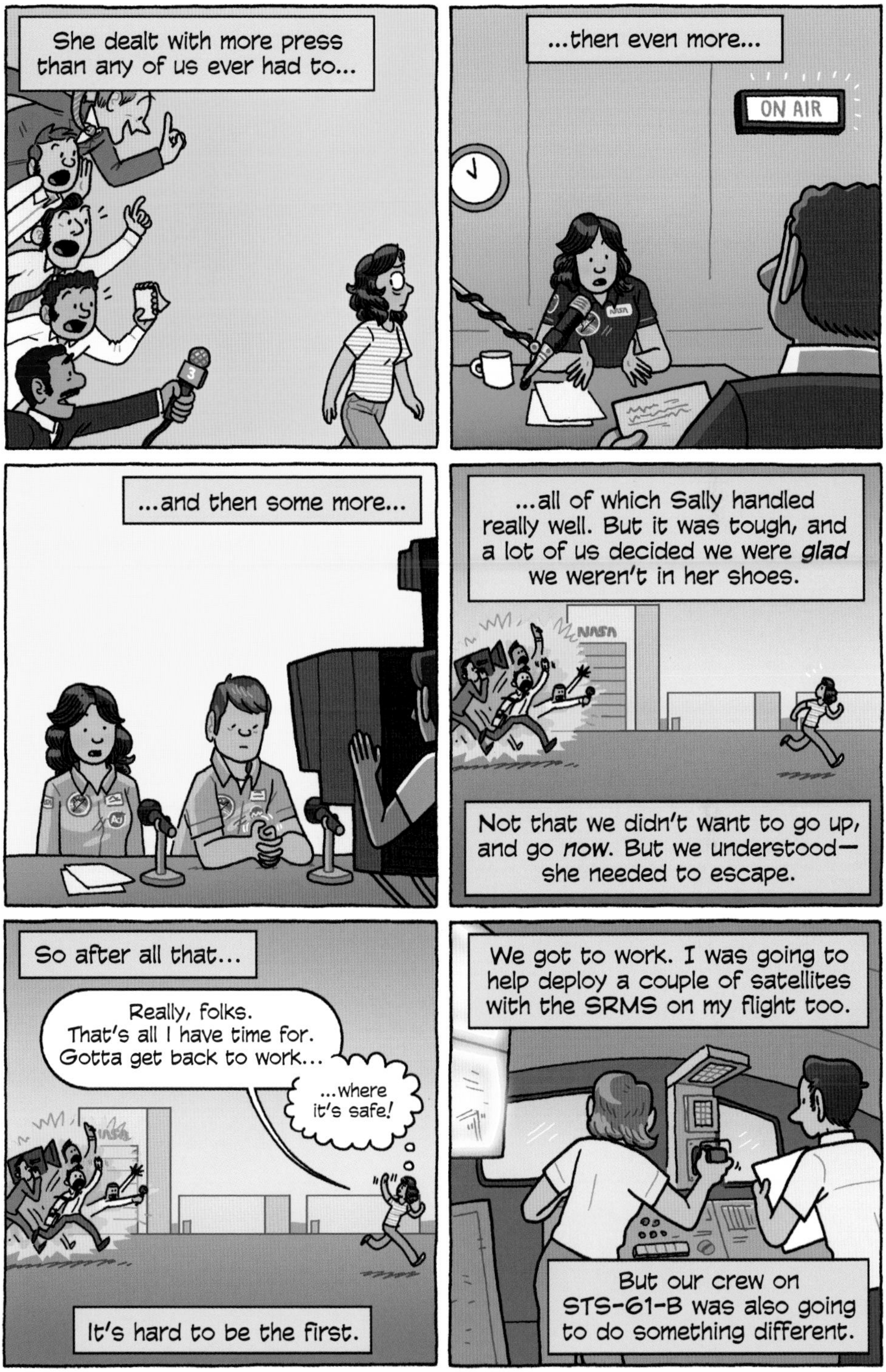

She dealt with more press than any of us ever had to...
3
...then even more...
ON AIR
NASA
...and then some more...
...all of which Sally handled really well. But it was tough, and a lot of us decided we were *glad* we weren't in her shoes.
NASA
Not that we didn't want to go up, and go *now*. But we understood—she needed to escape.
So after all that...
Really, folks. That's all I have time for. Gotta get back to work...
...where it's safe!
NASA
It's hard to be the first.
We got to work. I was going to help deploy a couple of satellites with the SRMS on my flight too.
But our crew on STS-61-B was also going to do something different.

We were going to start practicing to build the International Space Station.

Cleared the payload bay. Looking good.

That meant *astronauts* on the other end of that 50-foot arm you're moving.

Compared to a satellite they're relatively light, even when you add in over 250 pounds of spacesuit.

But when you add in the cost of the EVA suit and training, astronauts aren't cheap.

A little to the right, and...

Not to mention that they— we—are, ya know, *people!*

CLANG CLANG

Nope, you just banged him into the side of the shuttle. High chance of suit puncture—that's gonna make this a *baaaad* day.

CLANG CLANG

I didn't practice on *real* people.

Rats. I should have seen that one coming. Sorry.

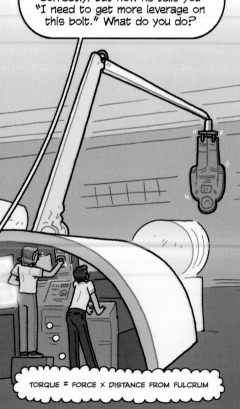

Okay, great, Mary. Captain Cardboard is positioned correctly, but now he tells you "I need to get more leverage on this bolt." What do you do?

TORQUE = FORCE X DISTANCE FROM FULCRUM

Can't make him stronger, so I increase the distance like...this, so we create a longer lever arm.

Roger that. Nice.

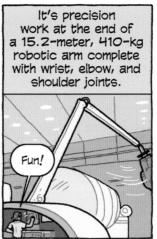

It's precision work at the end of a 15.2-meter, 410-kg robotic arm complete with wrist, elbow, and shoulder joints.

Fun!

Yeah, it is.

And it's a good thing you're having fun, because we're going to do it again.

And again.

And again.

And again, blindfolded, simulating a loss of visual contact.

ENEEEE
NEEEE
ENEEEE

ENEEEE
NEEEE

And again, simulating a Canadarm failure.

And again.

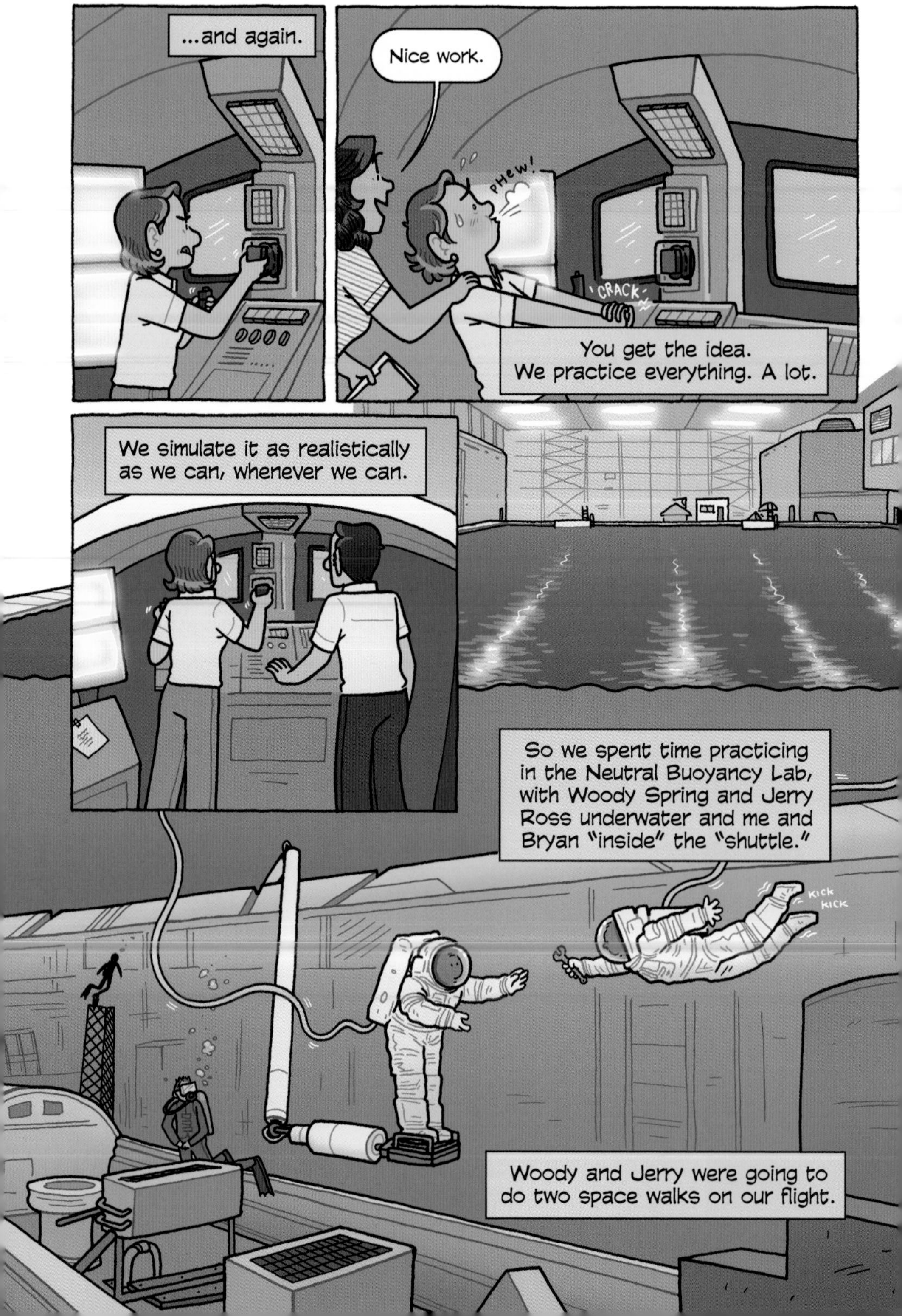
...and again.
Nice work.
PHEW!
CRACK
You get the idea.
We practice everything. A lot.
We simulate it as realistically as we can, whenever we can.
So we spent time practicing in the Neutral Buoyancy Lab, with Woody Spring and Jerry Ross underwater and me and Bryan "inside" the "shuttle."
KICK
KICK
Woody and Jerry were going to do two space walks on our flight.

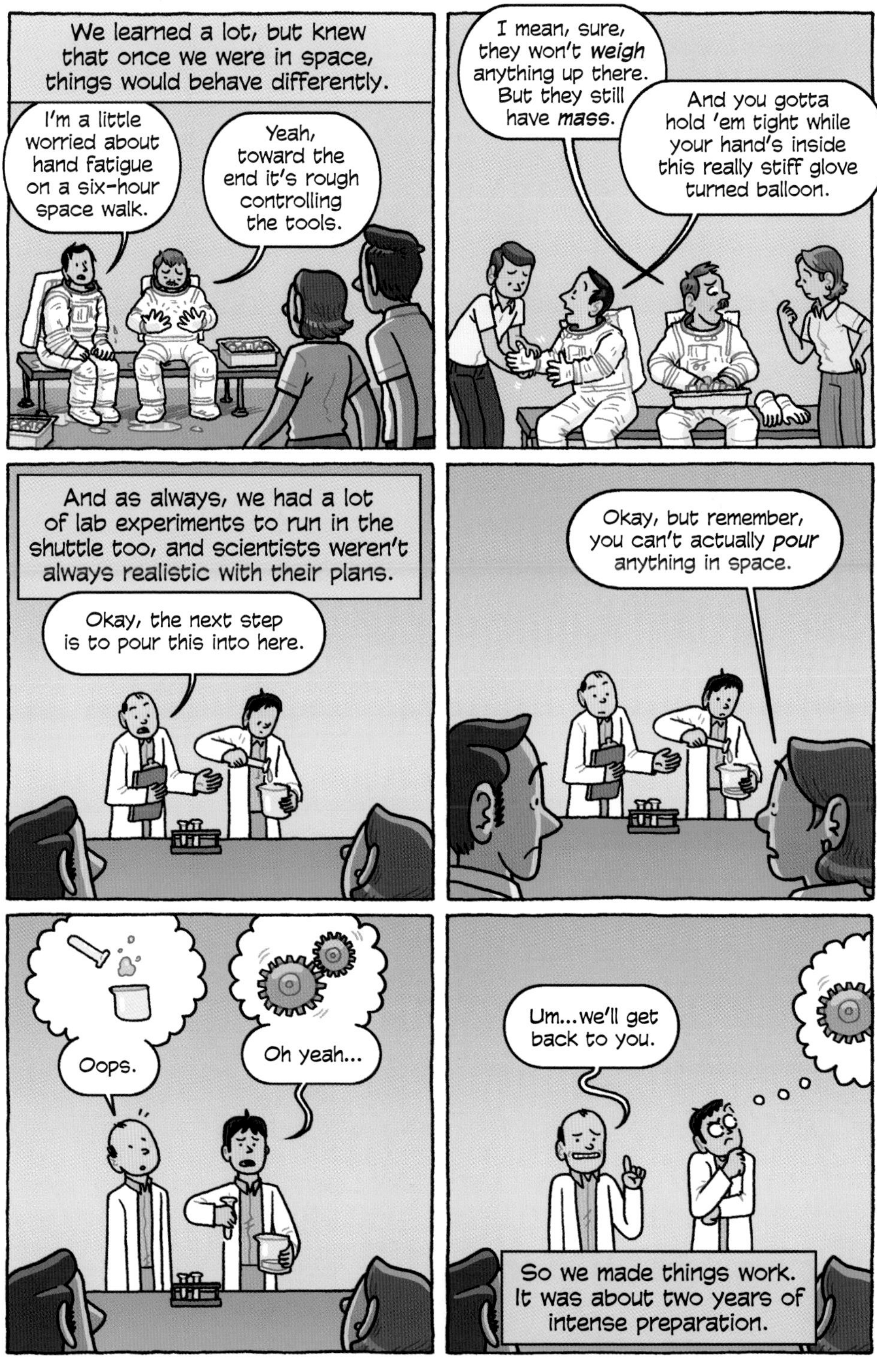
We learned a lot, but knew that once we were in space, things would behave differently.
I'm a little worried about hand fatigue on a six-hour space walk.
Yeah, toward the end it's rough controlling the tools.
I mean, sure, they won't *weigh* anything up there. But they still have *mass*.
And you gotta hold 'em tight while your hand's inside this really stiff glove turned balloon.
And as always, we had a lot of lab experiments to run in the shuttle too, and scientists weren't always realistic with their plans.
Okay, the next step is to pour this into here.
Okay, but remember, you can't actually *pour* anything in space.
Oops.
Oh yeah...
Um...we'll get back to you.
So we made things work. It was about two years of intense preparation.

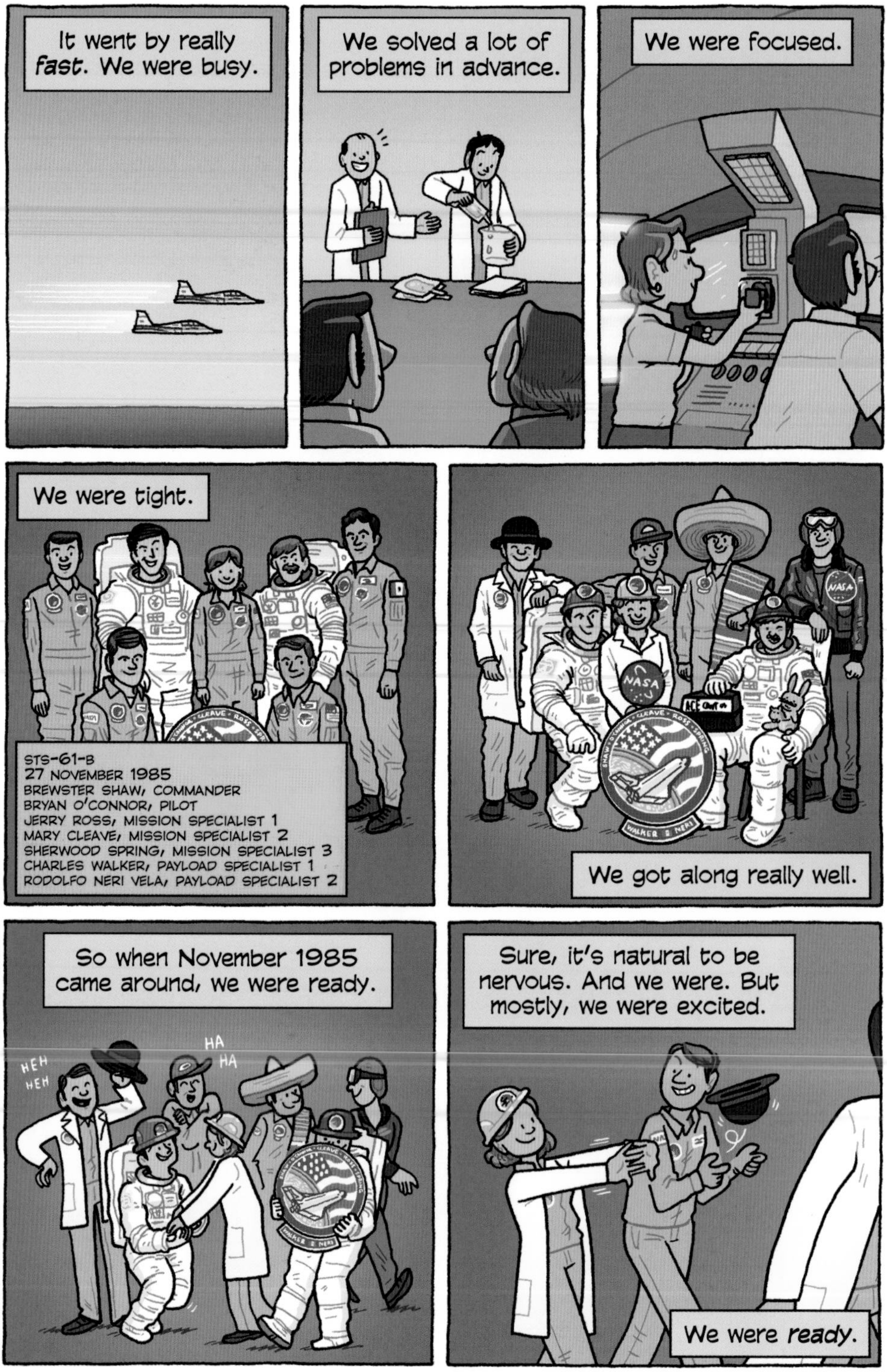
It went by really *fast*. We were busy.
We solved a lot of problems in advance.
We were focused.
We were tight.
STS-61-B
27 NOVEMBER 1985
BREWSTER SHAW, COMMANDER
BRYAN O'CONNOR, PILOT
JERRY ROSS, MISSION SPECIALIST 1
MARY CLEAVE, MISSION SPECIALIST 2
SHERWOOD SPRING, MISSION SPECIALIST 3
CHARLES WALKER, PAYLOAD SPECIALIST 1
RODOLFO NERI VELA, PAYLOAD SPECIALIST 2
NASA
We got along really well.
So when November 1985 came around, we were ready.
HEH HEH
HA HA
Sure, it's natural to be nervous. And we were. But mostly, we were excited.
We were *ready*.

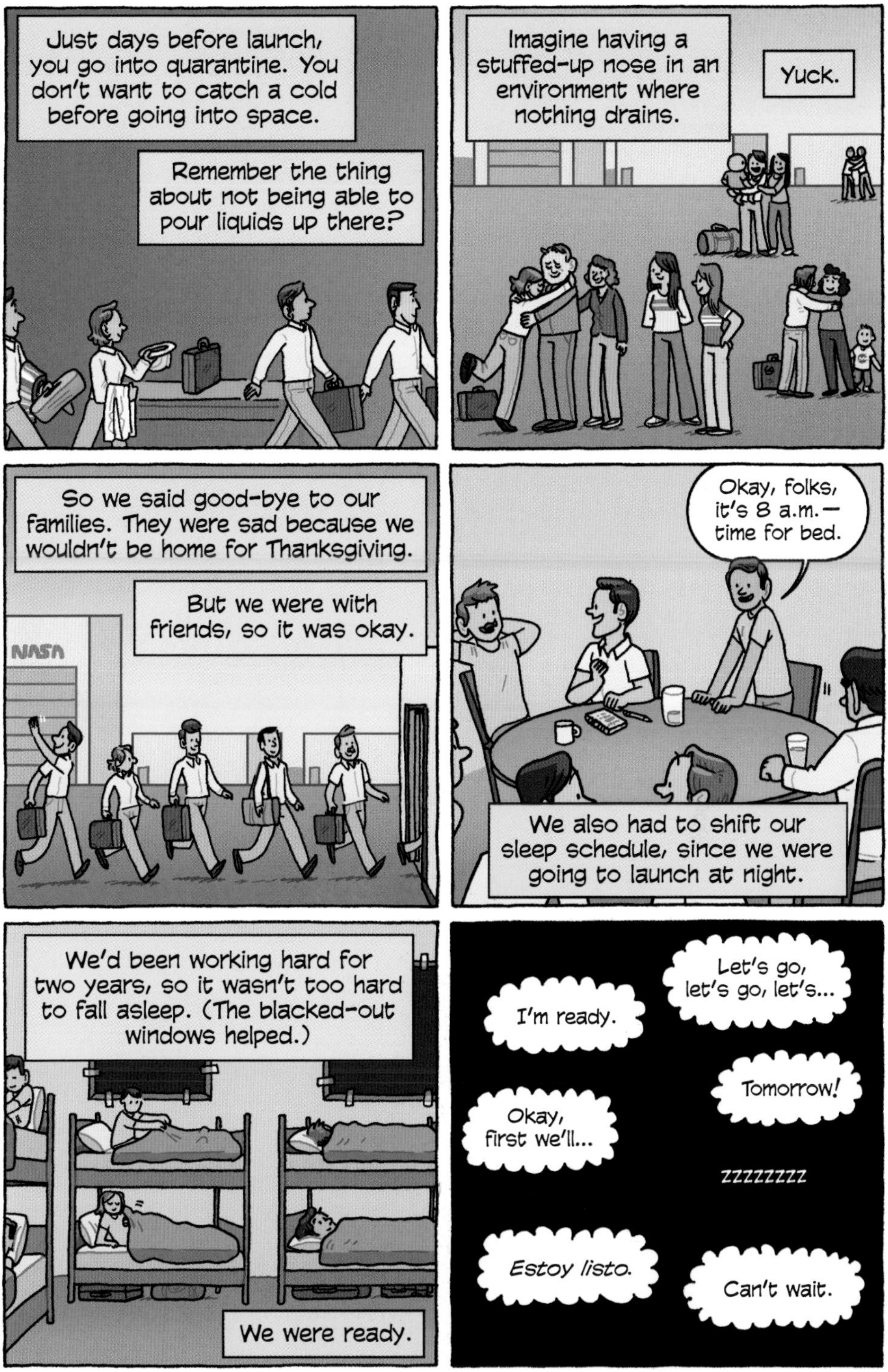
Just days before launch, you go into quarantine. You don't want to catch a cold before going into space.
Remember the thing about not being able to pour liquids up there?
Imagine having a stuffed-up nose in an environment where nothing drains.
Yuck.
So we said good-bye to our families. They were sad because we wouldn't be home for Thanksgiving.
But we were with friends, so it was okay.
NASA
Okay, folks, it's 8 a.m.— time for bed.
We also had to shift our sleep schedule, since we were going to launch at night.
We'd been working hard for two years, so it wasn't too hard to fall asleep. (The blacked-out windows helped.)
We were ready.
Let's go, let's go, let's...
I'm ready.
Tomorrow!
Okay, first we'll...
ZZZZZZZZ
Estoy listo.
Can't wait.

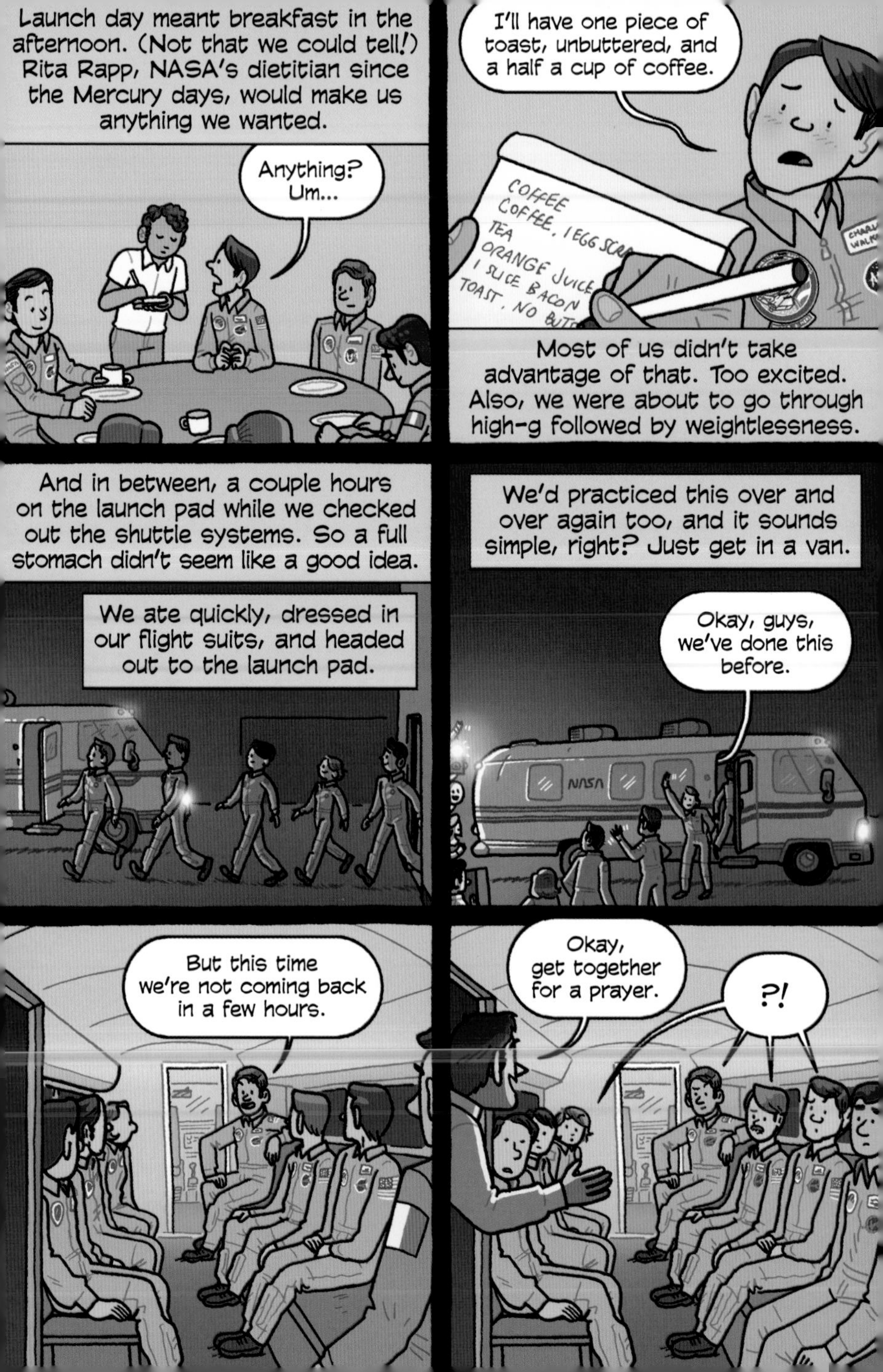
Launch day meant breakfast in the afternoon. (Not that we could tell!) Rita Rapp, NASA's dietitian since the Mercury days, would make us anything we wanted.
Anything? Um...
I'll have one piece of toast, unbuttered, and a half a cup of coffee.
COFFEE
COFFEE, 1 EGG SCR
TEA
ORANGE JUICE
1 SLICE BACON
TOAST, NO BUT
Most of us didn't take advantage of that. Too excited. Also, we were about to go through high-g followed by weightlessness.
And in between, a couple hours on the launch pad while we checked out the shuttle systems. So a full stomach didn't seem like a good idea.
We ate quickly, dressed in our flight suits, and headed out to the launch pad.
We'd practiced this over and over again too, and it sounds simple, right? Just get in a van.
Okay, guys, we've done this before.
NASA
But this time we're not coming back in a few hours.
Okay, get together for a prayer.
?!

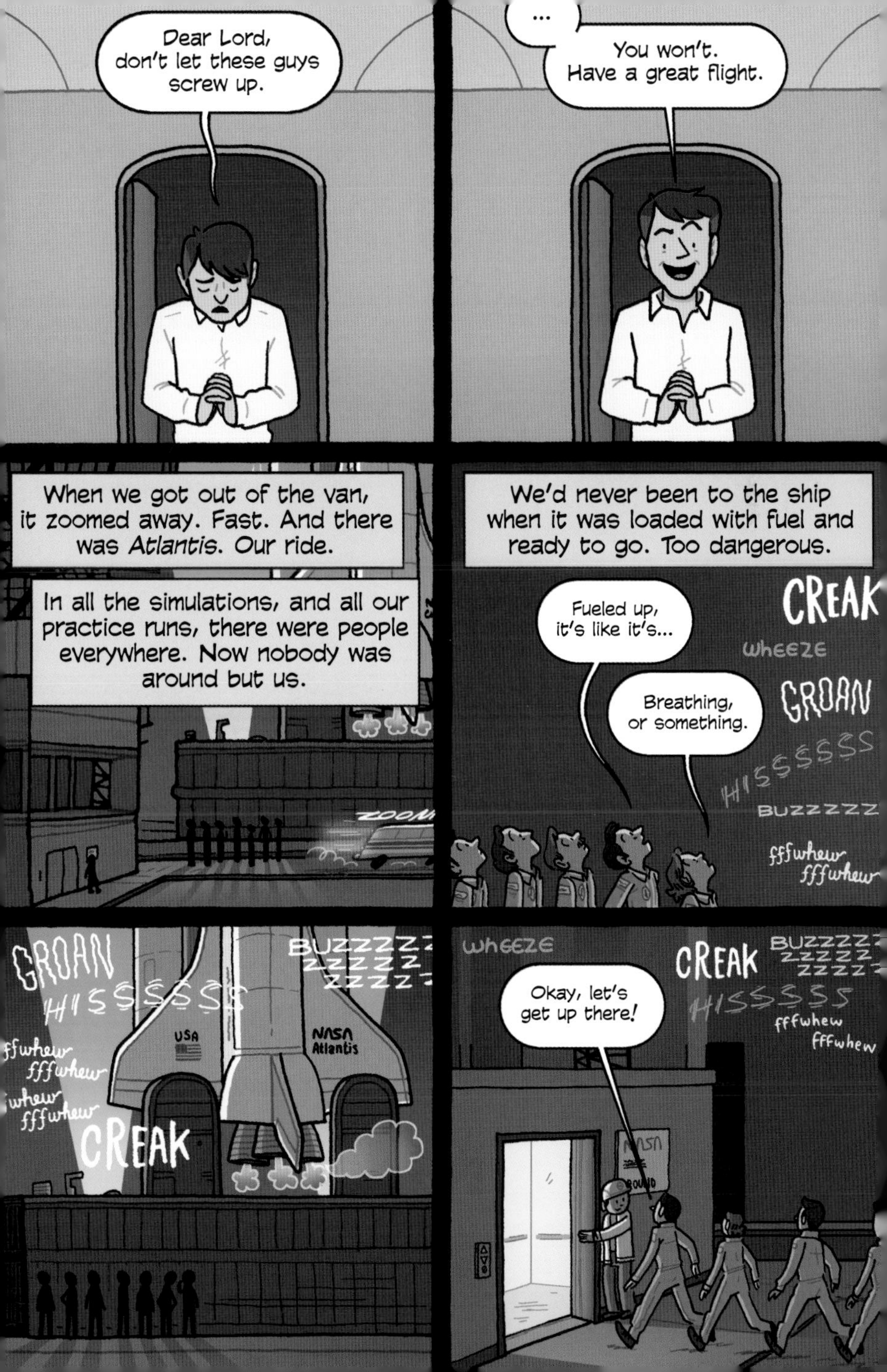
Dear Lord, don't let these guys screw up.
...
You won't. Have a great flight.
When we got out of the van, it zoomed away. Fast. And there was *Atlantis*. Our ride.
In all the simulations, and all our practice runs, there were people everywhere. Now nobody was around but us.
ZOOM
We'd never been to the ship when it was loaded with fuel and ready to go. Too dangerous.
Fueled up, it's like it's...
Breathing, or something.
CREAK
WHEEZE
GROAN
HISSSSSS
BUZZZZZ
fffwhew fffwhew
GROAN
HISSSSSS
BUZZZZZ ZZZZZ ZZZZ
USA
NASA Atlantis
fffwhew
fffwhew
whew
fffwhew
CREAK
WHEEZE
CREAK
BUZZZZZ ZZZZZ ZZZZ
HISSSSSS
fffwhew fffwhew
Okay, let's get up there!
NASA

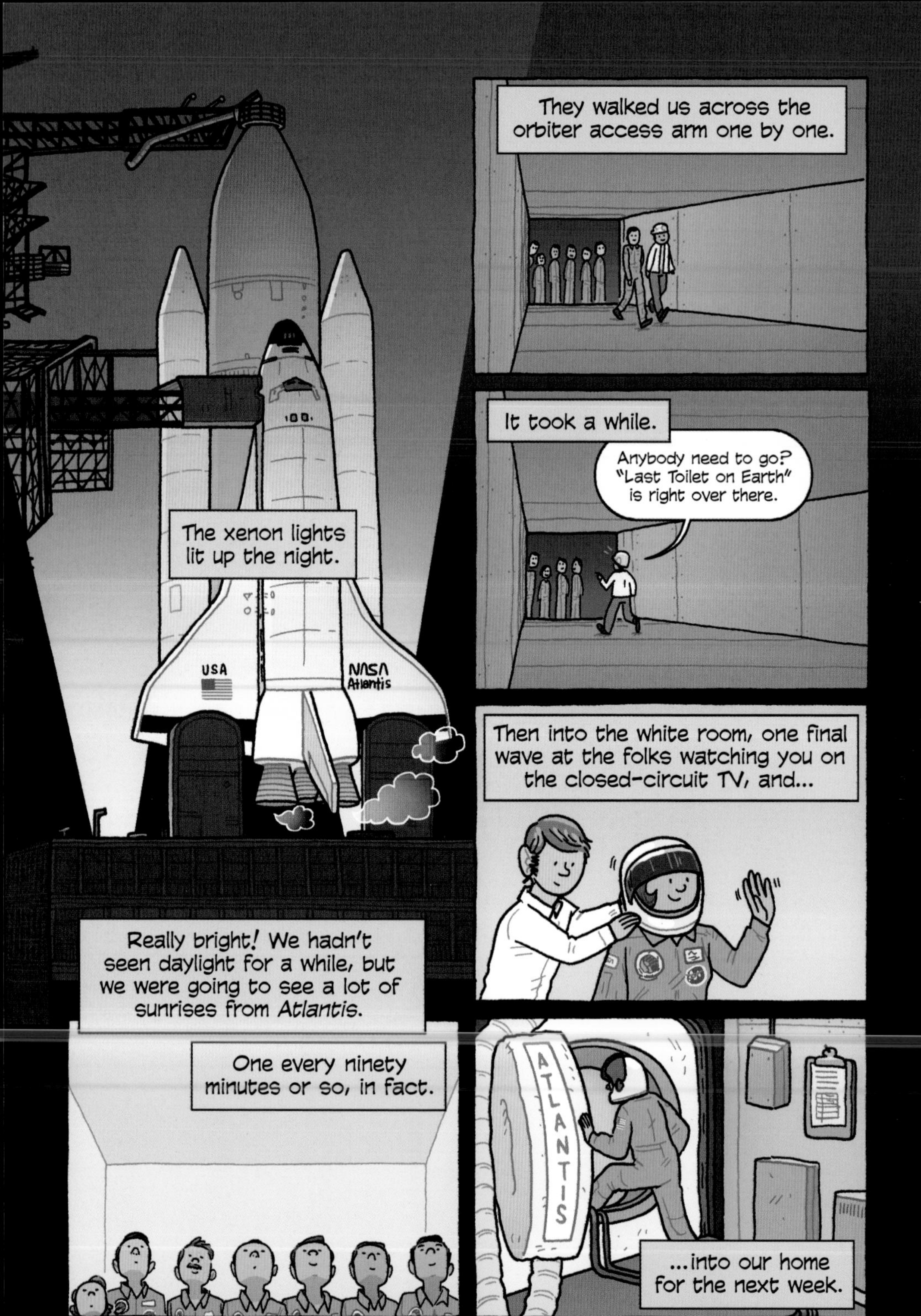
The xenon lights lit up the night.
USA
NASA Atlantis
Really bright! We hadn't seen daylight for a while, but we were going to see a lot of sunrises from *Atlantis*.
One every ninety minutes or so, in fact.
They walked us across the orbiter access arm one by one.
It took a while.
Anybody need to go? "Last Toilet on Earth" is right over there.
Then into the white room, one final wave at the folks watching you on the closed-circuit TV, and...
ATLANTIS
...into our home for the next week.

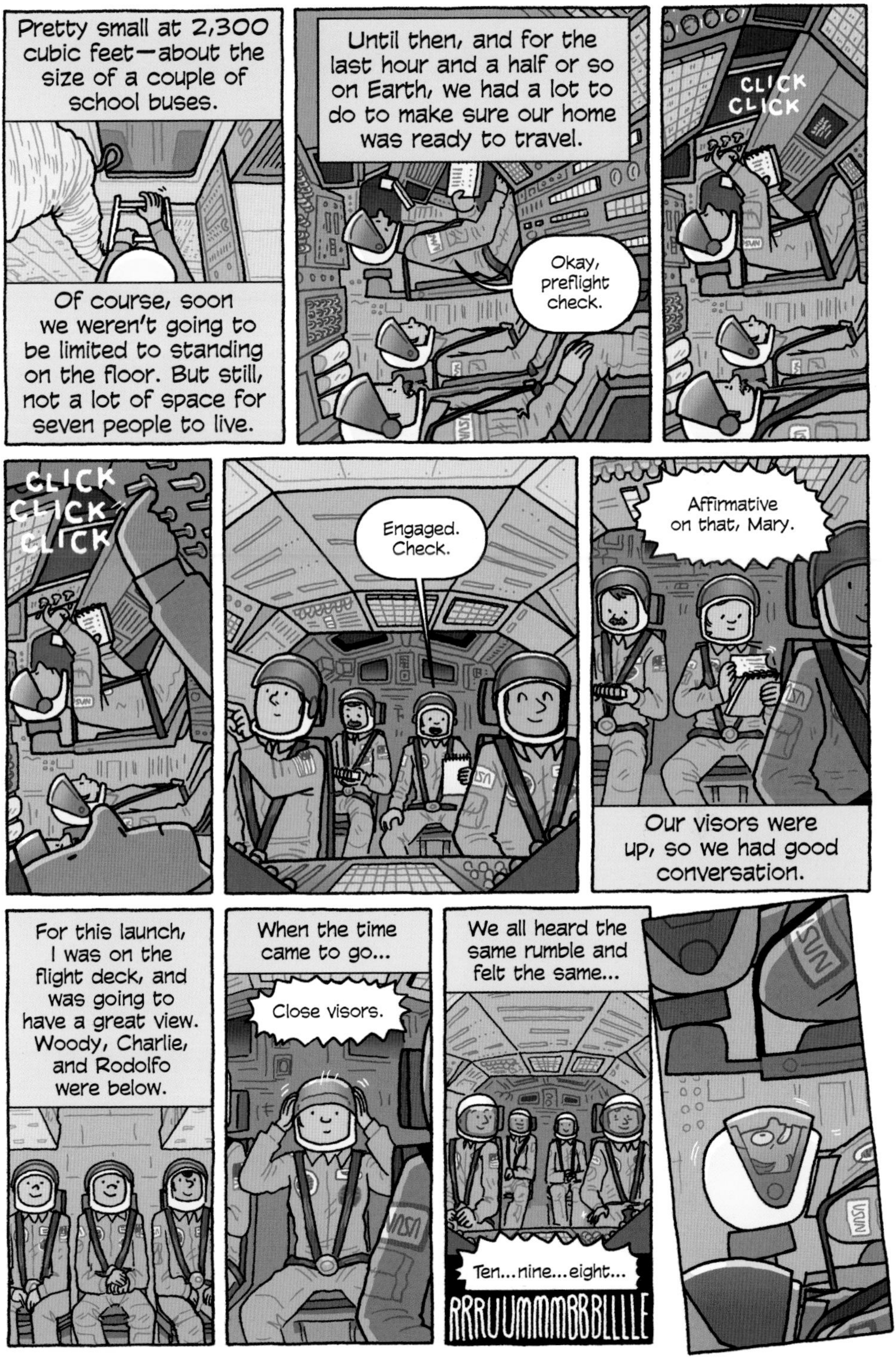
Pretty small at 2,300 cubic feet—about the size of a couple of school buses.
Of course, soon we weren't going to be limited to standing on the floor. But still, not a lot of space for seven people to live.
Until then, and for the last hour and a half or so on Earth, we had a lot to do to make sure our home was ready to travel.
Okay, preflight check.
CLICK CLICK
CLICK CLICK CLICK
Engaged. Check.
Affirmative on that, Mary.
Our visors were up, so we had good conversation.
For this launch, I was on the flight deck, and was going to have a great view. Woody, Charlie, and Rodolfo were below.
When the time came to go...
Close visors.
We all heard the same rumble and felt the same...
Ten...nine...eight...
RRRUUMMMBBBLLLLE

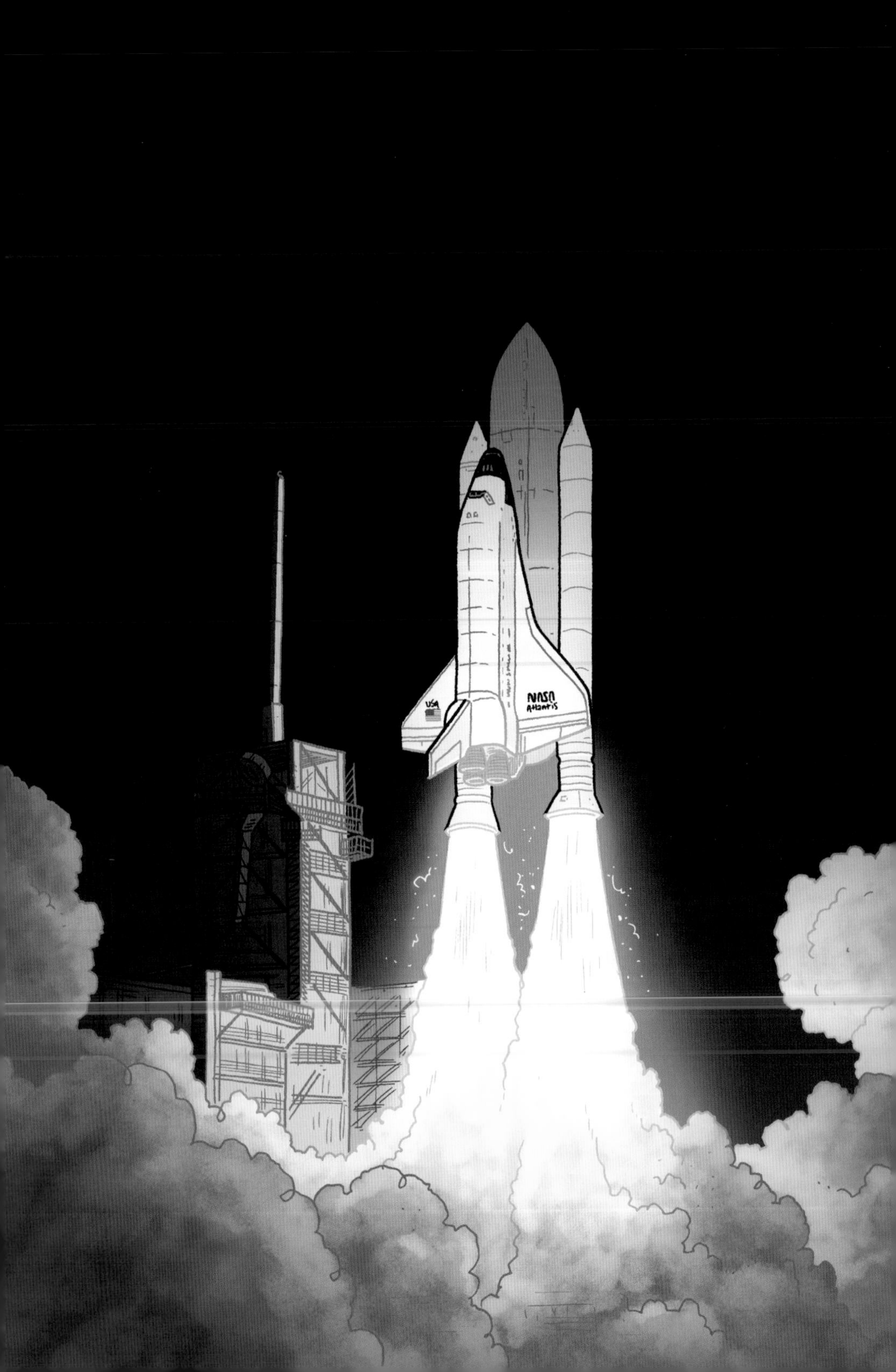
USA
NASA
Atlantis

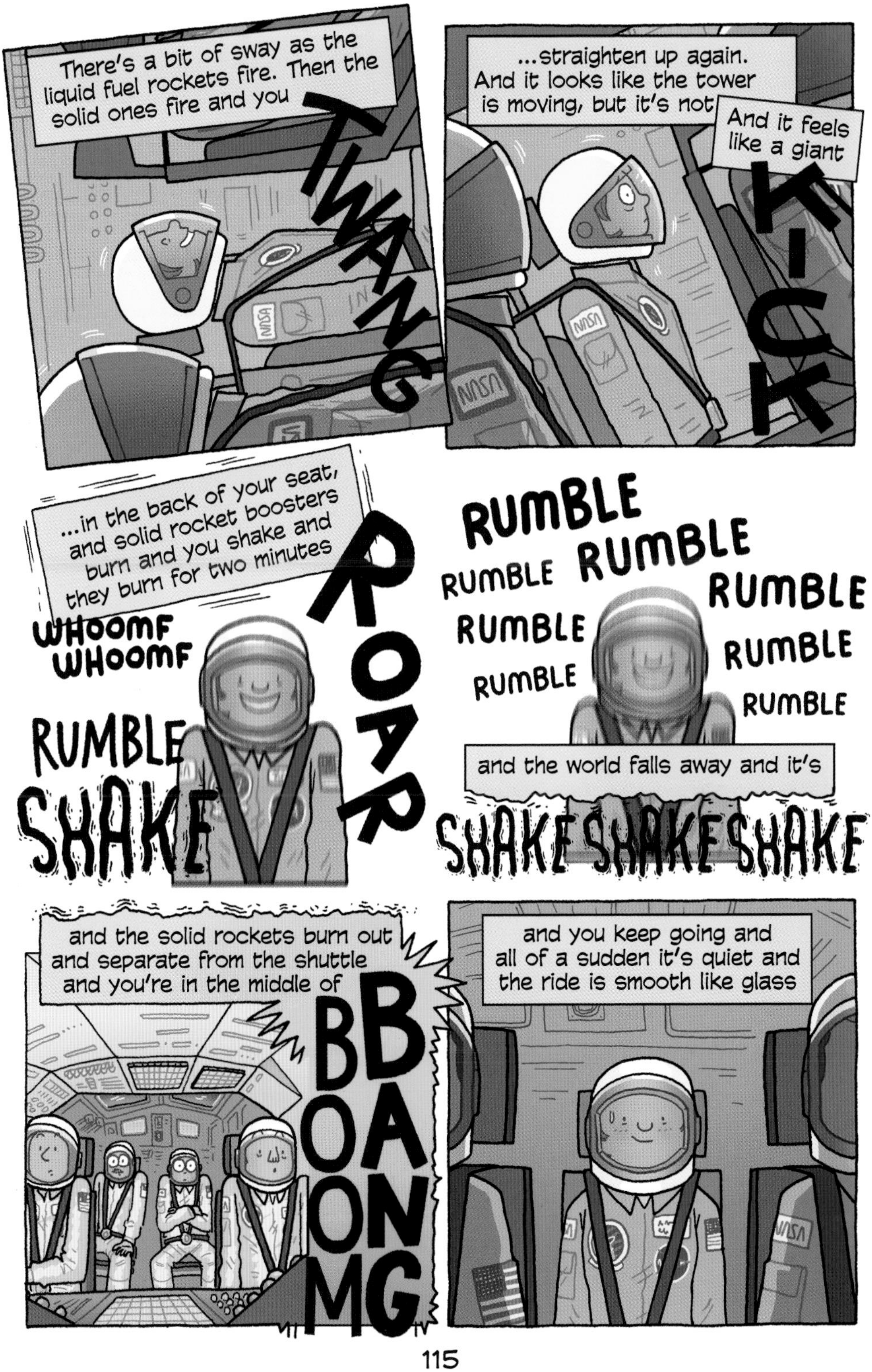

There's a bit of sway as the liquid fuel rockets fire. Then the solid ones fire and you
TWANG
...straighten up again. And it looks like the tower is moving, but it's not
And it feels like a giant
KICK
...in the back of your seat, and solid rocket boosters burn and you shake and they burn for two minutes
WHOOMF
WHOOMF
ROAR
RUMBLE
SHAKE
RUMBLE
RUMBLE RUMBLE
RUMBLE
RUMBLE
RUMBLE
RUMBLE
RUMBLE
RUMBLE
and the world falls away and it's
SHAKE SHAKE SHAKE
and the solid rockets burn out and separate from the shuttle and you're in the middle of
BOOOMG
BBANG
and you keep going and all of a sudden it's quiet and the ride is smooth like glass

and we're not done yet because we're not in orbit, so the engines pick back up again and acceleration builds and pressure

and it's like a big monkey sitting on your chest and the monkey gets heavier

and heavier

and heavier

and heavier

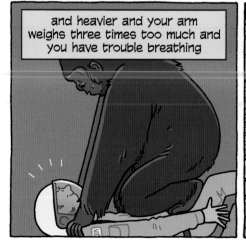

and heavier and your arm weighs three times too much and you have trouble breathing

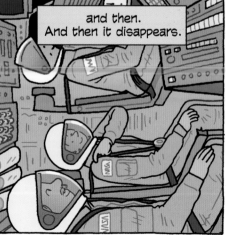

and then.
And then it disappears.

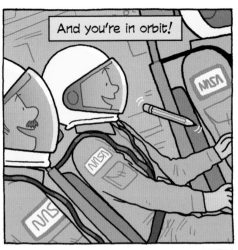

And you're in orbit!

We enjoyed weightlessness for a few minutes.

Along with the view.

Wow.

¡Padrísimo!

"Father?..."

Idiom, Mary. It means it's *fantastic*.

Yeah. You can say that again.

It really was fantastic. It was also time to get to work.

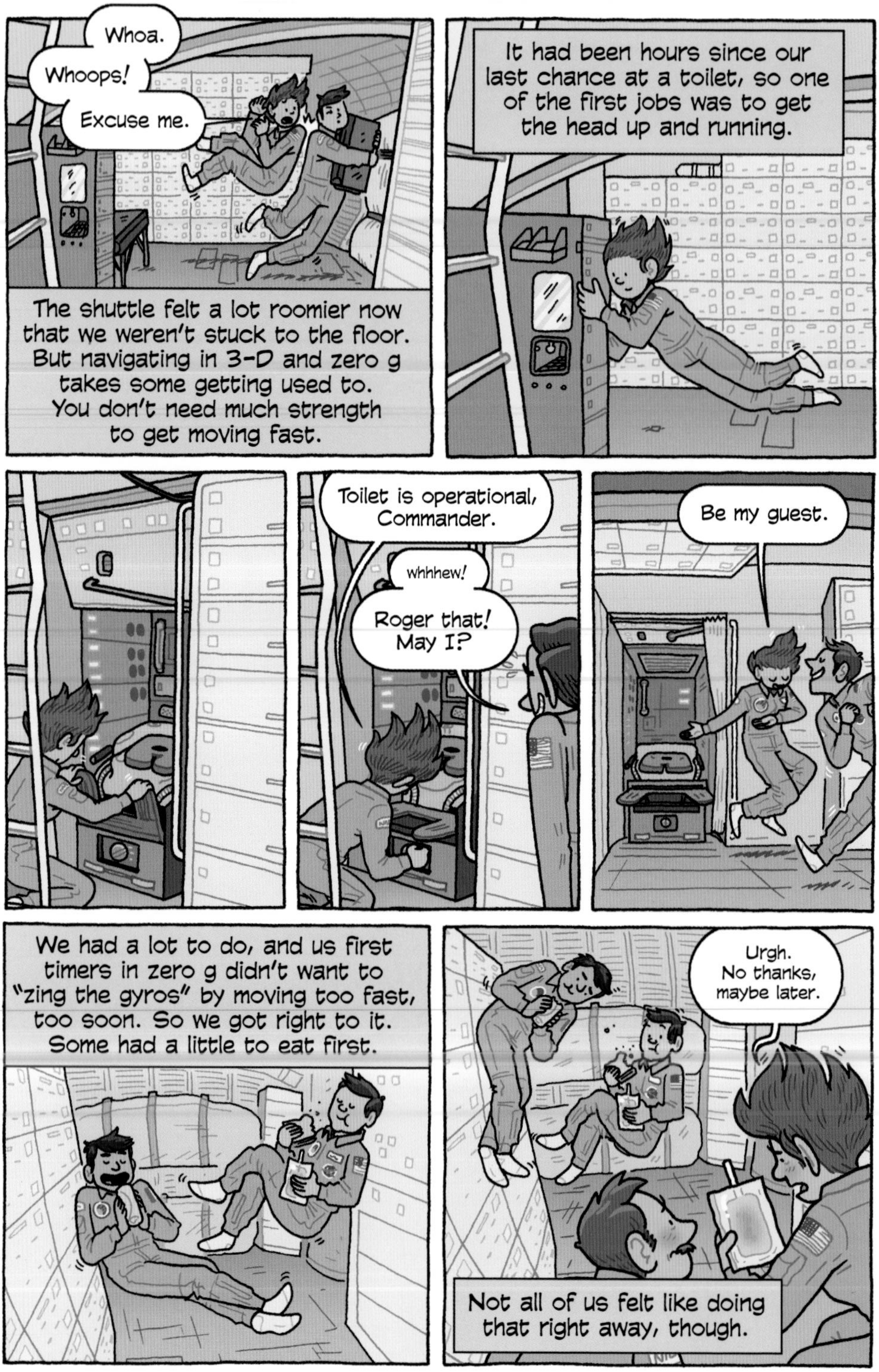
Whoa.
Whoops!
Excuse me.
The shuttle felt a lot roomier now that we weren't stuck to the floor. But navigating in 3-D and zero g takes some getting used to. You don't need much strength to get moving fast.
It had been hours since our last chance at a toilet, so one of the first jobs was to get the head up and running.
Toilet is operational, Commander.
whhhew!
Roger that! May I?
Be my guest.
We had a lot to do, and us first timers in zero g didn't want to "zing the gyros" by moving too fast, too soon. So we got right to it. Some had a little to eat first.
Urgh. No thanks, maybe later.
Not all of us felt like doing that right away, though.

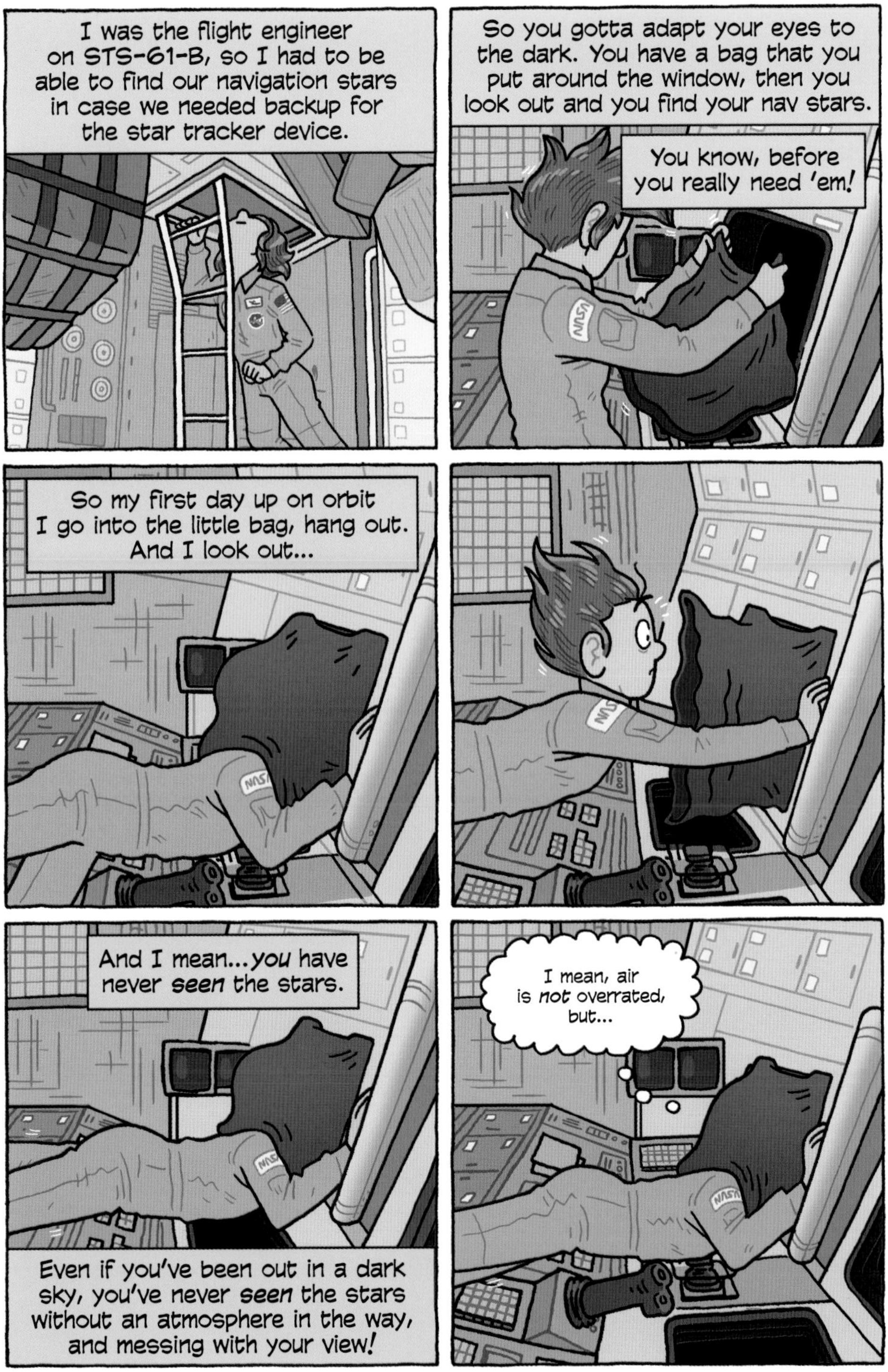

I was the flight engineer on STS-61-B, so I had to be able to find our navigation stars in case we needed backup for the star tracker device.
So you gotta adapt your eyes to the dark. You have a bag that you put around the window, then you look out and you find your nav stars.
You know, before you really need 'em!
NASA
So my first day up on orbit I go into the little bag, hang out. And I look out...
NASA
NASA
And I mean...*you* have never *seen* the stars.
NASA
Even if you've been out in a dark sky, you've never *seen* the stars without an atmosphere in the way, and messing with your view!
I mean, air is *not* overrated, but...
NASA

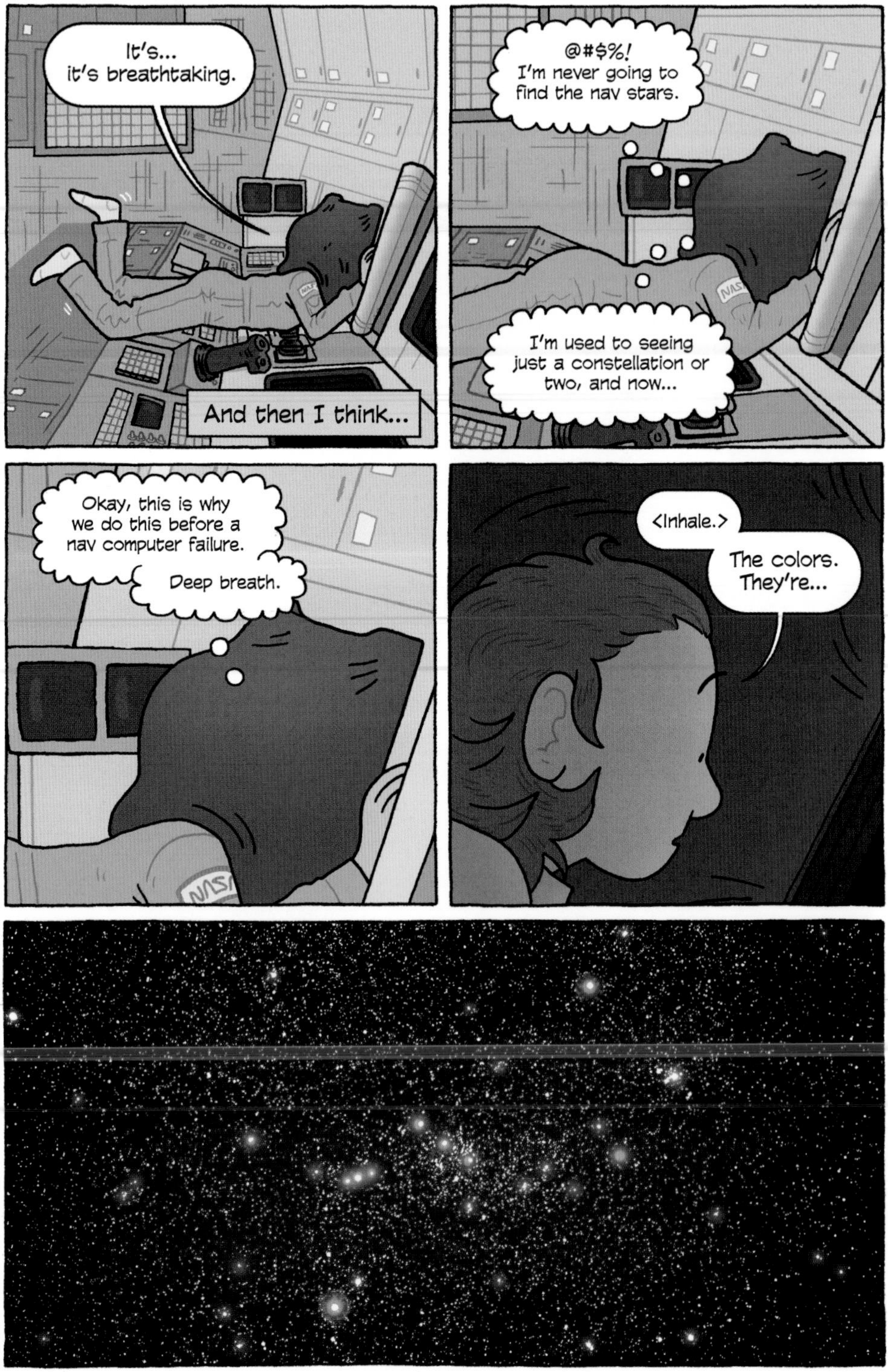
It's... it's breathtaking.
And then I think...
@#$%! I'm never going to find the nav stars.
I'm used to seeing just a constellation or two, and now...
Okay, this is why we do this before a nav computer failure.
Deep breath.
<Inhale.>
The colors. They're...

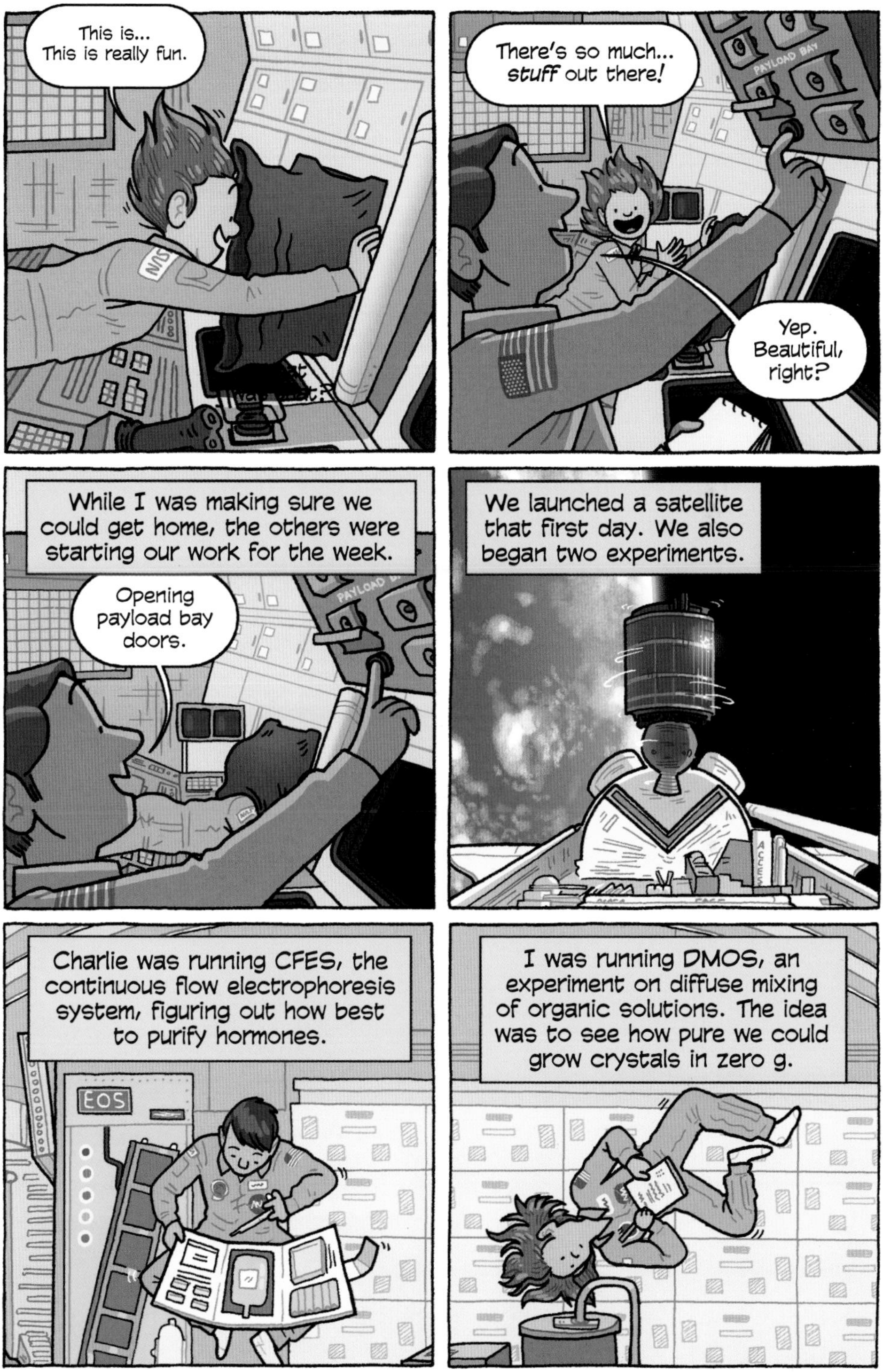
This is...
This is really fun.
There's so much...
stuff out there!
Yep. Beautiful, right?
While I was making sure we could get home, the others were starting our work for the week.
Opening payload bay doors.
We launched a satellite that first day. We also began two experiments.
Charlie was running CFES, the continuous flow electrophoresis system, figuring out how best to purify hormones.
I was running DMOS, an experiment on diffuse mixing of organic solutions. The idea was to see how pure we could grow crystals in zero g.

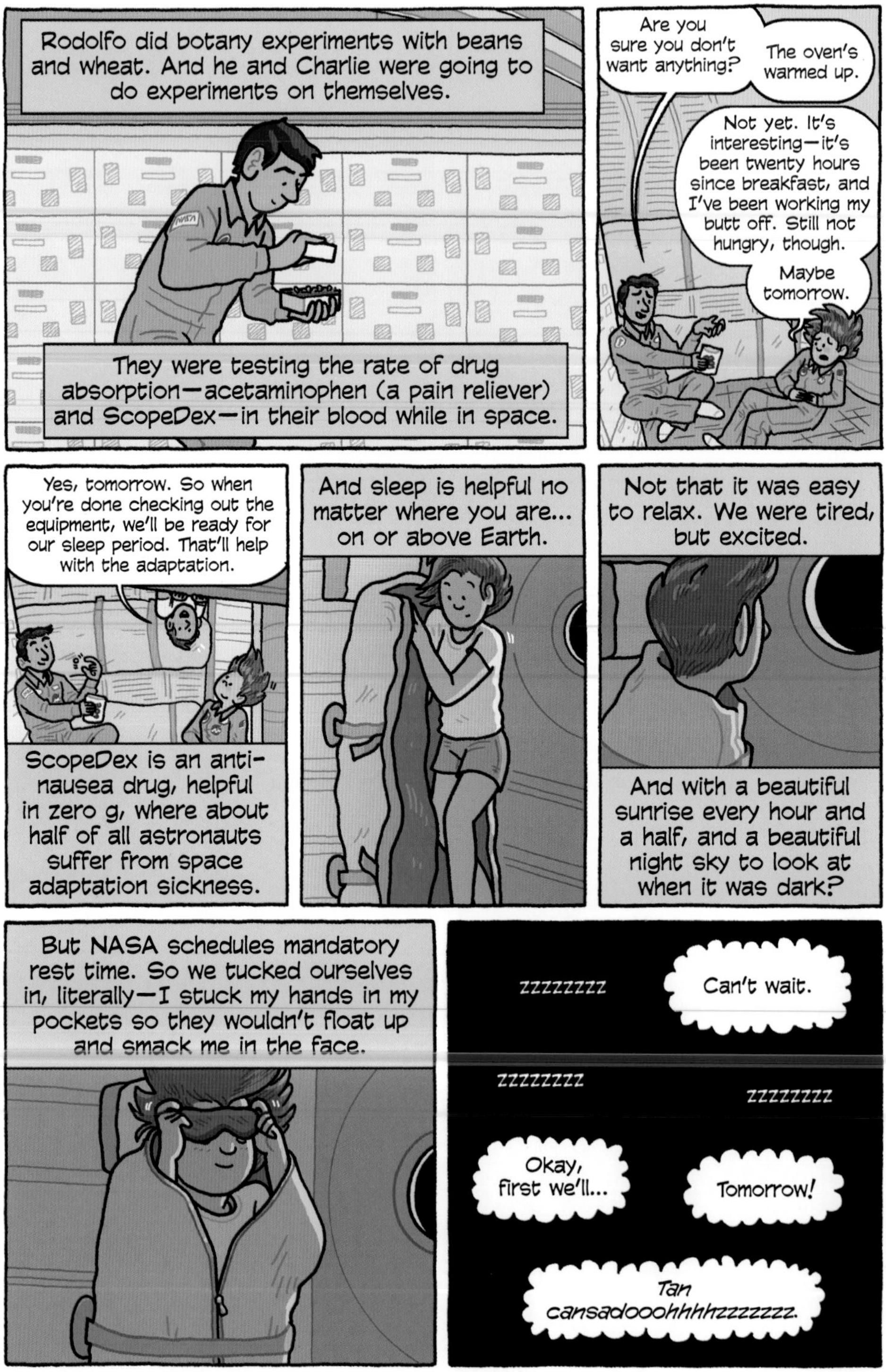

Rodolfo did botany experiments with beans and wheat. And he and Charlie were going to do experiments on themselves.
They were testing the rate of drug absorption—acetaminophen (a pain reliever) and ScopeDex—in their blood while in space.
Are you sure you don't want anything?
The oven's warmed up.
Not yet. It's interesting—it's been twenty hours since breakfast, and I've been working my butt off. Still not hungry, though.
Maybe tomorrow.
Yes, tomorrow. So when you're done checking out the equipment, we'll be ready for our sleep period. That'll help with the adaptation.
ScopeDex is an anti-nausea drug, helpful in zero g, where about half of all astronauts suffer from space adaptation sickness.
And sleep is helpful no matter where you are... on or above Earth.
Not that it was easy to relax. We were tired, but excited.
And with a beautiful sunrise every hour and a half, and a beautiful night sky to look at when it was dark?
But NASA schedules mandatory rest time. So we tucked ourselves in, literally—I stuck my hands in my pockets so they wouldn't float up and smack me in the face.
ZZZZZZZZ
Can't wait.
ZZZZZZZZ
ZZZZZZZZ
Okay, first we'll...
Tomorrow!
Tan cansadooohhhhzzzzzzz.

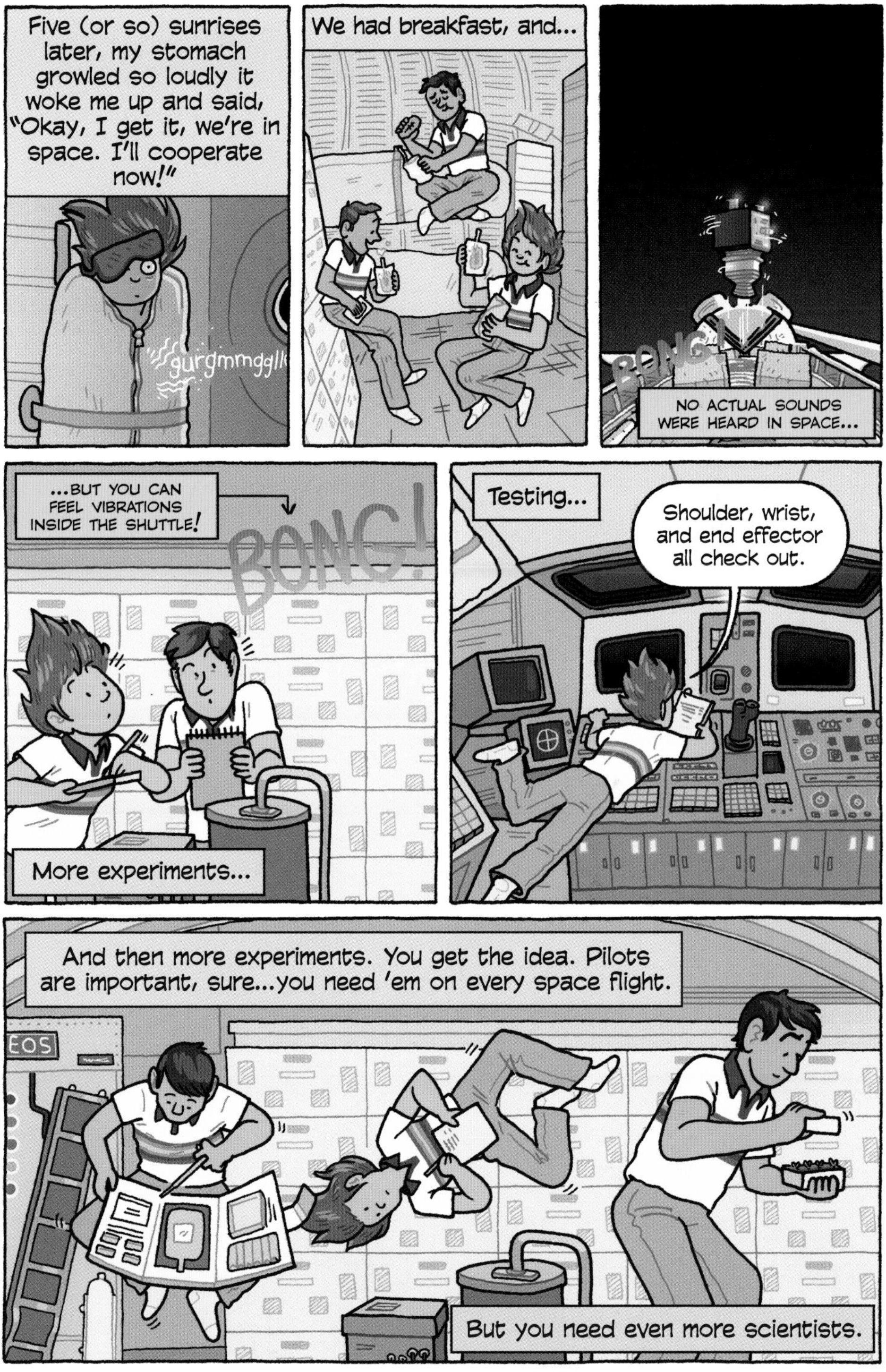
Five (or so) sunrises later, my stomach growled so loudly it woke me up and said, "Okay, I get it, we're in space. I'll cooperate now!"
gurgmmggllk
We had breakfast, and...
BONG!
NO ACTUAL SOUNDS WERE HEARD IN SPACE...
...BUT YOU CAN FEEL VIBRATIONS INSIDE THE SHUTTLE!
BONG!
More experiments...
Testing...
Shoulder, wrist, and end effector all check out.
And then more experiments. You get the idea. Pilots are important, sure...you need 'em on every space flight.
EOS
But you need even more scientists.

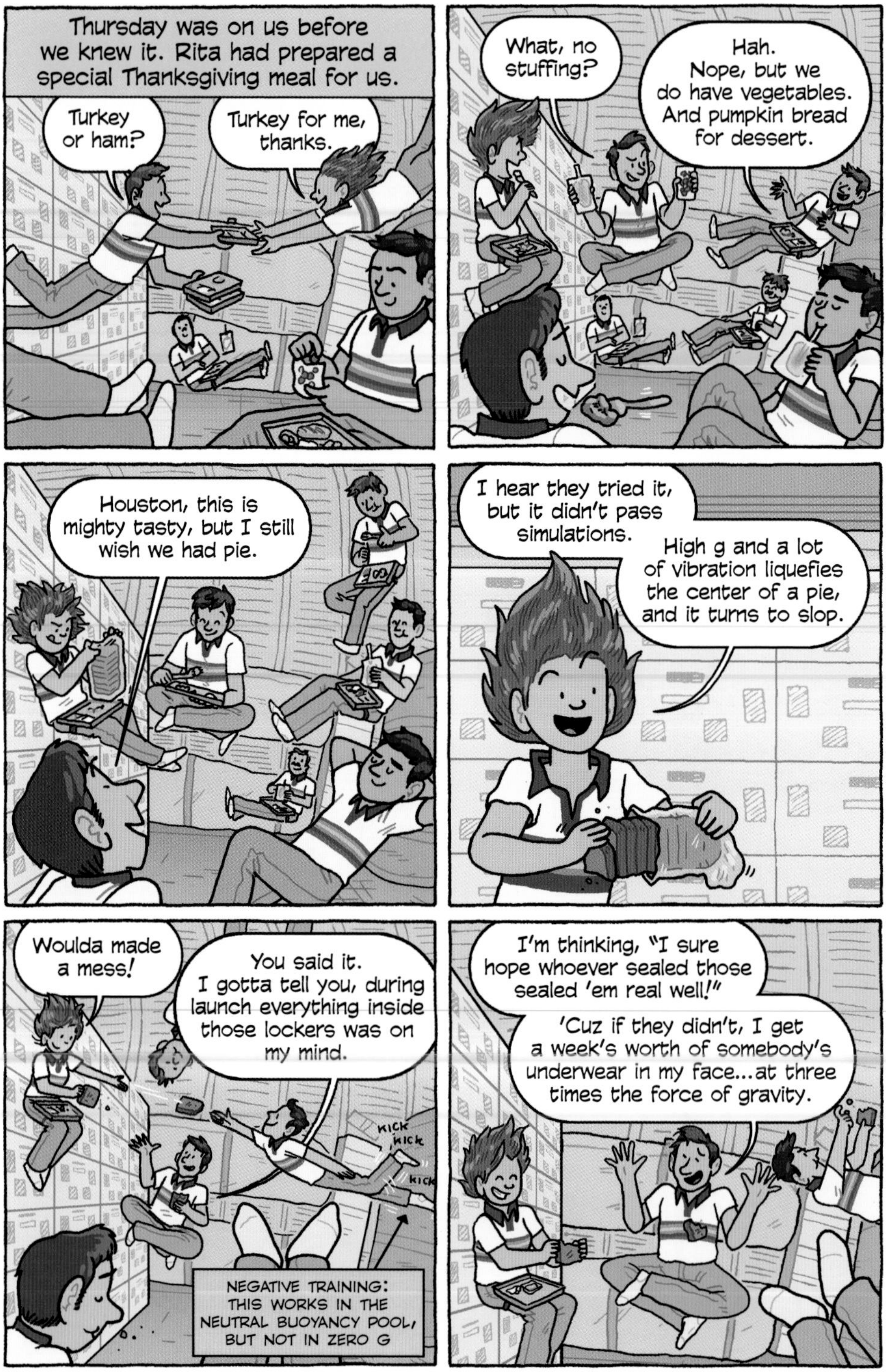

Thursday was on us before we knew it. Rita had prepared a special Thanksgiving meal for us.
Turkey or ham?
Turkey for me, thanks.
What, no stuffing?
Hah. Nope, but we do have vegetables. And pumpkin bread for dessert.
Houston, this is mighty tasty, but I still wish we had pie.
I hear they tried it, but it didn't pass simulations.
High g and a lot of vibration liquefies the center of a pie, and it turns to slop.
Woulda made a mess!
You said it. I gotta tell you, during launch everything inside those lockers was on my mind.
KICK
KICK
KICK
NEGATIVE TRAINING: THIS WORKS IN THE NEUTRAL BUOYANCY POOL, BUT NOT IN ZERO G
I'm thinking, "I sure hope whoever sealed those sealed 'em real well!"
'Cuz if they didn't, I get a week's worth of somebody's underwear in my face...at three times the force of gravity.

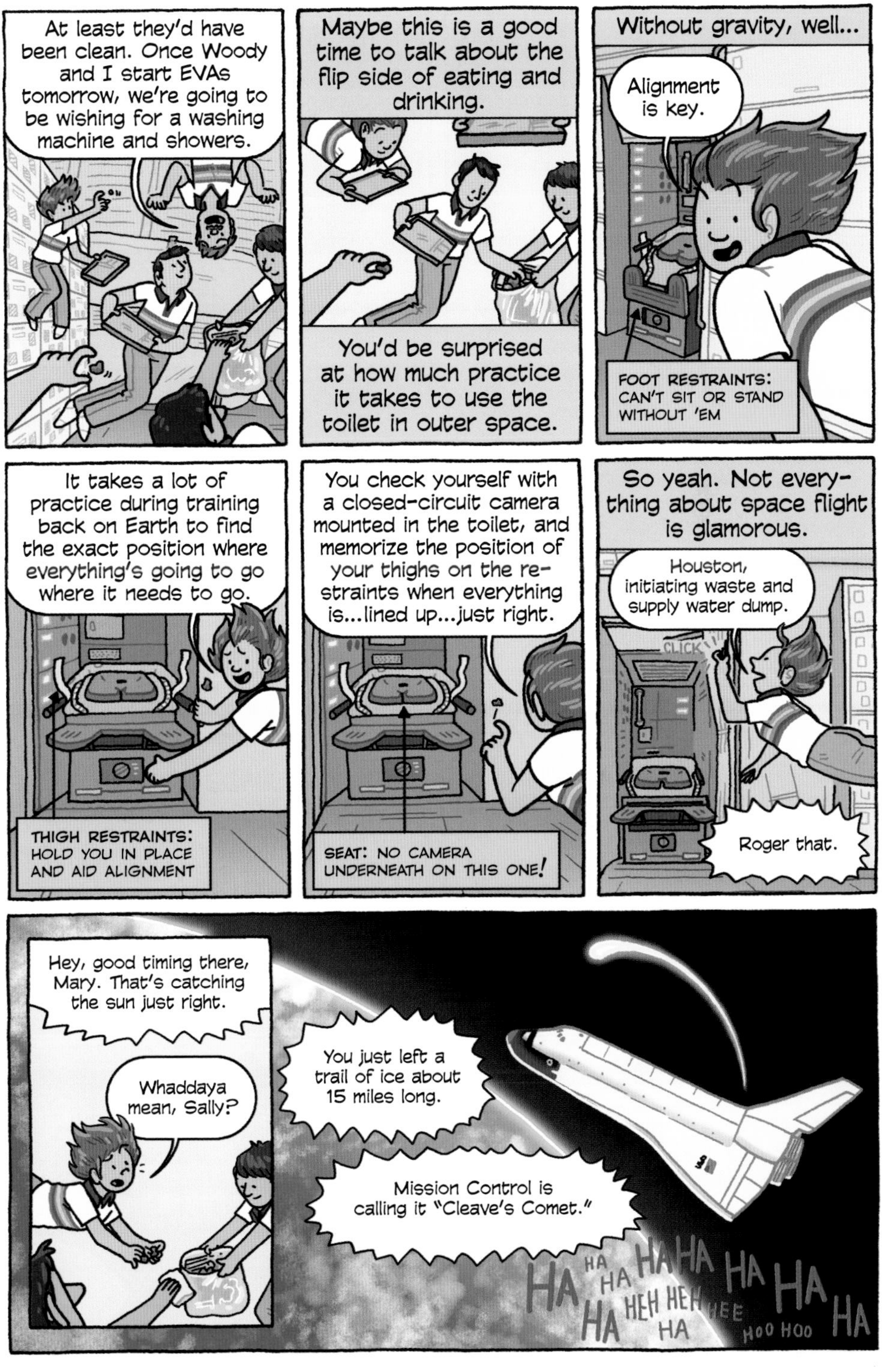

At least they'd have been clean. Once Woody and I start EVAs tomorrow, we're going to be wishing for a washing machine and showers.
Maybe this is a good time to talk about the flip side of eating and drinking.
You'd be surprised at how much practice it takes to use the toilet in outer space.
Without gravity, well...
Alignment is key.
FOOT RESTRAINTS: CAN'T SIT OR STAND WITHOUT 'EM
It takes a lot of practice during training back on Earth to find the exact position where everything's going to go where it needs to go.
THIGH RESTRAINTS: HOLD YOU IN PLACE AND AID ALIGNMENT
You check yourself with a closed-circuit camera mounted in the toilet, and memorize the position of your thighs on the restraints when everything is...lined up...just right.
SEAT: NO CAMERA UNDERNEATH ON THIS ONE!
So yeah. Not everything about space flight is glamorous.
Houston, initiating waste and supply water dump.
CLICK
Roger that.
Hey, good timing there, Mary. That's catching the sun just right.
Whaddaya mean, Sally?
You just left a trail of ice about 15 miles long.
Mission Control is calling it "Cleave's Comet."
HA HA HA HA HA HA HA HA HA HA HEH HEH HEE HA HOO HOO HA

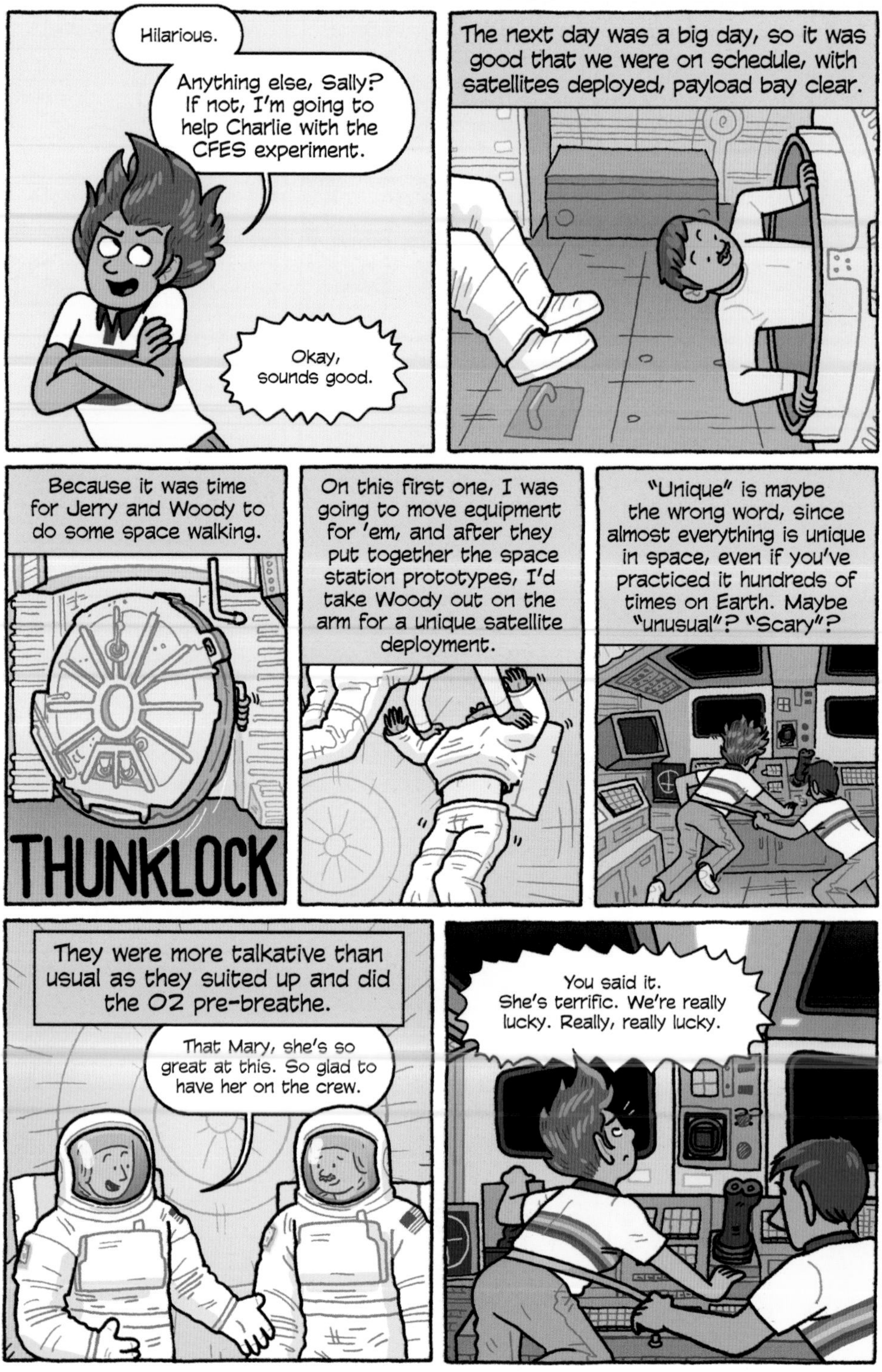
Hilarious.
Anything else, Sally? If not, I'm going to help Charlie with the CFES experiment.
Okay, sounds good.
The next day was a big day, so it was good that we were on schedule, with satellites deployed, payload bay clear.
Because it was time for Jerry and Woody to do some space walking.
THUNKLOCK
On this first one, I was going to move equipment for 'em, and after they put together the space station prototypes, I'd take Woody out on the arm for a unique satellite deployment.
"Unique" is maybe the wrong word, since almost everything is unique in space, even if you've practiced it hundreds of times on Earth. Maybe "unusual"? "Scary"?
They were more talkative than usual as they suited up and did the O2 pre-breathe.
That Mary, she's so great at this. So glad to have her on the crew.
You said it. She's terrific. We're really lucky. Really, really lucky.

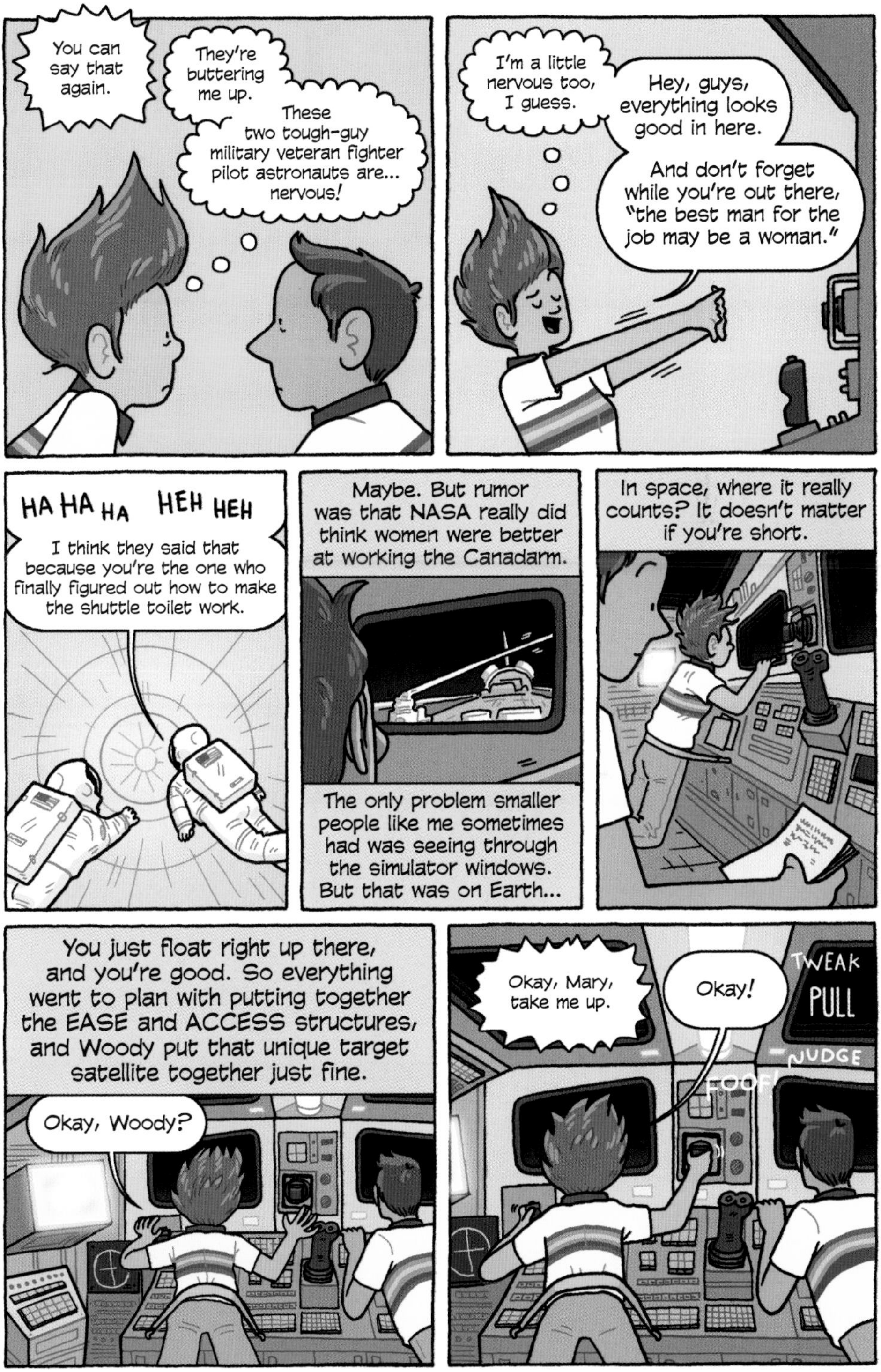
You can say that again.
They're buttering me up.
These two tough-guy military veteran fighter pilot astronauts are... nervous!
I'm a little nervous too, I guess.
Hey, guys, everything looks good in here.
And don't forget while you're out there, "the best man for the job may be a woman."
HA HA HA HEH HEH
I think they said that because you're the one who finally figured out how to make the shuttle toilet work.
Maybe. But rumor was that NASA really did think women were better at working the Canadarm.
The only problem smaller people like me sometimes had was seeing through the simulator windows. But that was on Earth...
In space, where it really counts? It doesn't matter if you're short.
You just float right up there, and you're good. So everything went to plan with putting together the EASE and ACCESS structures, and Woody put that unique target satellite together just fine.
Okay, Woody?
Okay, Mary, take me up.
Okay!
TWEAK
PULL
NUDGE
FOOF!

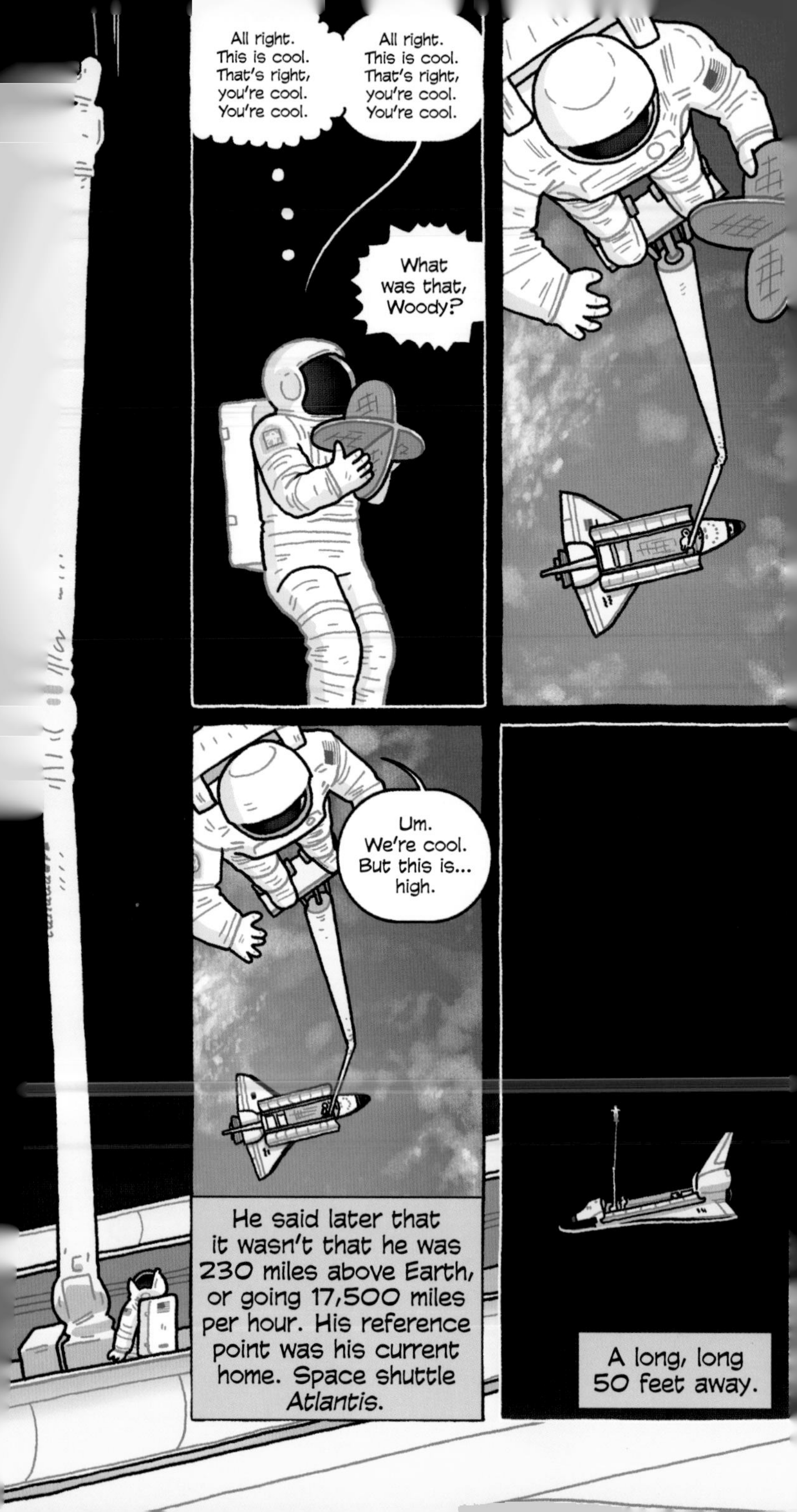
All right. This is cool. That's right, you're cool. You're cool.
All right. This is cool. That's right, you're cool. You're cool.
What was that, Woody?
Um. We're cool. But this is... high.
He said later that it wasn't that he was 230 miles above Earth, or going 17,500 miles per hour. His reference point was his current home. Space shuttle *Atlantis*.
A long, long 50 feet away.

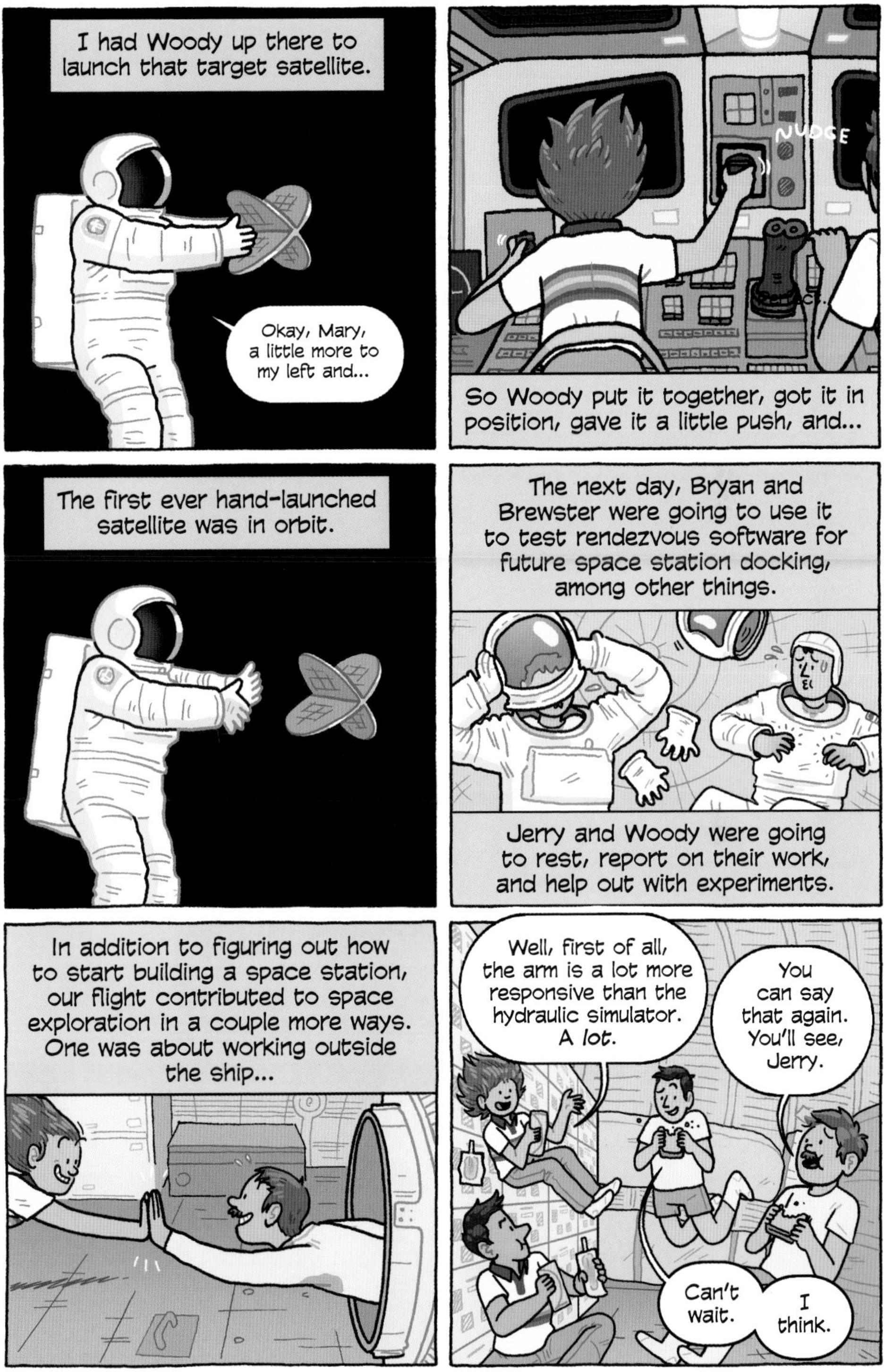

I had Woody up there to launch that target satellite.
Okay, Mary, a little more to my left and...
NUDGE
So Woody put it together, got it in position, gave it a little push, and...
The first ever hand-launched satellite was in orbit.
The next day, Bryan and Brewster were going to use it to test rendezvous software for future space station docking, among other things.
Jerry and Woody were going to rest, report on their work, and help out with experiments.
In addition to figuring out how to start building a space station, our flight contributed to space exploration in a couple more ways. One was about working outside the ship...
Well, first of all, the arm is a lot more responsive than the hydraulic simulator. A *lot*.
You can say that again. You'll see, Jerry.
Can't wait.
I think.

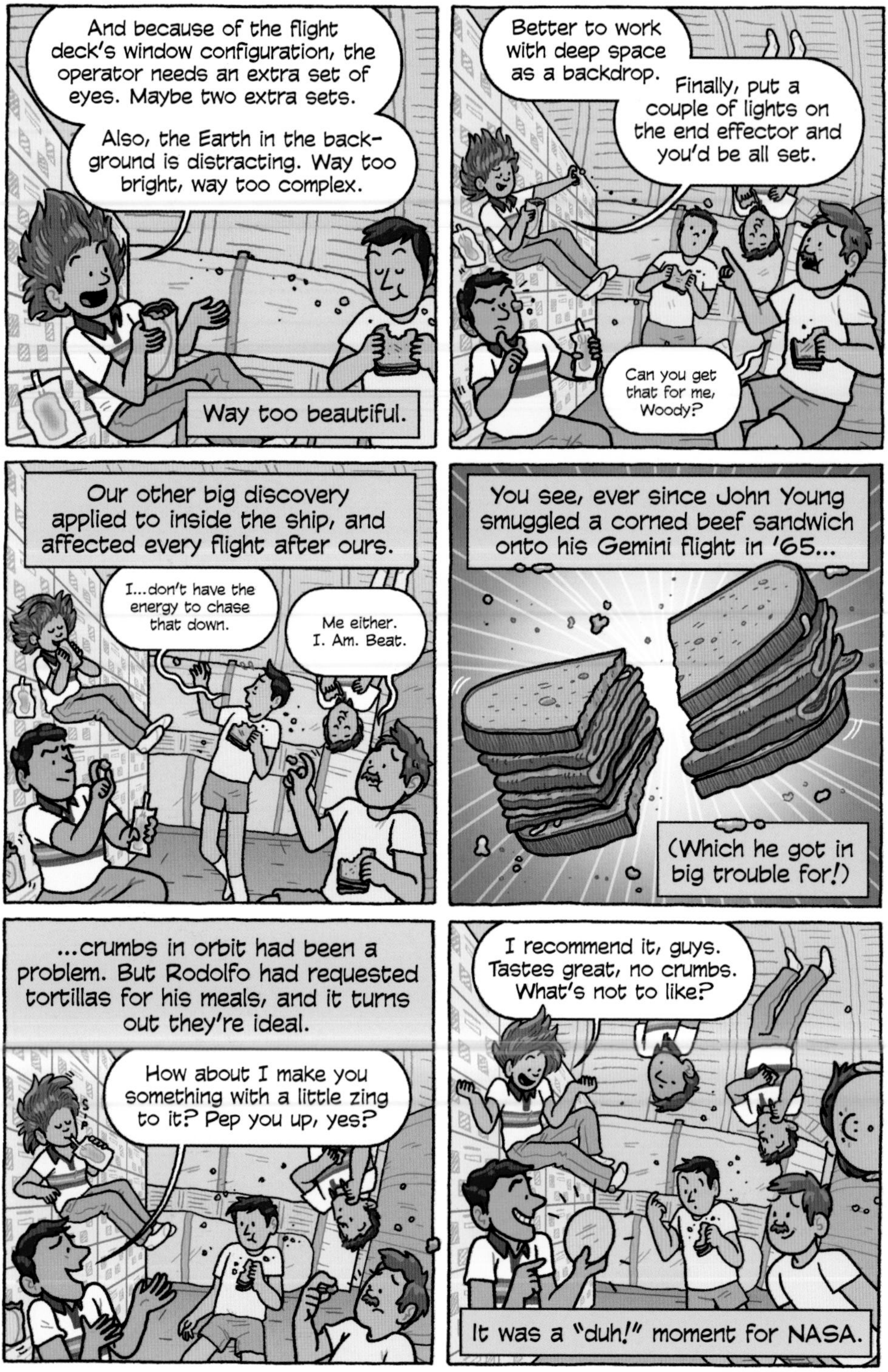

And because of the flight deck's window configuration, the operator needs an extra set of eyes. Maybe two extra sets.
Also, the Earth in the background is distracting. Way too bright, way too complex.
Way too beautiful.
Better to work with deep space as a backdrop.
Finally, put a couple of lights on the end effector and you'd be all set.
Can you get that for me, Woody?
Our other big discovery applied to inside the ship, and affected every flight after ours.
I...don't have the energy to chase that down.
Me either. I. Am. Beat.
You see, ever since John Young smuggled a corned beef sandwich onto his Gemini flight in '65...
(Which he got in big trouble for!)
...crumbs in orbit had been a problem. But Rodolfo had requested tortillas for his meals, and it turns out they're ideal.
S I P
How about I make you something with a little zing to it? Pep you up, yes?
I recommend it, guys. Tastes great, no crumbs. What's not to like?
It was a "duh!" moment for NASA.

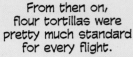

From then on, flour tortillas were pretty much standard for every flight.

Try one, Charlie.

And they make great cabin frisbees, too.

Anyway, after a day of rest for Jerry and Woody, science for Charlie, Rodolfo, and me, and rendezvous software testing for Brewster and Bryan...

Woody and Jerry were back in the airlock, getting ready for EVA 2.

It takes a long time to get outside in space. You can't just push open the door and go.

Mary sure is good at this. She's really a great guy.

So while they suited up and did their O2 pre-breathing—and buttering me up—I went over the plan again.

ACCESS

"Great guy"?

Yeah, be nice or I'll, ya know, flick my wrist and send you...

Assemble nine bays of ACCESS, pack component carrier, then move Jerry to the top to construct the last bay.

Maintenance, repair, disassembly.

Repeat with EASE structure: Unstow, move, attach, connect to form the 23.5 ft, 130 lb beam.

Okay, boys, that's enough goldbricking.

Ace Construction Company is back on the job.

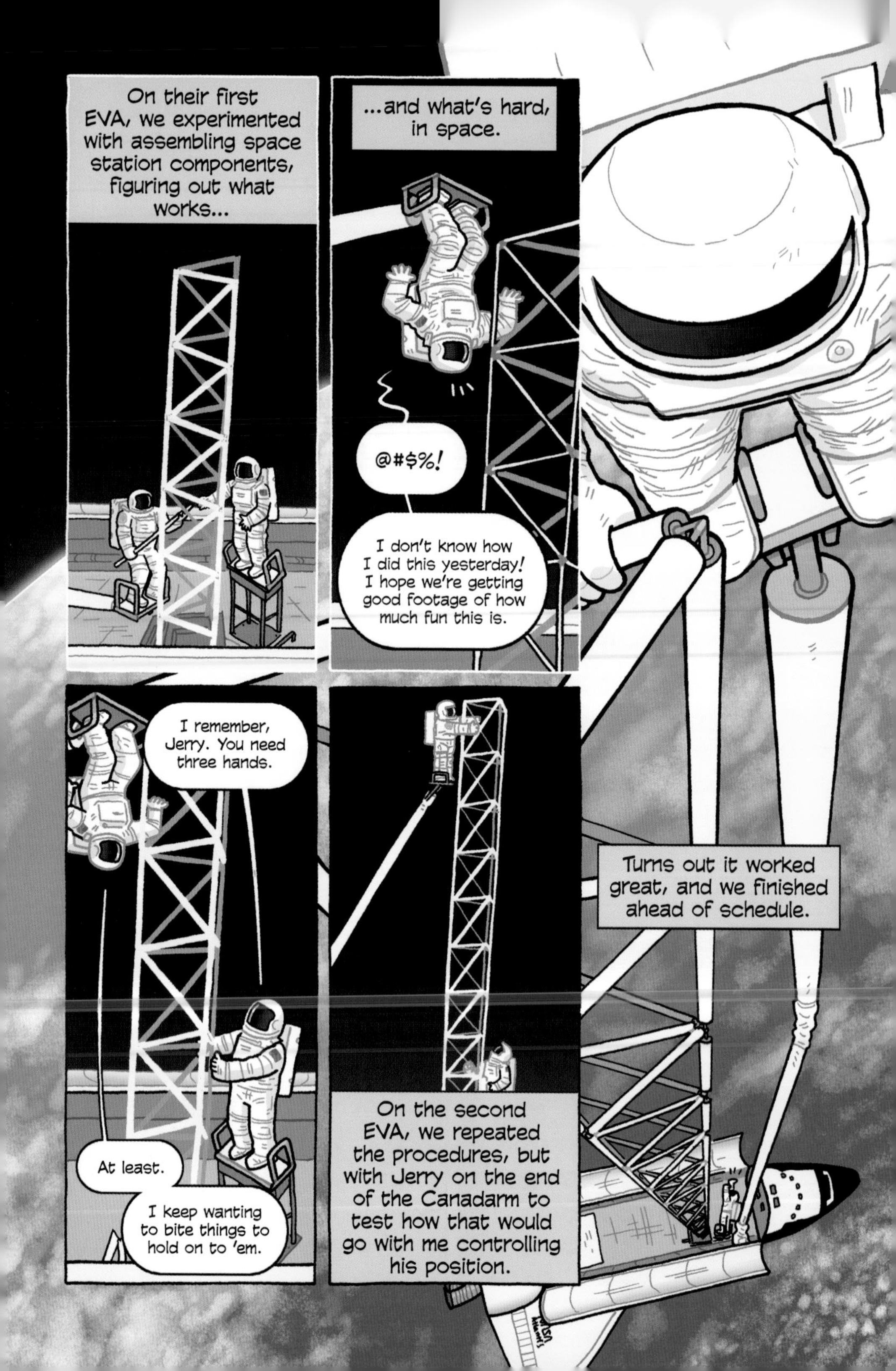

On their first EVA, we experimented with assembling space station components, figuring out what works...
...and what's hard, in space.
@#$%!
I don't know how I did this yesterday! I hope we're getting good footage of how much fun this is.
I remember, Jerry. You need three hands.
At least.
I keep wanting to bite things to hold on to 'em.
On the second EVA, we repeated the procedures, but with Jerry on the end of the Canadarm to test how that would go with me controlling his position.
Turns out it worked great, and we finished ahead of schedule.

So we had time at the end for me to pull him all the way back. So far back that he couldn't see the shuttle.

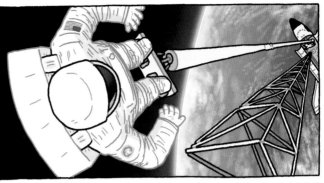

I did it slowly in case anybody got upset—which these guys would never admit to.

He was up there all by himself and couldn't take reference on the spaceship at all.

And then I rolled the wrist of the Canadarm and he was all by himself. And...

twist

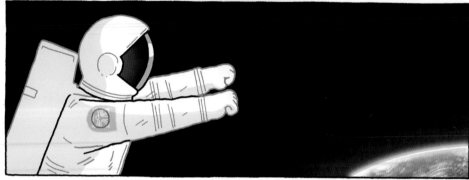

Look! Up in the sky! It's a bird...it's a plane...

It was cute.

No, it was great.

Okay, it was both.

1% power... time to go home!

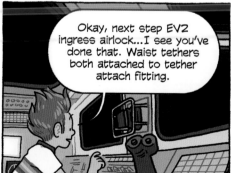

Okay, next step EV2 ingress airlock...I see you've done that. Waist tethers both attached to tether attach fitting.

Getting back in takes almost as long as going out. Again, it's a lot more than grabbing the handle and yelling, "Hey, guys, I'm home!"

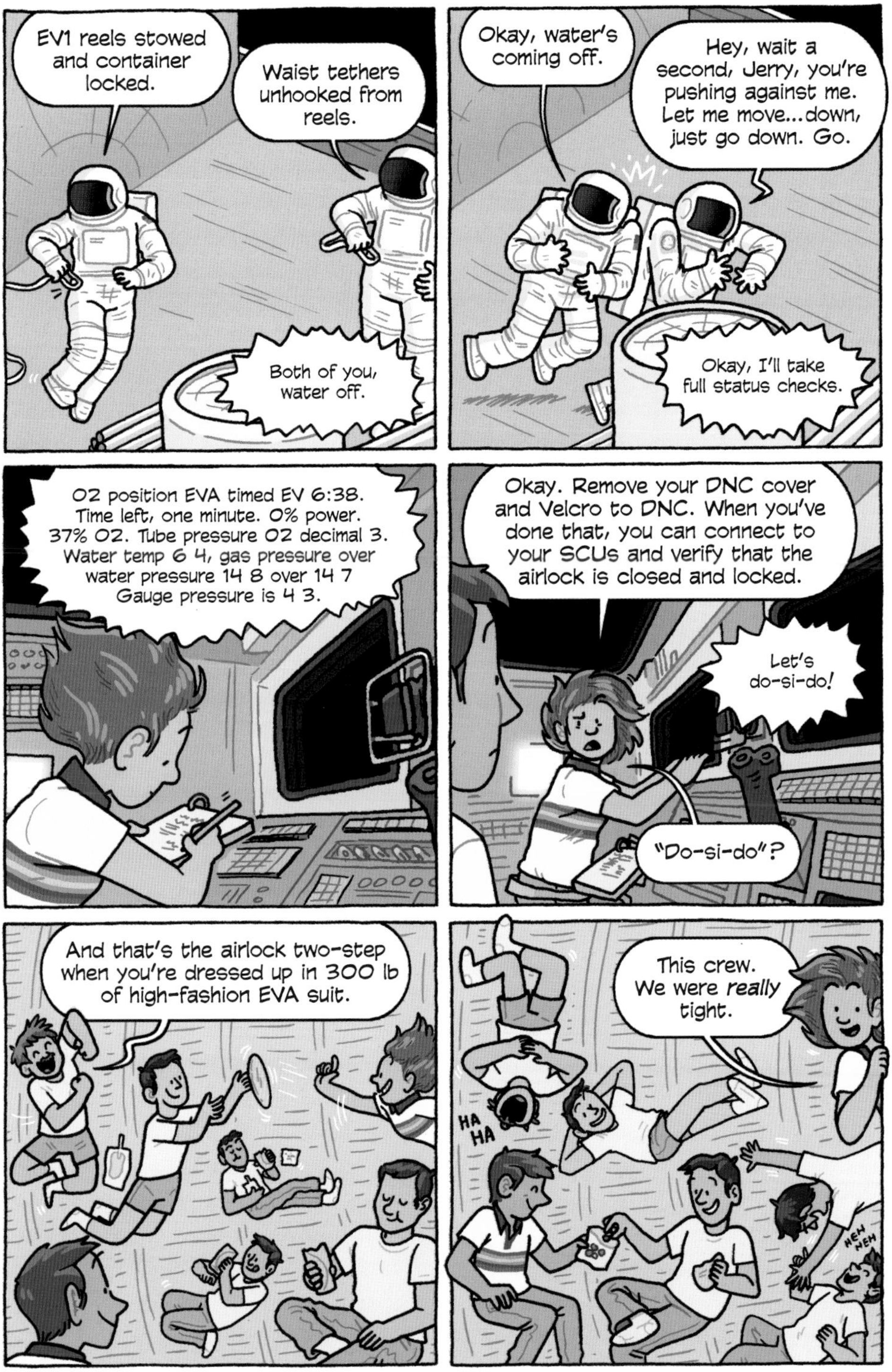
EV1 reels stowed and container locked.
Waist tethers unhooked from reels.
Both of you, water off.
Okay, water's coming off.
Hey, wait a second, Jerry, you're pushing against me. Let me move...down, just go down. Go.
Okay, I'll take full status checks.
O2 position EVA timed EV 6:38. Time left, one minute. 0% power. 37% O2. Tube pressure O2 decimal 3. Water temp 6 4, gas pressure over water pressure 14 8 over 14 7 Gauge pressure is 4 3.
Okay. Remove your DNC cover and Velcro to DNC. When you've done that, you can connect to your SCUs and verify that the airlock is closed and locked.
Let's do-si-do!
"Do-si-do"?
And that's the airlock two-step when you're dressed up in 300 lb of high-fashion EVA suit.
This crew. We were *really* tight.
HA HA
HEH HEH

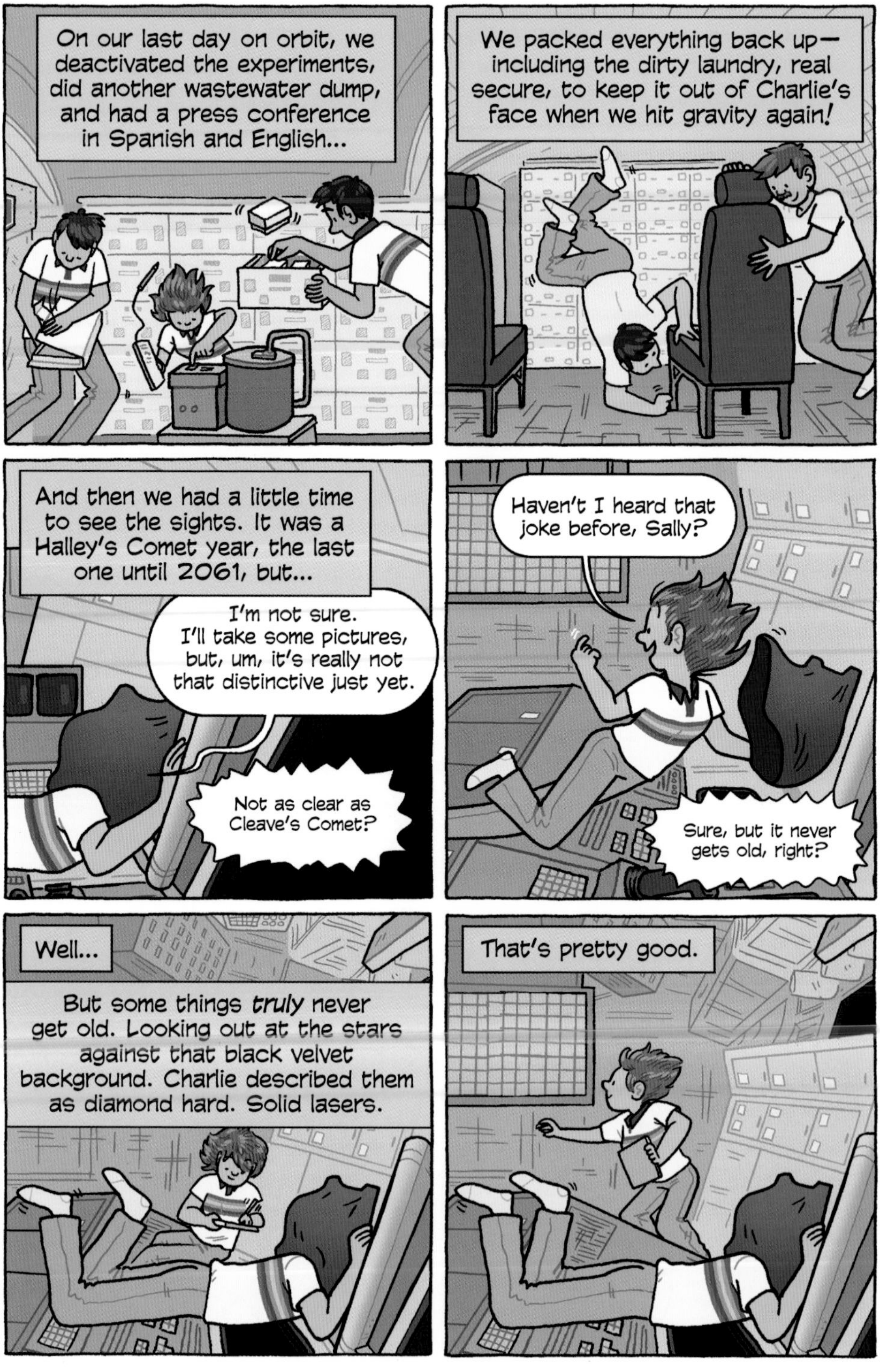
On our last day on orbit, we deactivated the experiments, did another wastewater dump, and had a press conference in Spanish and English...
We packed everything back up—including the dirty laundry, real secure, to keep it out of Charlie's face when we hit gravity again!
And then we had a little time to see the sights. It was a Halley's Comet year, the last one until 2061, but...
I'm not sure. I'll take some pictures, but, um, it's really not that distinctive just yet.
Not as clear as Cleave's Comet?
Haven't I heard that joke before, Sally?
Sure, but it never gets old, right?
Well...
But some things *truly* never get old. Looking out at the stars against that black velvet background. Charlie described them as diamond hard. Solid lasers.
That's pretty good.

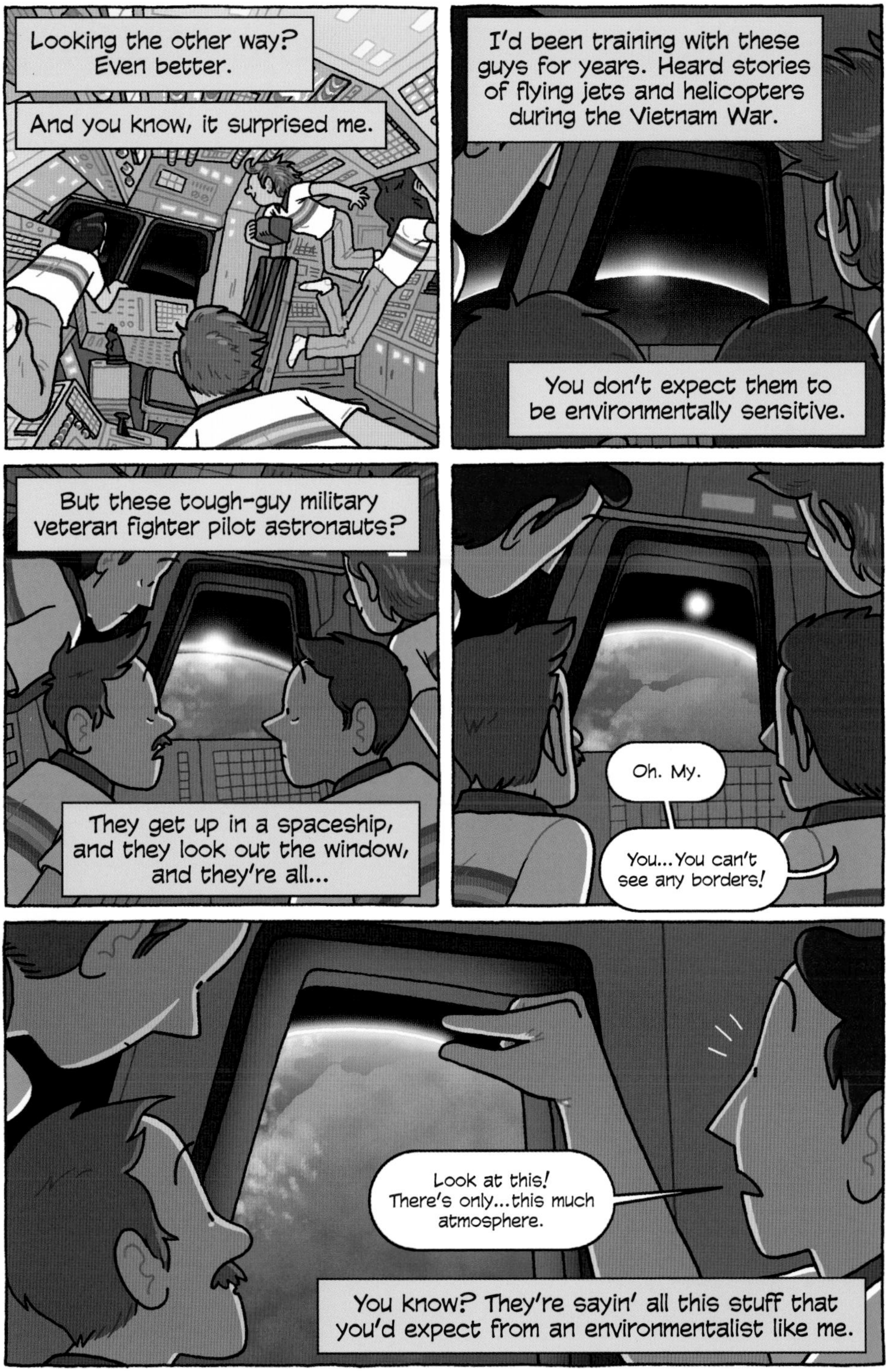
Looking the other way? Even better.
And you know, it surprised me.
I'd been training with these guys for years. Heard stories of flying jets and helicopters during the Vietnam War.
You don't expect them to be environmentally sensitive.
But these tough-guy military veteran fighter pilot astronauts?
They get up in a spaceship, and they look out the window, and they're all...
Oh. My.
You...You can't see any borders!
Look at this! There's only...this much atmosphere.
You know? They're sayin' all this stuff that you'd expect from an environmentalist like me.

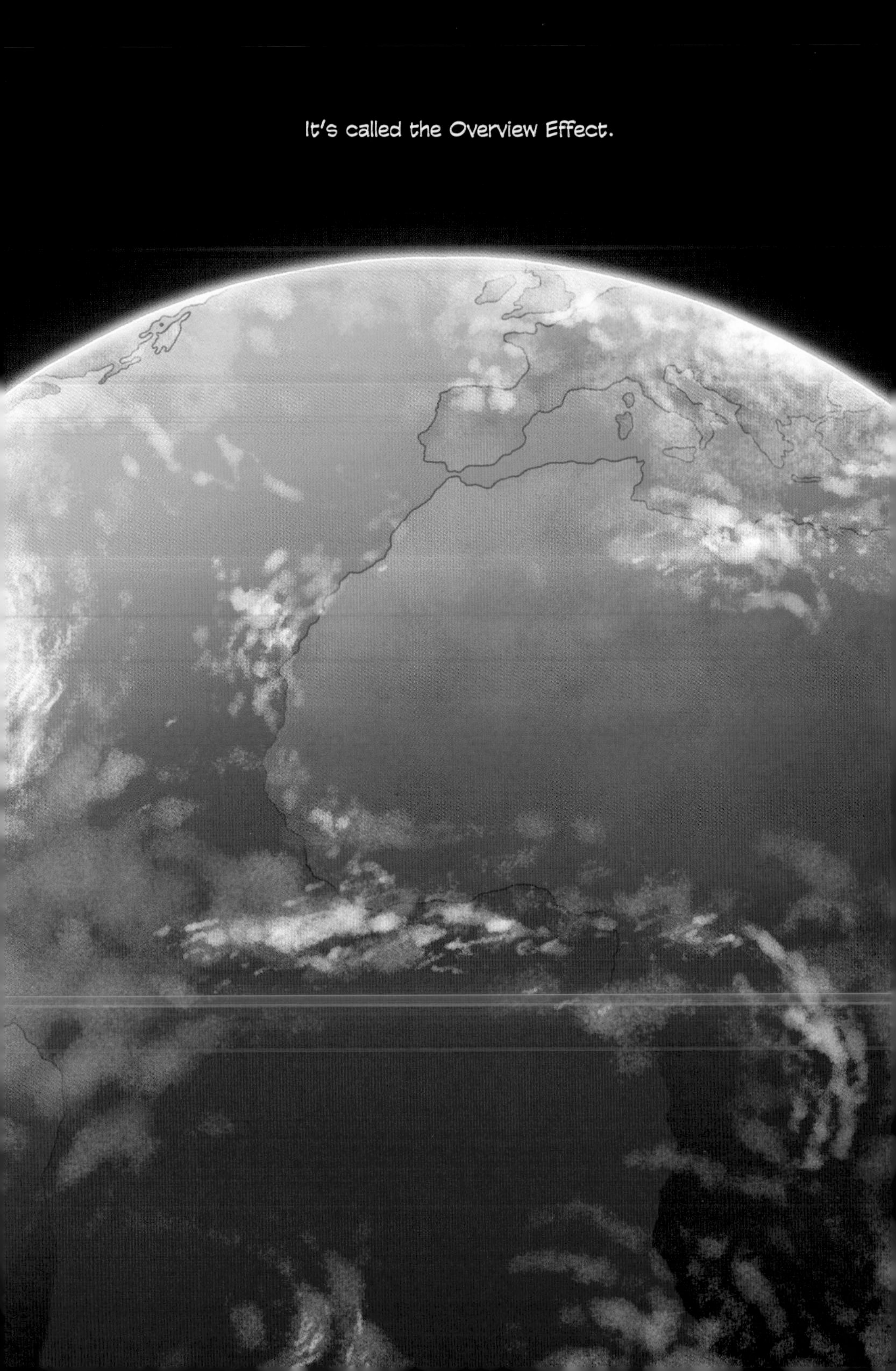
It's called the Overview Effect.

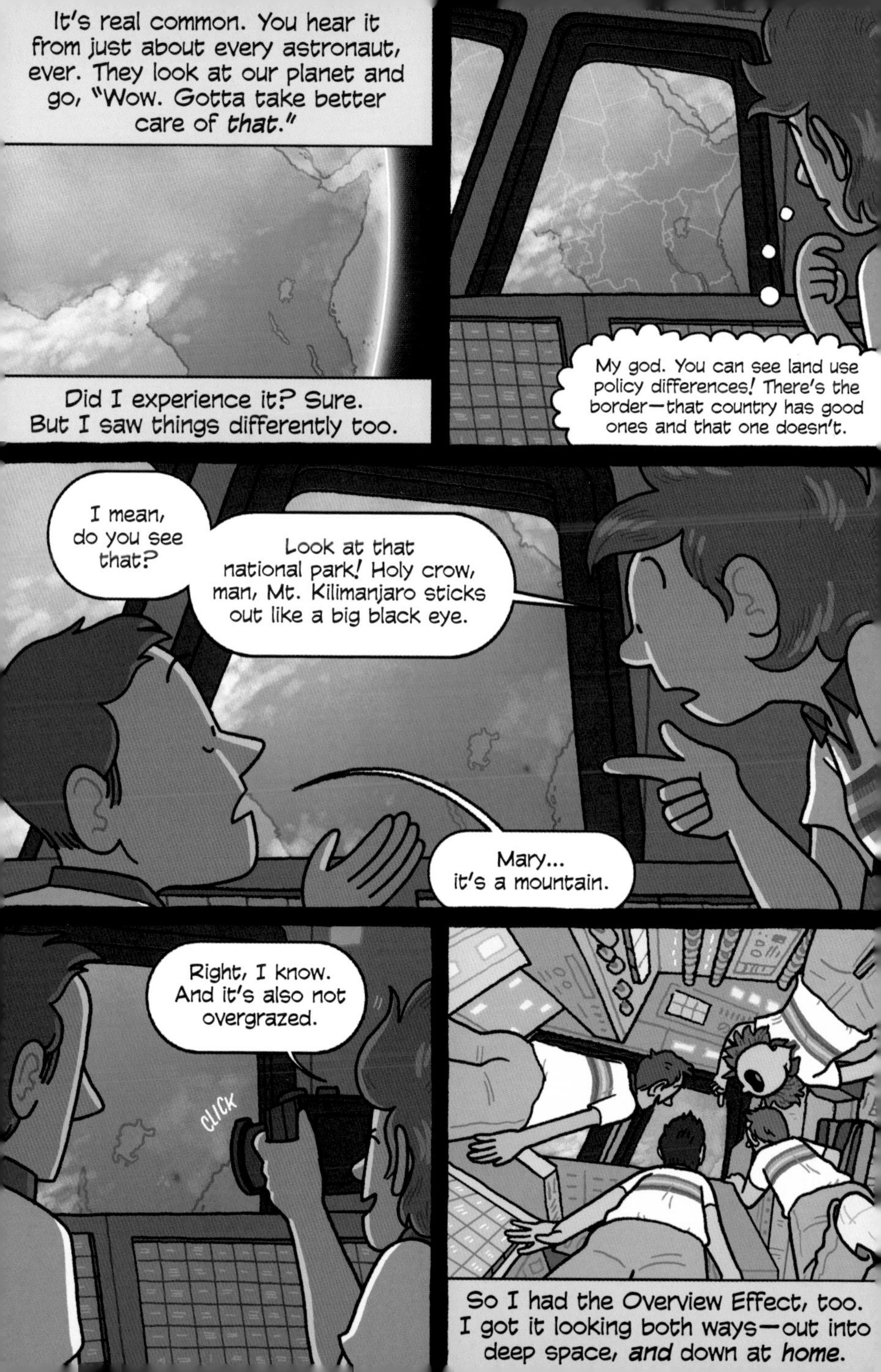
It's real common. You hear it from just about every astronaut, ever. They look at our planet and go, "Wow. Gotta take better care of *that*."
Did I experience it? Sure. But I saw things differently too.
My god. You can see land use policy differences! There's the border—that country has good ones and that one doesn't.
I mean, do you see that?
Look at that national park! Holy crow, man, Mt. Kilimanjaro sticks out like a big black eye.
Mary... it's a mountain.
Right, I know. And it's also not overgrazed.
CLICK
So I had the Overview Effect, too. I got it looking both ways—out into deep space, ***and*** down at ***home***.

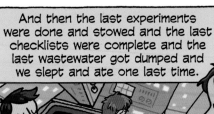

And then the last experiments were done and stowed and the last checklists were complete and the last wastewater got dumped and we slept and ate one last time.

And we returned to Earth.

Your mind can take it in as kinda soothing, that palette. But intellectually?

It's 3,000 degrees fahrenheit just a fraction of an inch beyond the outside of this window.

We're going 18,000 miles an hour.

We got quite a bit of vibration and a little bucking for the first time in well over a week.

Now, as soon as we pass transonic, it's going to go away again.

And it did.

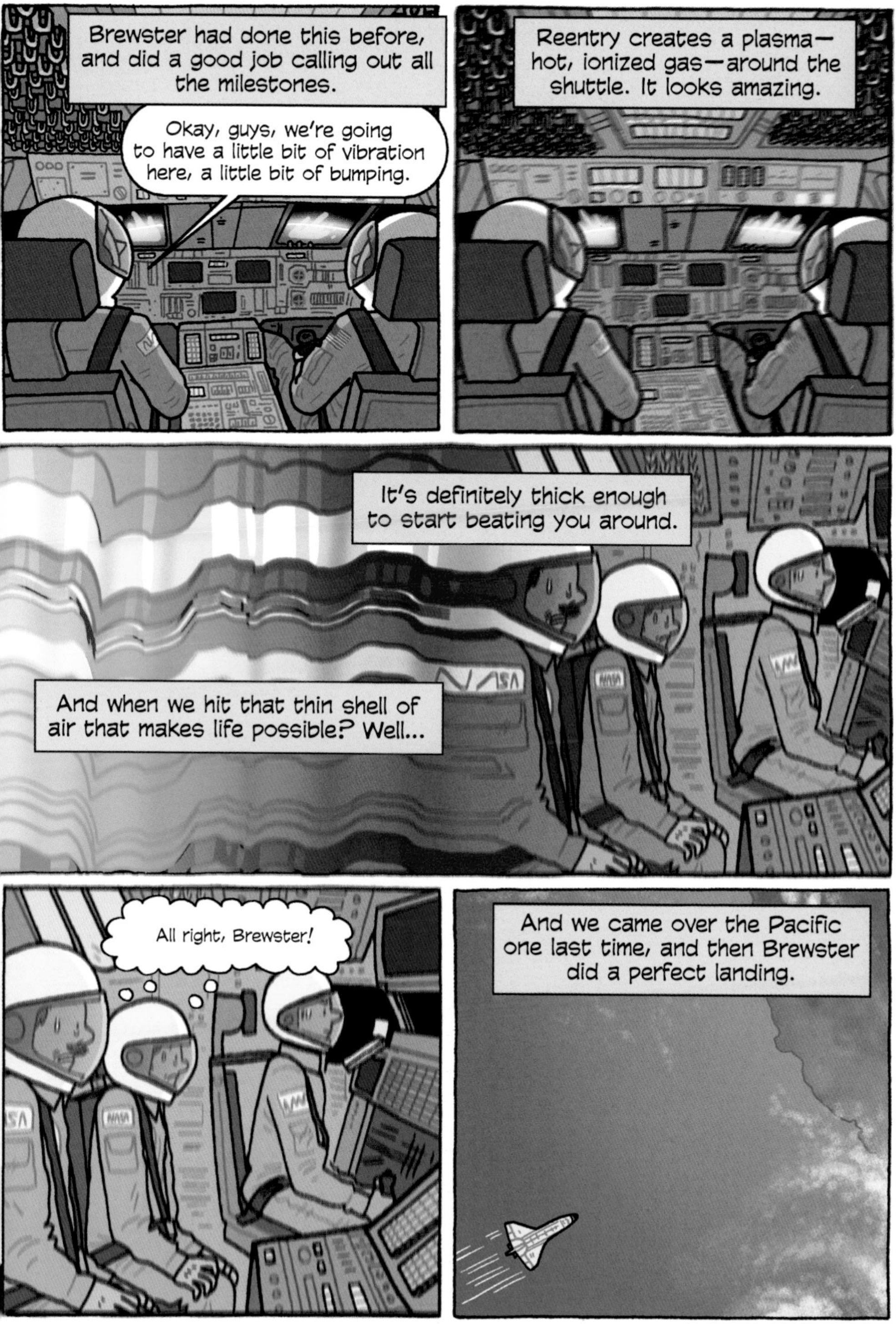
Brewster had done this before, and did a good job calling out all the milestones.
Okay, guys, we're going to have a little bit of vibration here, a little bit of bumping.
Reentry creates a plasma—hot, ionized gas—around the shuttle. It looks amazing.
It's definitely thick enough to start beating you around.
And when we hit that thin shell of air that makes life possible? Well...
All right, Brewster!
And we came over the Pacific one last time, and then Brewster did a perfect landing.

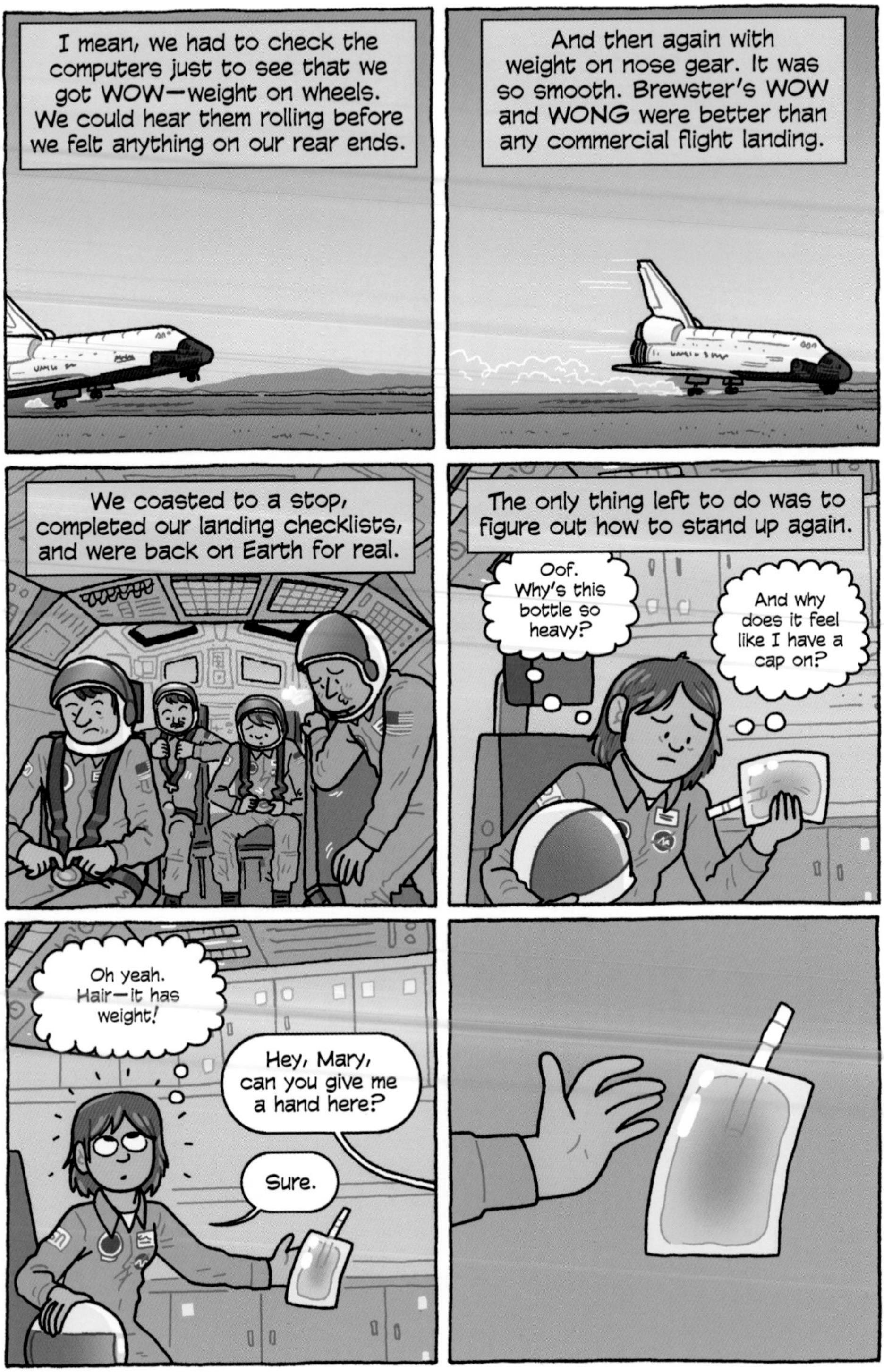
I mean, we had to check the computers just to see that we got WOW—weight on wheels. We could hear them rolling before we felt anything on our rear ends.
And then again with weight on nose gear. It was so smooth. Brewster's WOW and WONG were better than any commercial flight landing.
We coasted to a stop, completed our landing checklists, and were back on Earth for real.
The only thing left to do was to figure out how to stand up again.
Oof. Why's this bottle so heavy?
And why does it feel like I have a cap on?
Oh yeah. Hair—it has weight!
Hey, Mary, can you give me a hand here?
Sure.

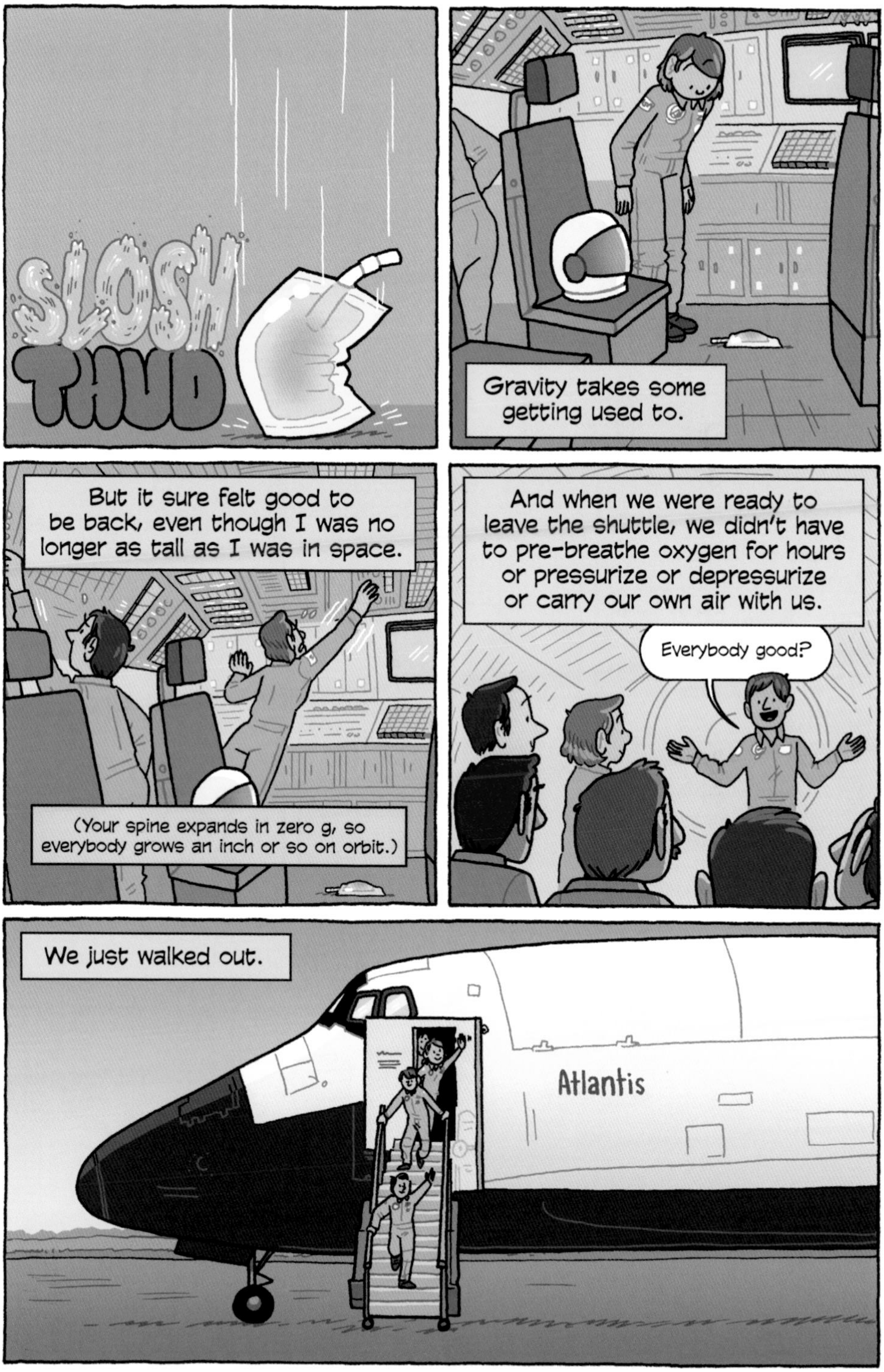
SLOSH
THUD
Gravity takes some getting used to.
But it sure felt good to be back, even though I was no longer as tall as I was in space.
(Your spine expands in zero g, so everybody grows an inch or so on orbit.)
And when we were ready to leave the shuttle, we didn't have to pre-breathe oxygen for hours or pressurize or depressurize or carry our own air with us.
Everybody good?
We just walked out.
Atlantis

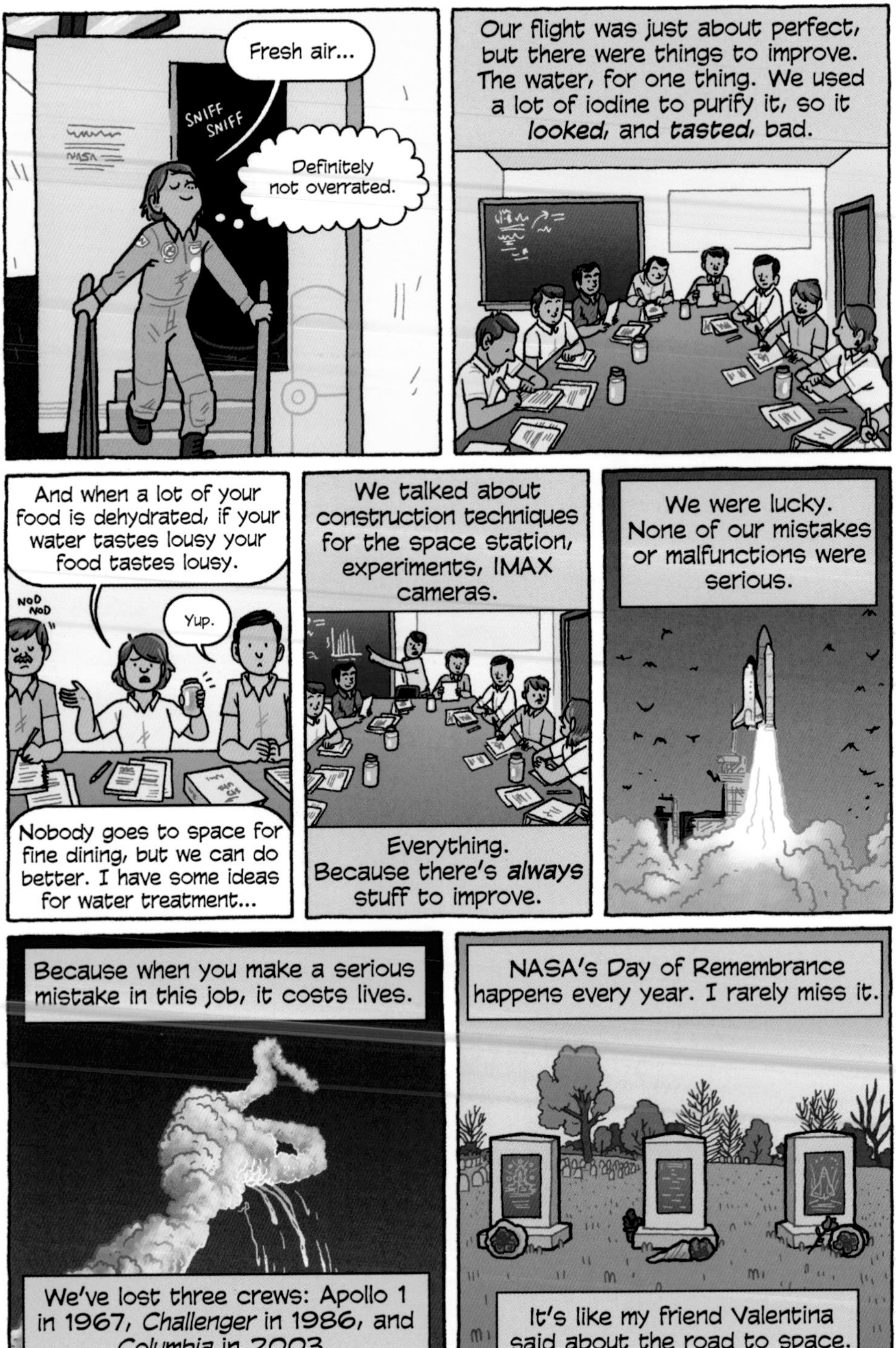

Fresh air...
SNIFF SNIFF
NASA
Definitely not overrated.
Our flight was just about perfect, but there were things to improve. The water, for one thing. We used a lot of iodine to purify it, so it *looked*, and *tasted*, bad.
And when a lot of your food is dehydrated, if your water tastes lousy your food tastes lousy.
NOD NOD
Yup.
Nobody goes to space for fine dining, but we can do better. I have some ideas for water treatment...
We talked about construction techniques for the space station, experiments, IMAX cameras.
Everything. Because there's *always* stuff to improve.
We were lucky. None of our mistakes or malfunctions were serious.
Because when you make a serious mistake in this job, it costs lives.
We've lost three crews: Apollo 1 in 1967, *Challenger* in 1986, and *Columbia* in 2003.
NASA's Day of Remembrance happens every year. I rarely miss it.
It's like my friend Valentina said about the road to space.

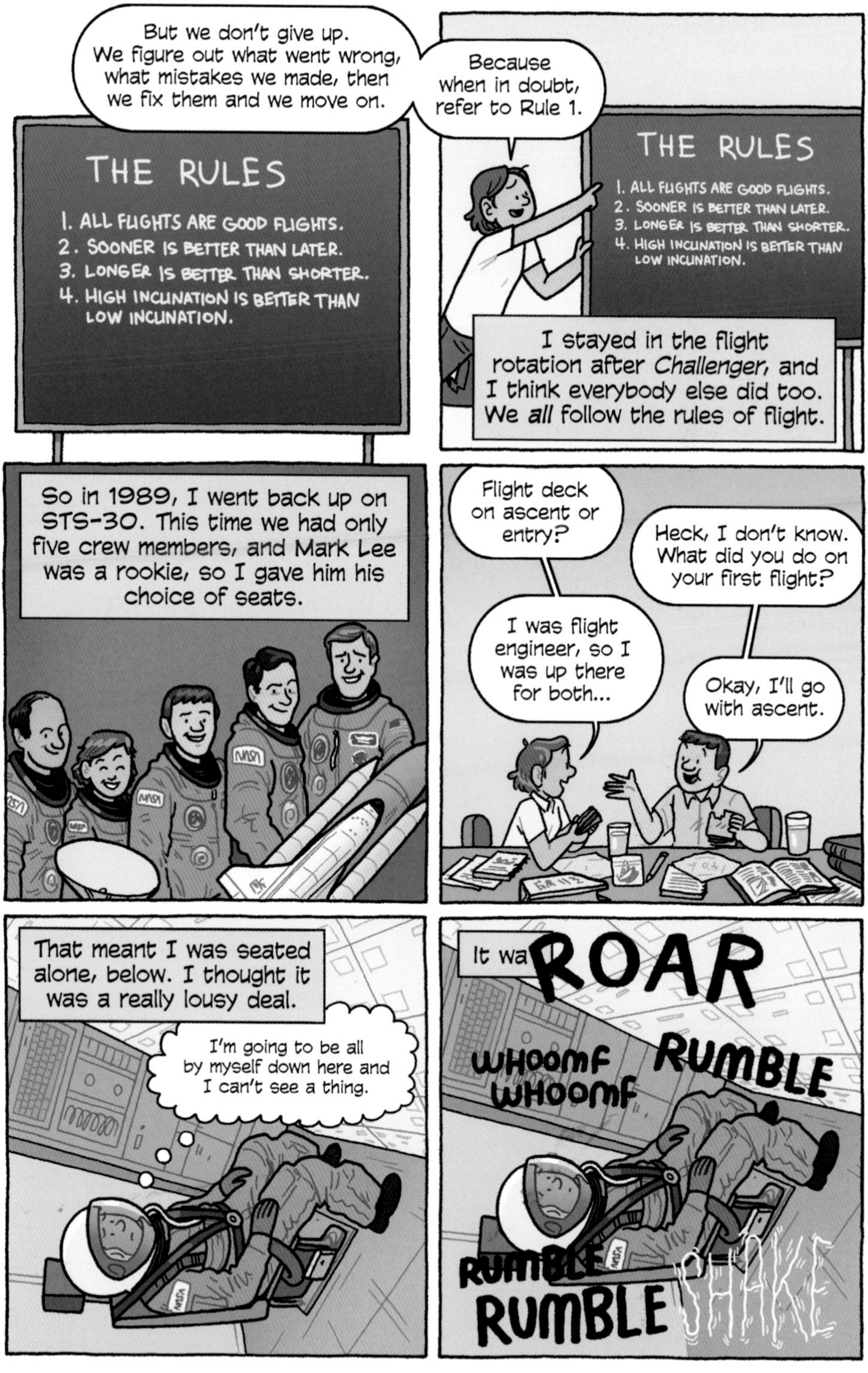
But we don't give up. We figure out what went wrong, what mistakes we made, then we fix them and we move on.
THE RULES
1. ALL FLIGHTS ARE GOOD FLIGHTS.
2. SOONER IS BETTER THAN LATER.
3. LONGER IS BETTER THAN SHORTER.
4. HIGH INCLINATION IS BETTER THAN LOW INCLINATION.
Because when in doubt, refer to Rule 1.
THE RULES
1. ALL FLIGHTS ARE GOOD FLIGHTS.
2. SOONER IS BETTER THAN LATER.
3. LONGER IS BETTER THAN SHORTER.
4. HIGH INCLINATION IS BETTER THAN LOW INCLINATION.
I stayed in the flight rotation after *Challenger*, and I think everybody else did too. We *all* follow the rules of flight.
So in 1989, I went back up on STS-30. This time we had only five crew members, and Mark Lee was a rookie, so I gave him his choice of seats.
Flight deck on ascent or entry?
Heck, I don't know. What did you do on your first flight?
I was flight engineer, so I was up there for both...
Okay, I'll go with ascent.
That meant I was seated alone, below. I thought it was a really lousy deal.
I'm going to be all by myself down here and I can't see a thing.
It wa
ROAR
WHOOMF
WHOOMF
RUMBLE
RUMBLE
RUMBLE
SHAKE

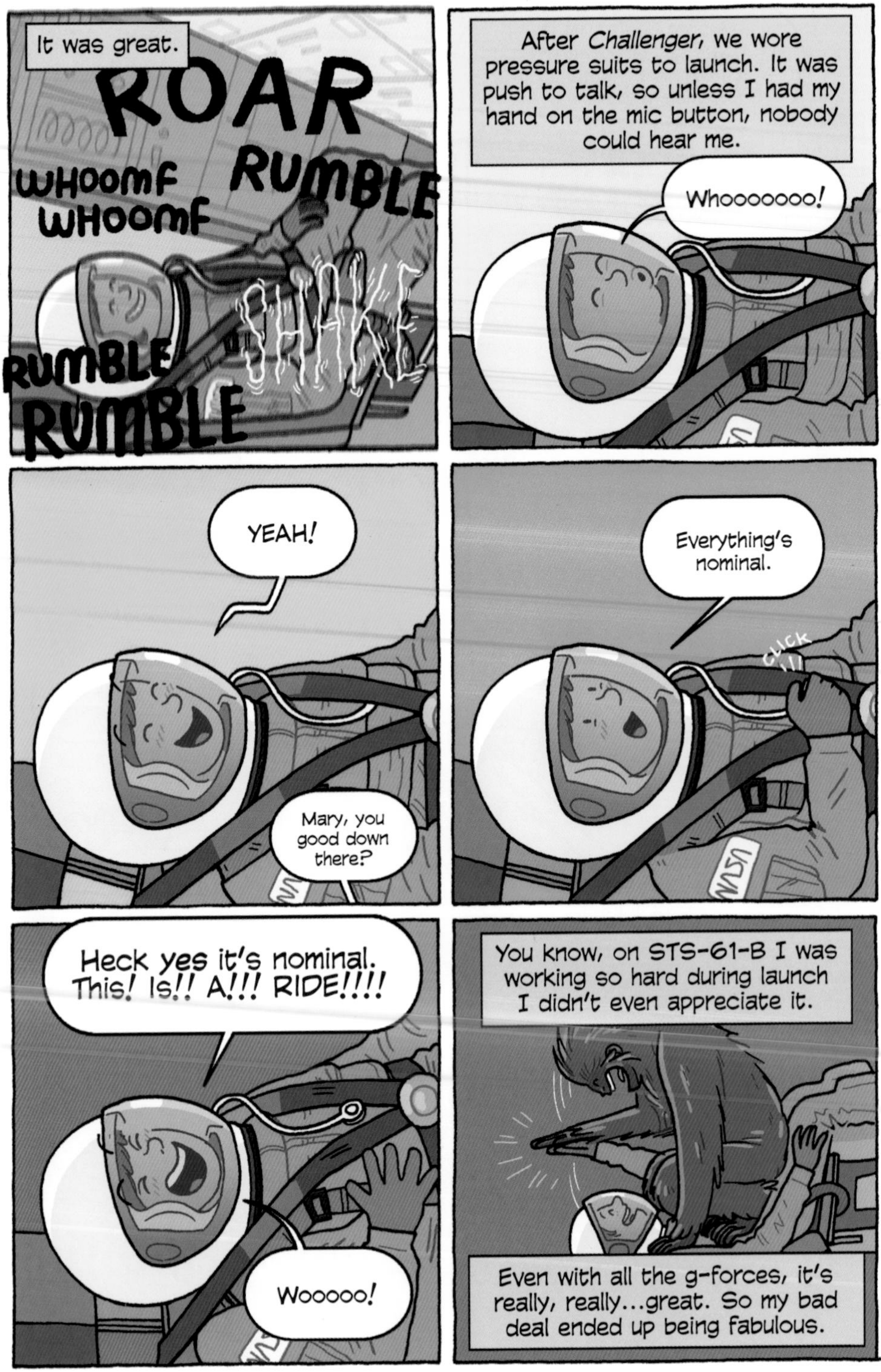
It was great.
ROAR
WHOOMF WHOOMF
RUMBLE
SHAKE
RUMBLE RUMBLE
After *Challenger*, we wore pressure suits to launch. It was push to talk, so unless I had my hand on the mic button, nobody could hear me.
Whooooooo!
YEAH!
Mary, you good down there?
Everything's nominal.
CLICK
Heck yes it's nominal. This! Is!! A!!! RIDE!!!!
Wooooo!
You know, on STS-61-B I was working so hard during launch I didn't even appreciate it.
Even with all the g-forces, it's really, really...great. So my bad deal ended up being fabulous.

Our primary mission was to launch *Magellan*, which was going to do radar imaging of Venus's surface.

Understanding a planet where greenhouse gases took over is important, and *Magellan* did great work. That kinda got me interested in robotic spacecraft.

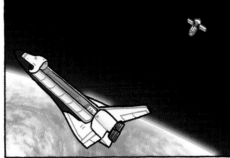

Mike Lee and I worked real hard until we deployed *Magellan*. First day, it's out of the payload bay. After that it belonged to the Jet Propulsion Lab engineers and scientists.

So we got rid of this thing, and then I got to do a lot more picture taking. I wasn't part of the flight crew, so I didn't have to worry about crew rest periods.

CLICK

As my officemate Mike Mullane says, "I can sleep back on Earth— how often can I look out the window from space?"

So basically for the rest of the mission, I didn't sleep too much. I was up taking pictures and just having a good time.

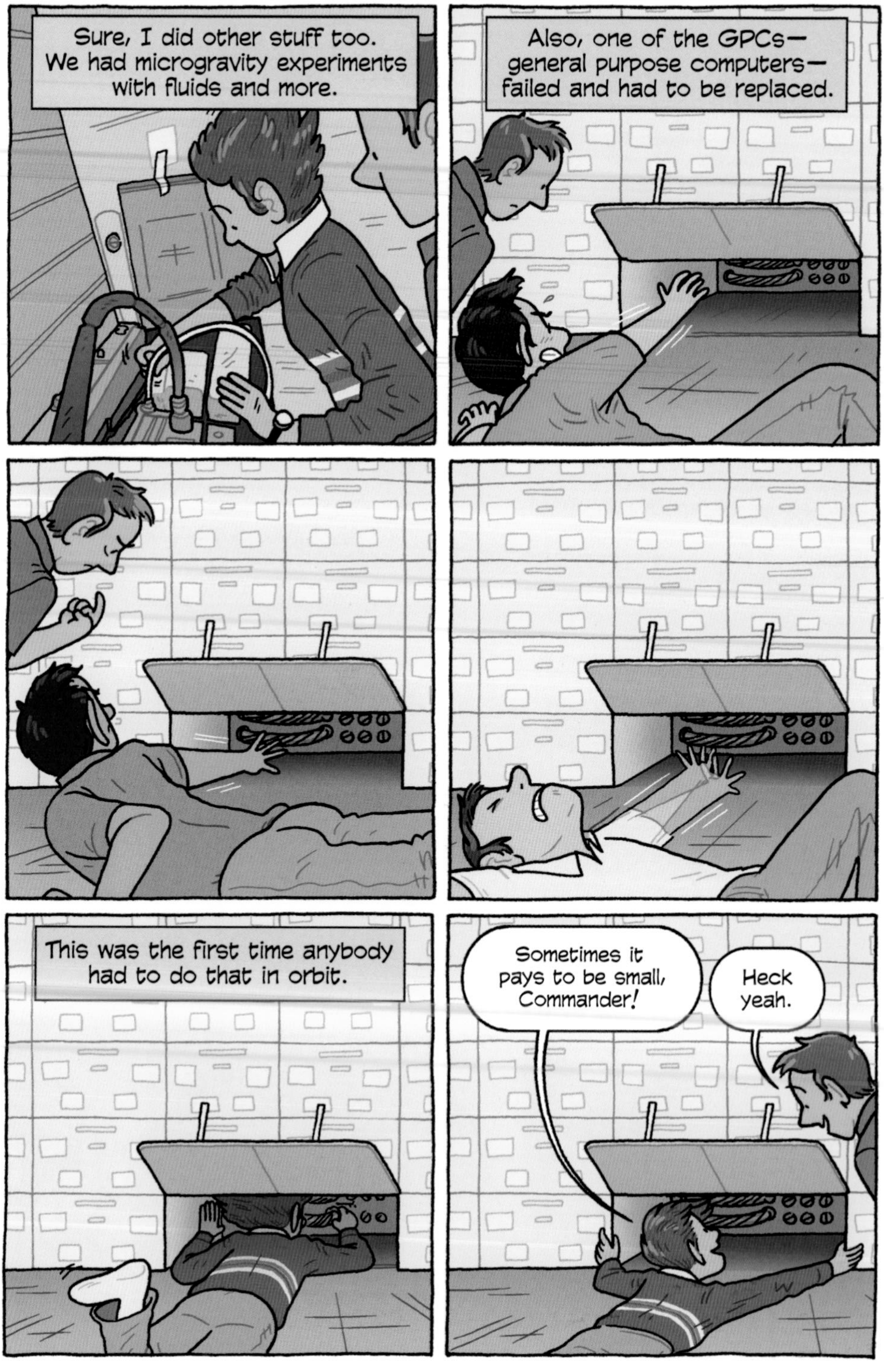

Sure, I did other stuff too. We had microgravity experiments with fluids and more.
Also, one of the GPCs—general purpose computers—failed and had to be replaced.
This was the first time anybody had to do that in orbit.
Sometimes it pays to be small, Commander!
Heck yeah.

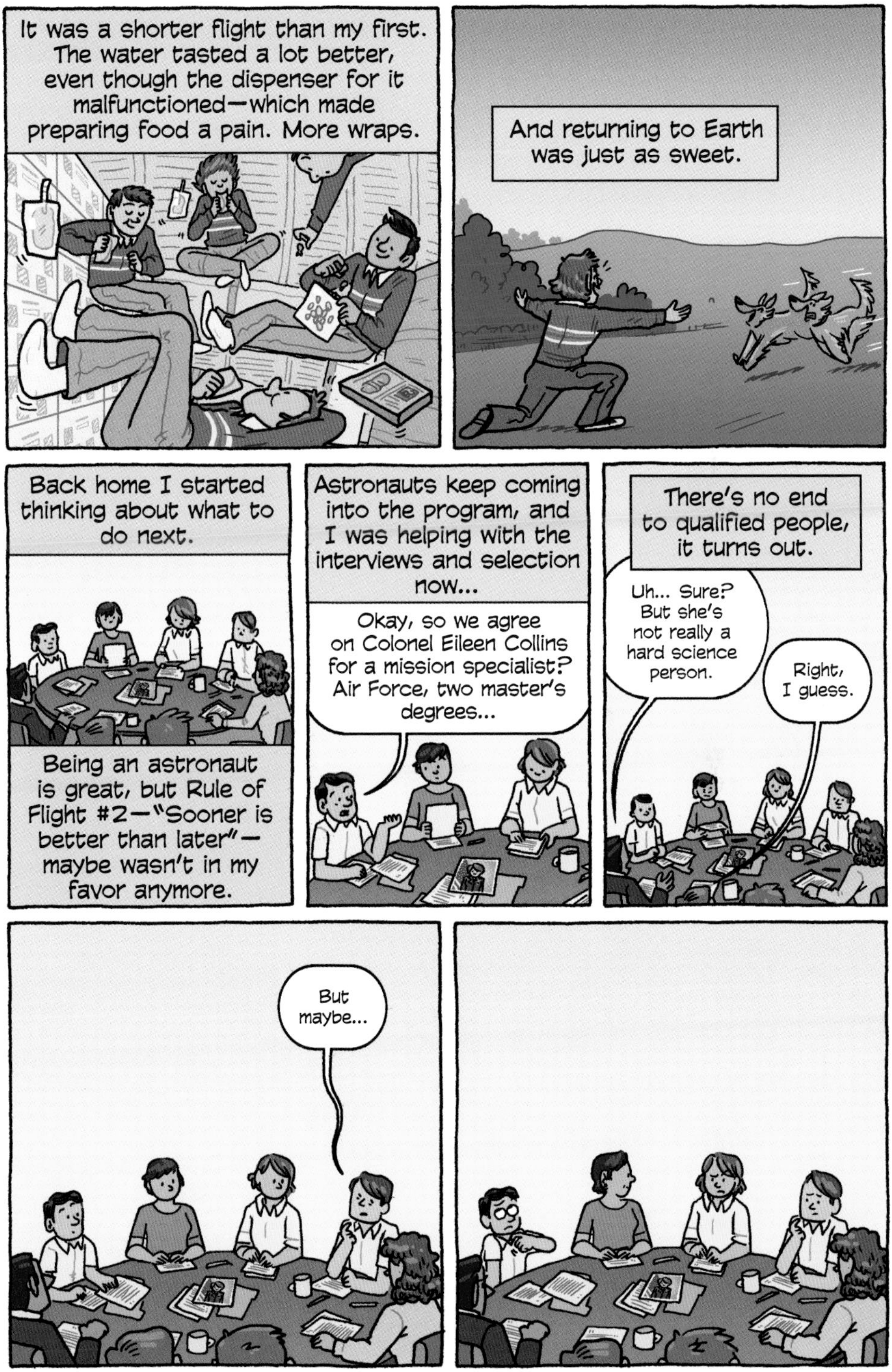

It was a shorter flight than my first. The water tasted a lot better, even though the dispenser for it malfunctioned—which made preparing food a pain. More wraps.
And returning to Earth was just as sweet.
Back home I started thinking about what to do next.
Being an astronaut is great, but Rule of Flight #2—"Sooner is better than later"—maybe wasn't in my favor anymore.
Astronauts keep coming into the program, and I was helping with the interviews and selection now...
Okay, so we agree on Colonel Eileen Collins for a mission specialist? Air Force, two master's degrees...
There's no end to qualified people, it turns out.
Uh... Sure? But she's not really a hard science person.
Right, I guess.
But maybe...

Guys, if nobody else will say it, I will.

Why don't we consider her as a pilot?

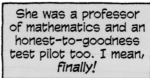

She was a professor of mathematics and an honest-to-goodness test pilot too. I mean, *finally!*

Of course!

Maybe...

I don't think...

Eileen ended up as the first woman commander. She headed up two missions, including the return to flight after the *Columbia* disaster. So it worked out.

And I was starting to get more involved in high-level decisions, obviously.

Thanks for the offer, but...

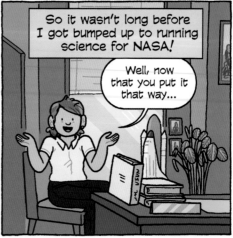

So it wasn't long before I got bumped up to running science for NASA!

Well, now that you put it that way...

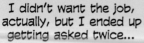

I didn't want the job, actually, but I ended up getting asked twice...

...and if the guy at the top asks you something, the second time you don't say no.

And it turns out running NASA's science program is fun!

With *Magellan* and all that, I'd gotten interested in astronomy and satellites. If I'd done that before engineering, I might have even ended up being an astrophysicist.

Though maybe not, because, well, astrophysicists are very *impressed* with themselves.

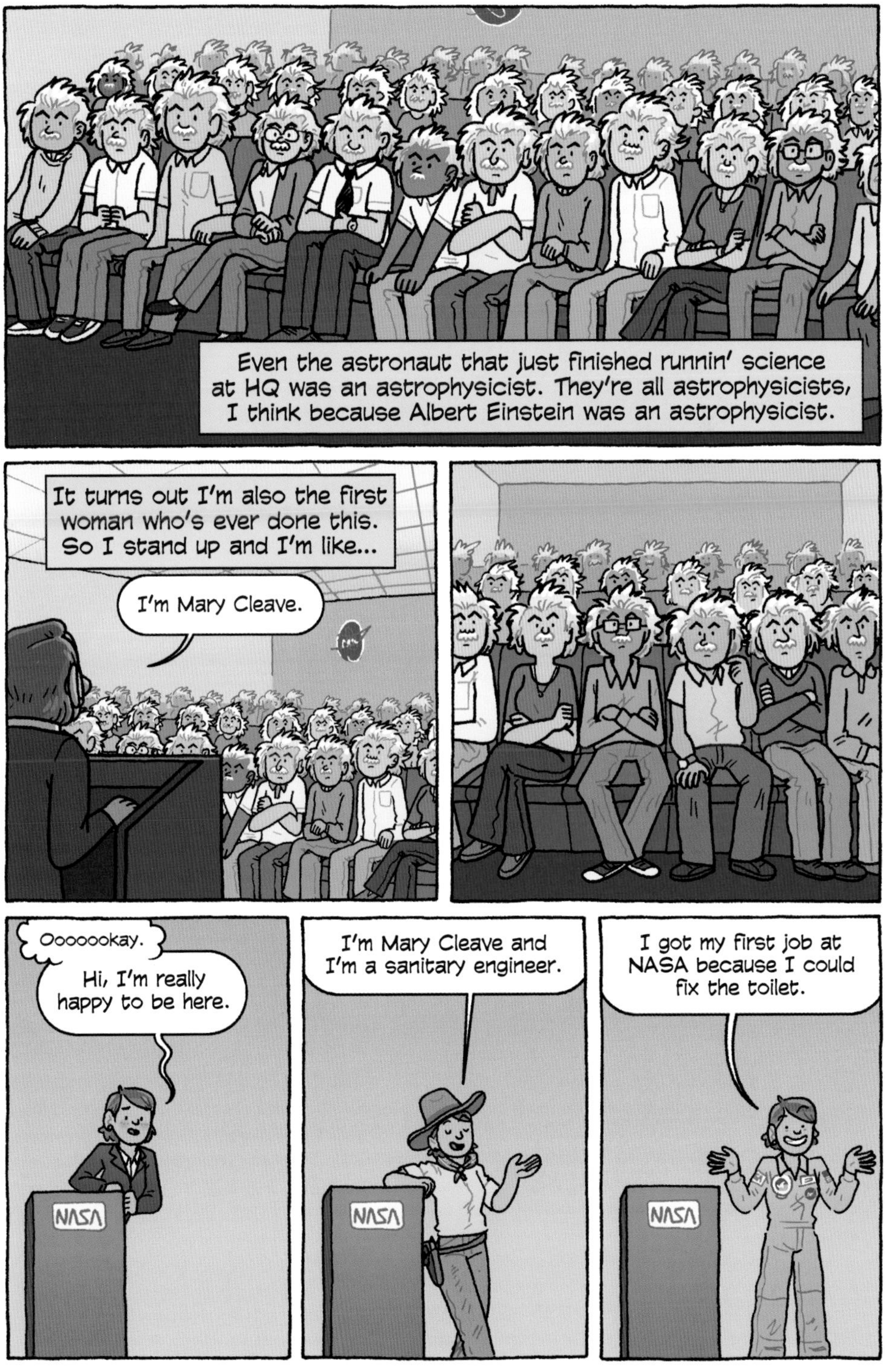
Even the astronaut that just finished runnin' science at HQ was an astrophysicist. They're all astrophysicists, I think because Albert Einstein was an astrophysicist.
It turns out I'm also the first woman who's ever done this. So I stand up and I'm like...
I'm Mary Cleave.
Oooooookay.
Hi, I'm really happy to be here.
NASA
I'm Mary Cleave and I'm a sanitary engineer.
NASA
I got my first job at NASA because I could fix the toilet.
NASA

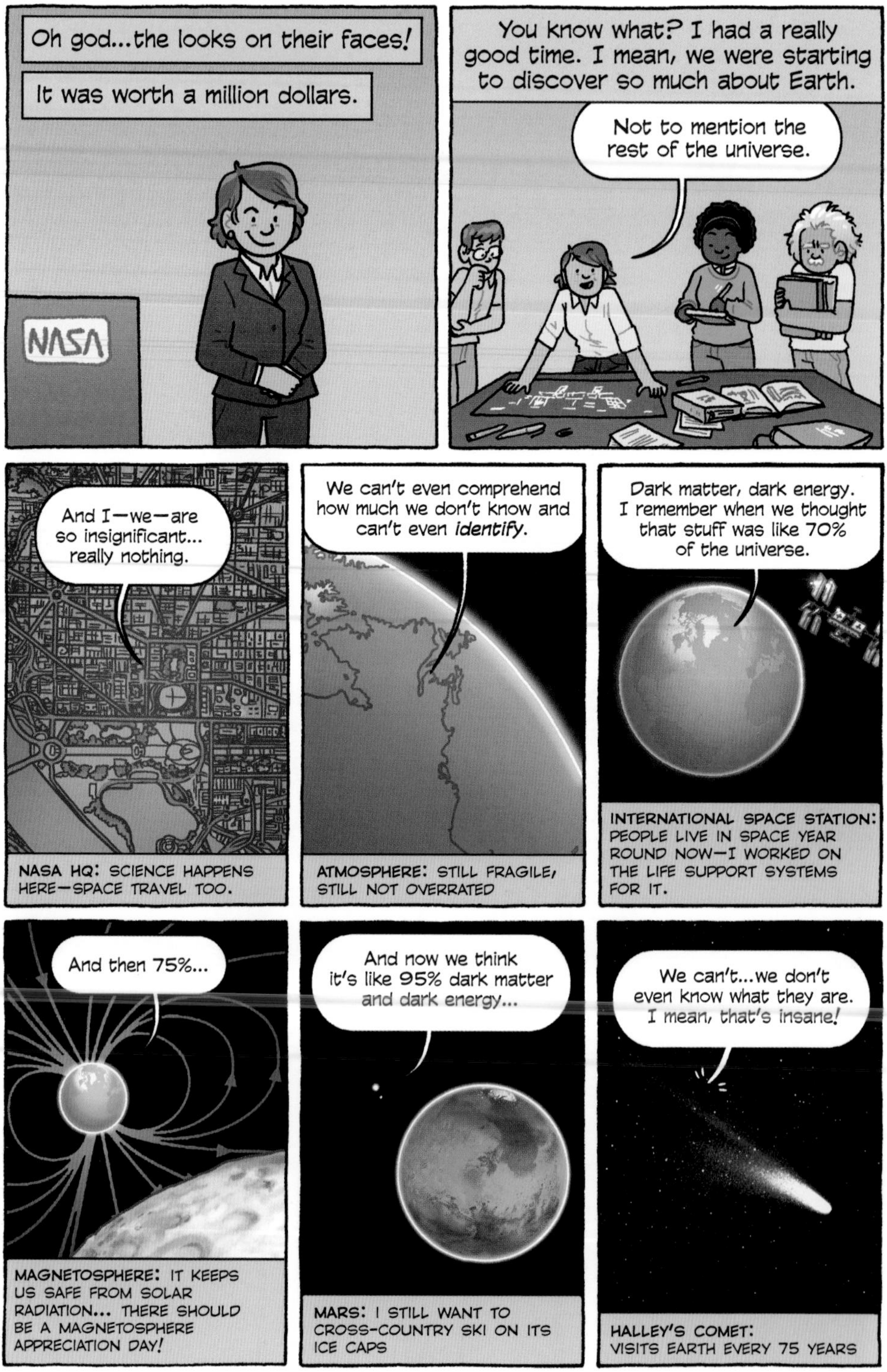

Oh god...the looks on their faces!
It was worth a million dollars.
NASA
You know what? I had a really good time. I mean, we were starting to discover so much about Earth.
Not to mention the rest of the universe.
And I—we—are so insignificant... really nothing.
NASA HQ: SCIENCE HAPPENS HERE—SPACE TRAVEL TOO.
We can't even comprehend how much we don't know and can't even *identify*.
ATMOSPHERE: STILL FRAGILE, STILL NOT OVERRATED
Dark matter, dark energy. I remember when we thought that stuff was like 70% of the universe.
INTERNATIONAL SPACE STATION: PEOPLE LIVE IN SPACE YEAR ROUND NOW—I WORKED ON THE LIFE SUPPORT SYSTEMS FOR IT.
And then 75%...
MAGNETOSPHERE: IT KEEPS US SAFE FROM SOLAR RADIATION... THERE SHOULD BE A MAGNETOSPHERE APPRECIATION DAY!
And now we think it's like 95% dark matter and dark energy...
MARS: I STILL WANT TO CROSS-COUNTRY SKI ON ITS ICE CAPS
We can't...we don't even know what they are. I mean, that's insane!
HALLEY'S COMET: VISITS EARTH EVERY 75 YEARS

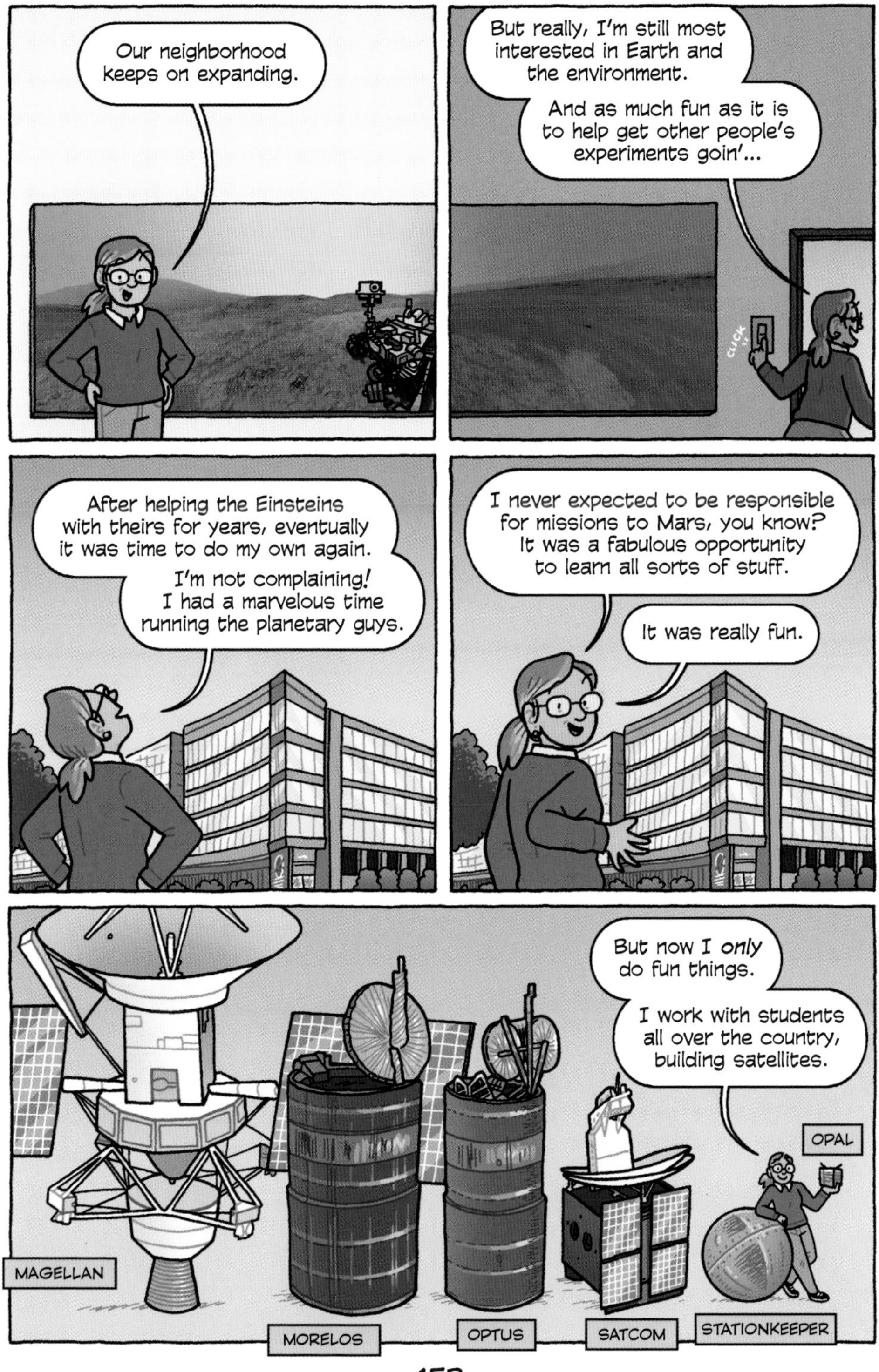

Our neighborhood keeps on expanding.
But really, I'm still most interested in Earth and the environment.
And as much fun as it is to help get other people's experiments goin'...
CLICK
After helping the Einsteins with theirs for years, eventually it was time to do my own again.
I'm not complaining! I had a marvelous time running the planetary guys.
I never expected to be responsible for missions to Mars, you know? It was a fabulous opportunity to learn all sorts of stuff.
It was really fun.
But now I *only* do fun things.
I work with students all over the country, building satellites.
MAGELLAN
MORELOS
OPTUS
SATCOM
STATIONKEEPER
OPAL

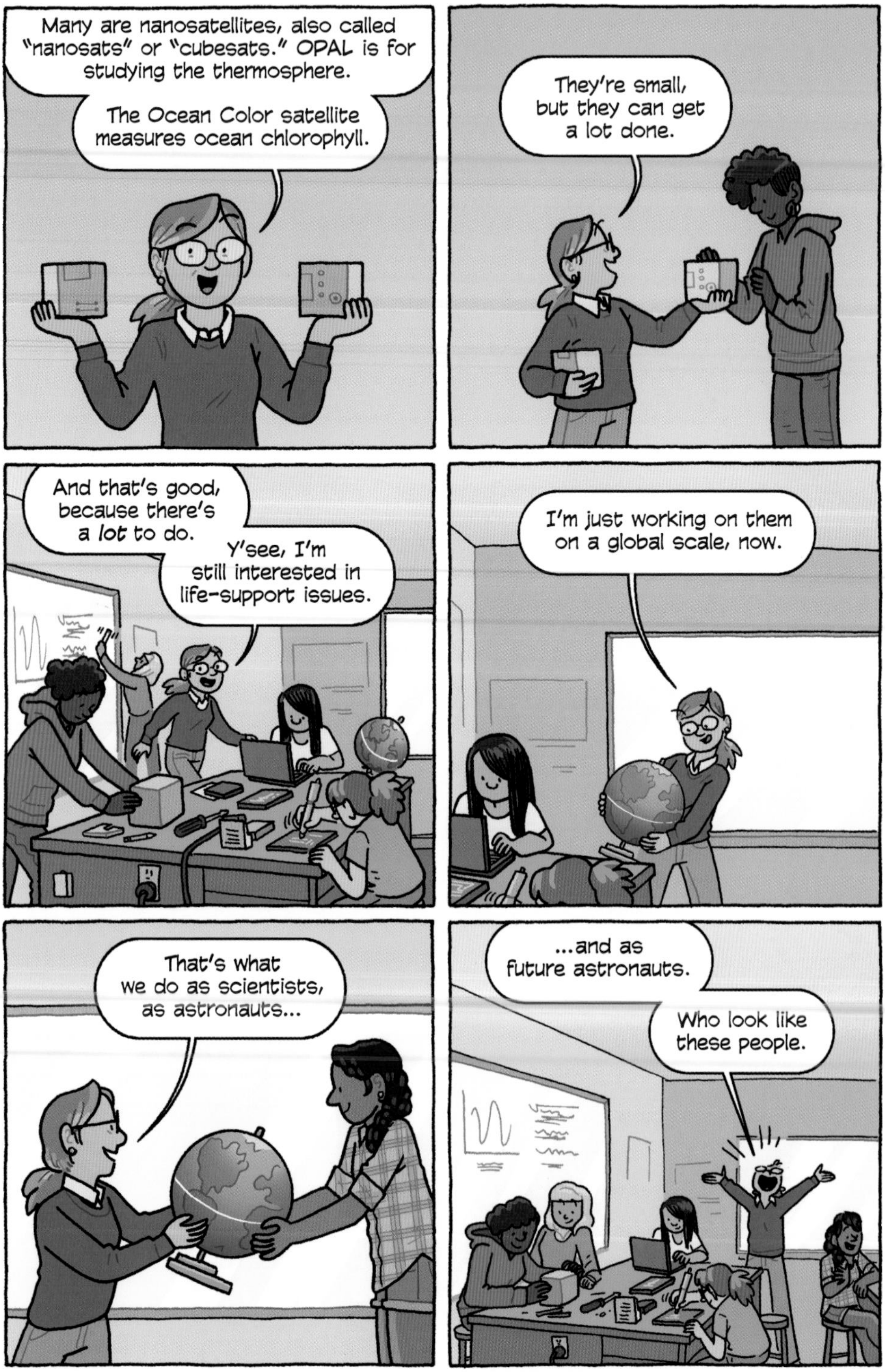
Many are nanosatellites, also called "nanosats" or "cubesats." OPAL is for studying the thermosphere.
The Ocean Color satellite measures ocean chlorophyll.
They're small, but they can get a lot done.
And that's good, because there's a *lot* to do.
Y'see, I'm still interested in life-support issues.
I'm just working on them on a global scale, now.
That's what we do as scientists, as astronauts...
...and as future astronauts.
Who look like these people.

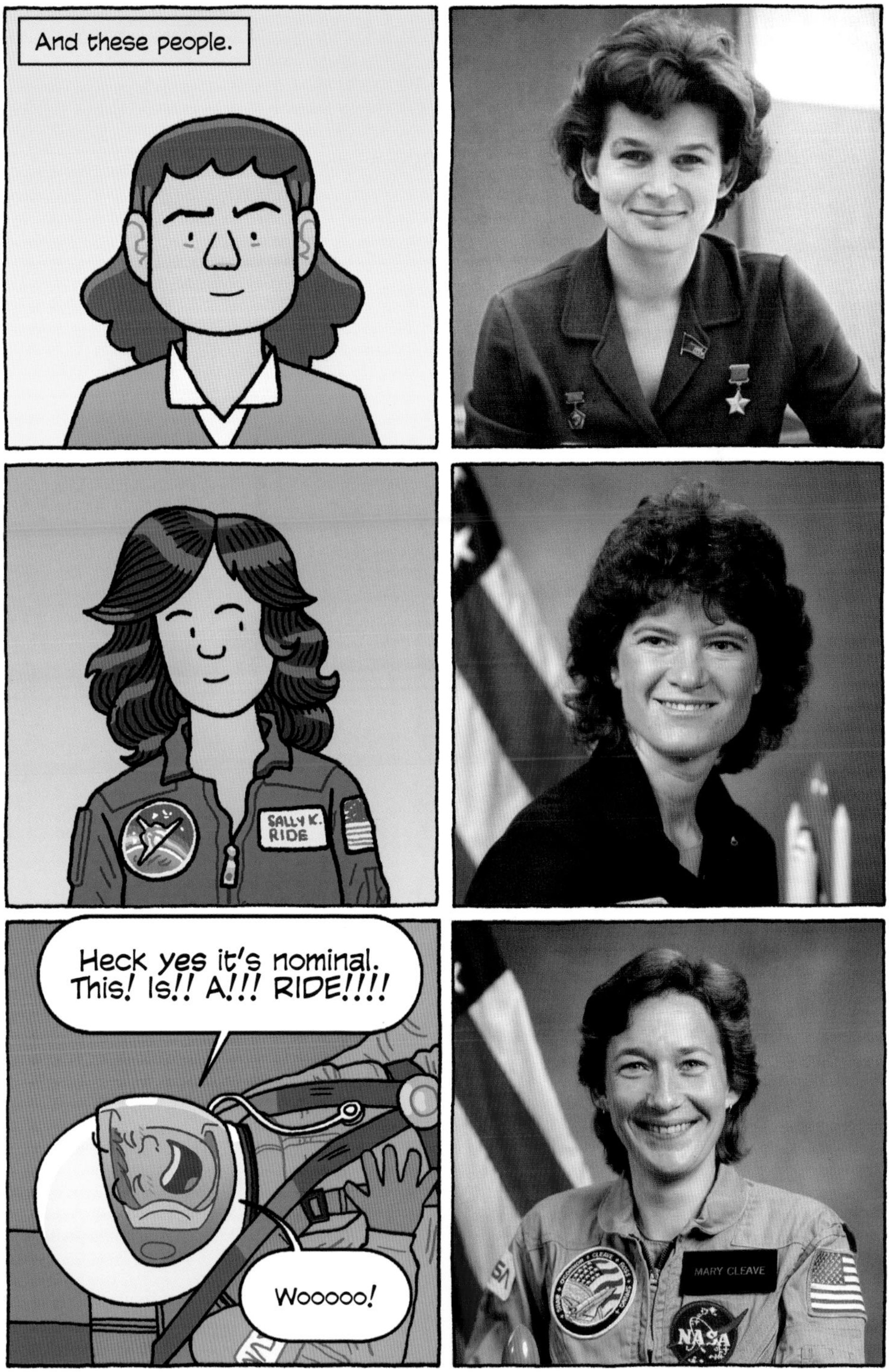
And these people.
SALLY K.
RIDE
Heck yes it's nominal.
This! Is!! A!!! RIDE!!!!
Wooooo!
MARY CLEAVE
NASA

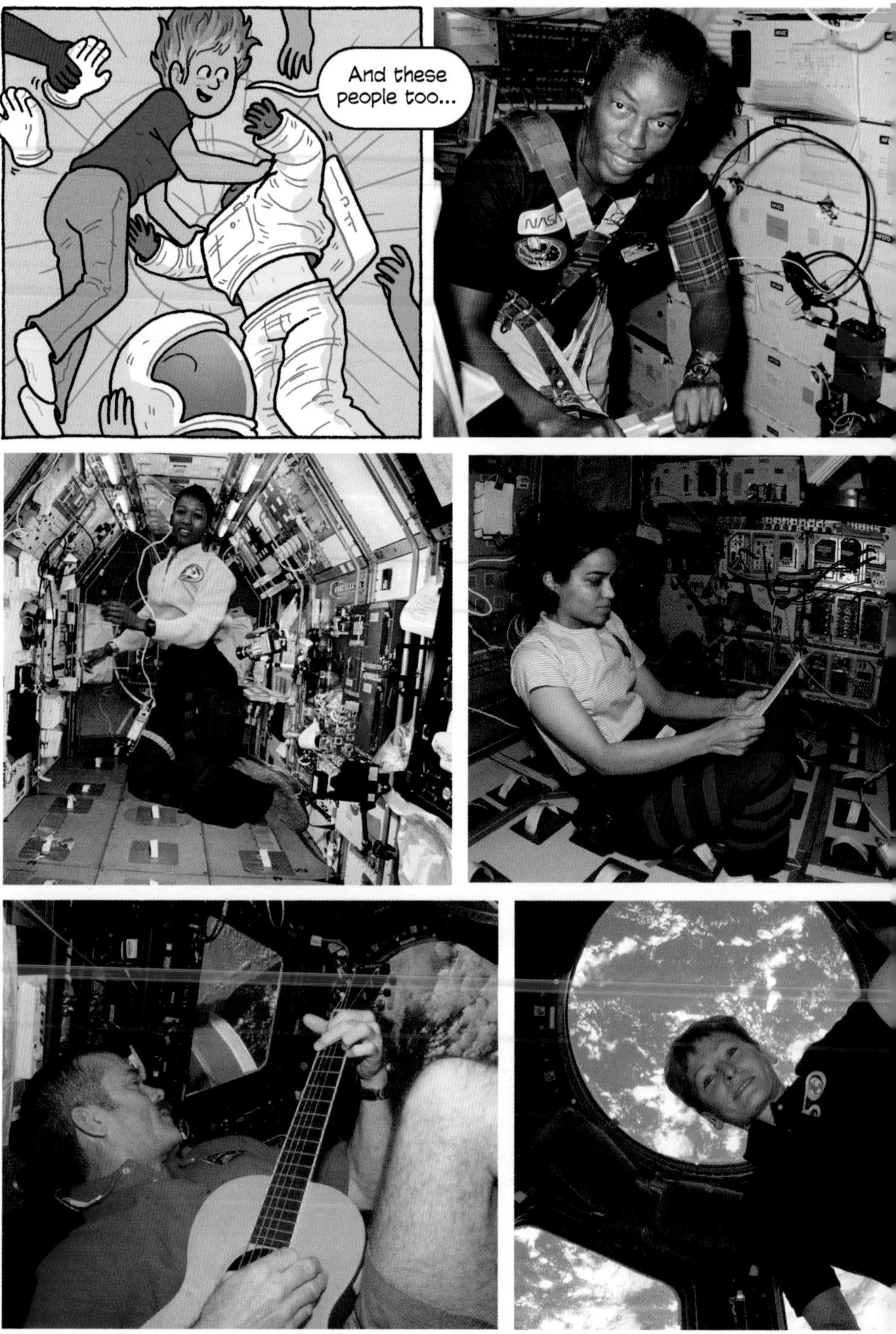
And these people too...

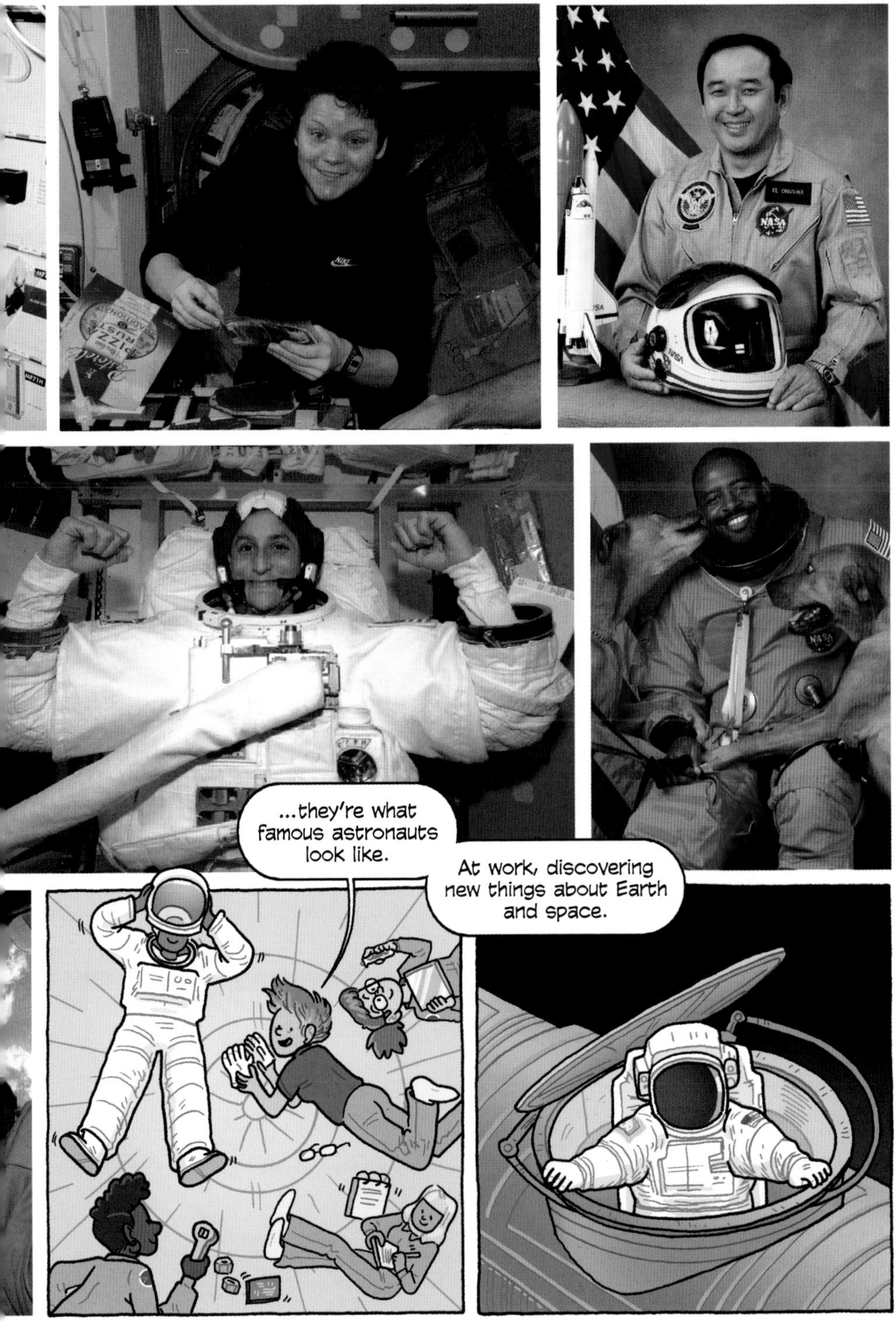
...they're what
famous astronauts
look like.
At work, discovering
new things about Earth
and space.

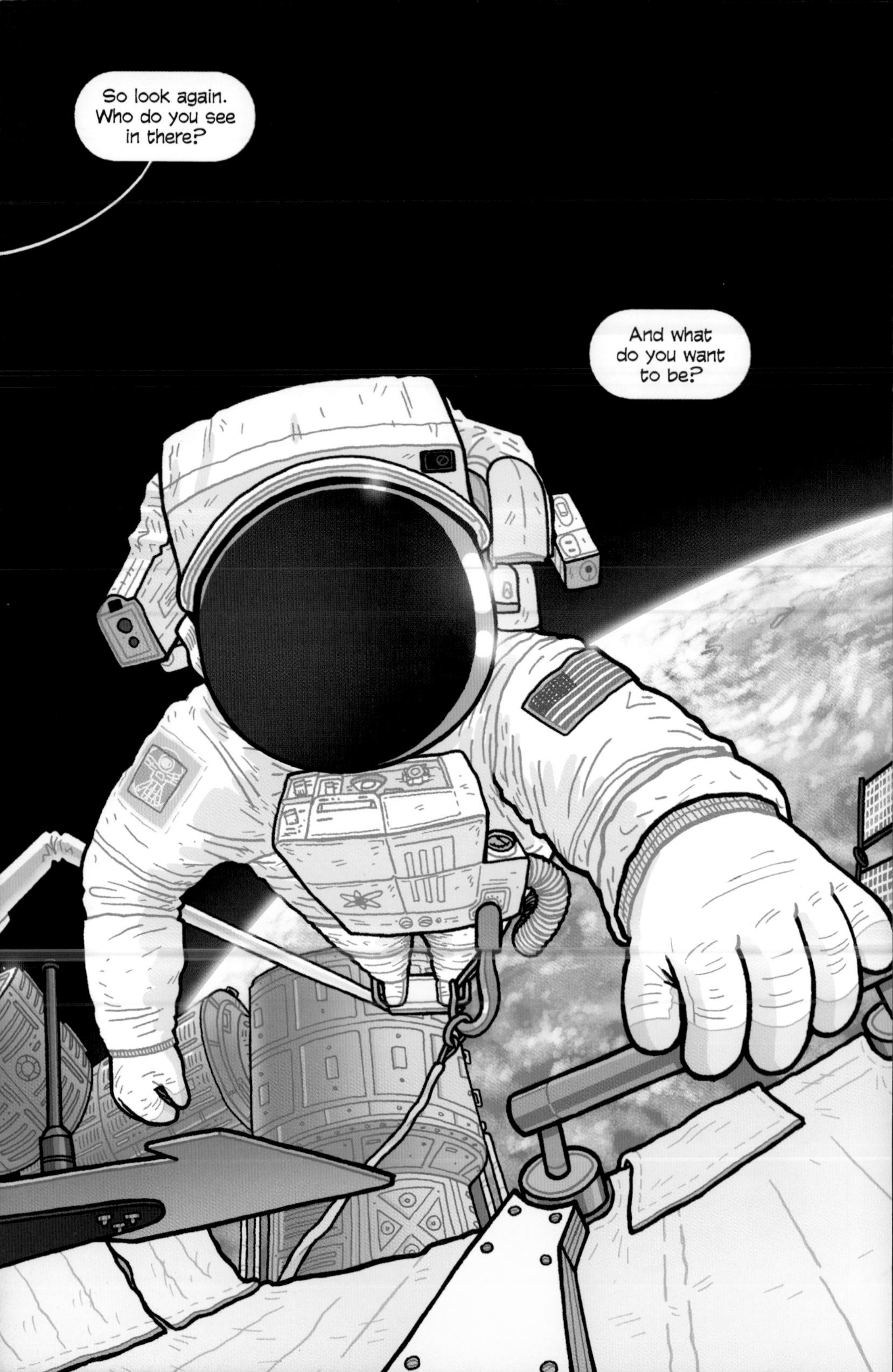
So look again. Who do you see in there?
And what do you want to be?

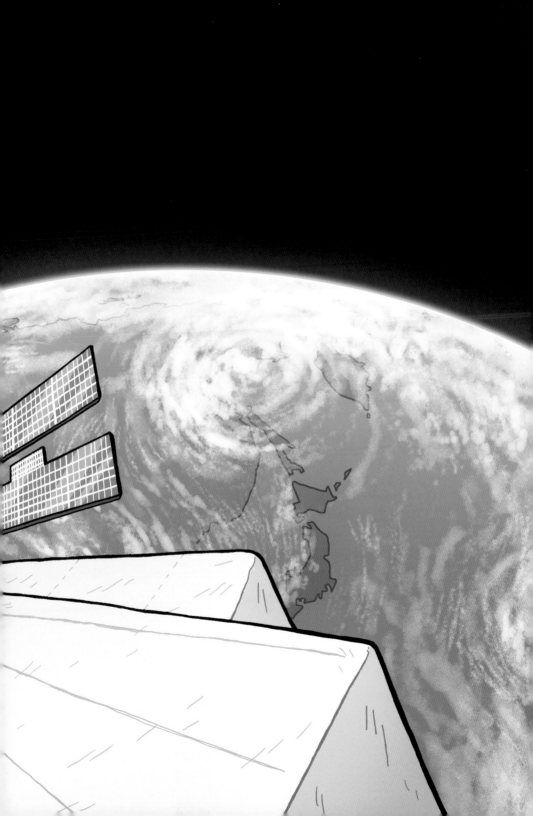

ACKNOWLEDGMENTS

First and foremost, thanks to Mary, who spent time talking, answering questions, and even showing us around her hometown—including a stop for some ale at a pub where George Washington, Thomas Jefferson, and Benjamin Franklin used to hang out.

In the book, you noticed that the Soviet scientists and cosmonauts speak...well, they almost seem to speak Russian! That's thanks to Kevin Cannon, who created the excellent faux-Cyrillic font for an earlier book about the space race he and Jim did together. And our friends Casey and Calista, etc., etc. are tops when it comes to turning scripts into stories and stories into comics.

AUTHOR'S NOTE

Space travel is wonderful in many ways, and one of them (at least for comic book creators) is that it's so well documented. You can listen in on trips to the Moon with Neil Armstrong and Buzz Aldrin and Michael Collins! You can hear Sally Ride make bad jokes as CAPCOM. You can read about missions and hear stories in the words of real astronauts and rocket scientists.

We did all those things for this book, and below you'll find a list of the most important resources we used to put this story together. So much got left out that we could do a bunch more graphic novels, though, and maybe we will; space is hard to get to and live in, but it's great for comics!

(Because people always ask about scenes we had to cut out because of space, here's maybe our biggest regret: We weren't able to fit in what happened the evening Cleave's Comet appeared over Houston. It turns out that the 911 switchboards lit up as emergency responders got overwhelmed with UFO reports. The police called NASA, and you can just imagine the conversation from their perspective:

"UFO sighting? When?"
"Uh-huh. Uh-huh."
"Okay, look. We know what that was, but...
   do you really want us to identify it?")

Even with all those references, there are a few things you won't be able to check out yourself. Specifically, the conversations we had with Mary Cleave and Carolyn Huntoon aren't published, so you'll have to take our word for what they said to us. Sorry about that, and thanks to Mary and Carolyn for their help, their support, and the great stories they told.

Speaking of which, the coolest things you saw in this book actually happened. But to keep the story moving along we sometimes made small changes that depart from the literal truth. One example is on the very first page, where Mary's gloves are a little different from what she actually wore. We substituted in a design used on later missions because those gloves would look more familiar, and we worried that showing the old kind would give you a "hey, wait a minute" moment when we didn't want you to pause. There are other examples (on page 66, we used the modern term for fans of people who boldly go, rather than "Trekker," which is what Trekkies called themselves back then), so we hope all of the space nerds (and we're space nerds too!) who had a "hey, wait a minute" moment were willing to accept some artistic license!

Sometimes we also had to put words into people's mouths, but you'd be surprised at which ones. (Hint: It's mostly the everyday stuff that glues scenes together.) When something in *Astronauts* was funny, it's almost always because that person really did say something that made us laugh! But you should know that not all characters represent just one person either. As you'll see below, we tapped into the experiences and voices of many astronauts, engineers, scientists, and NASA folks to create this story. Thousands of people work on each mission to space, and this book couldn't be thousands of pages long. That means sometimes we combined what happened to a bunch of individuals, at different times, into one person's story happening in the now of the book. So even though everything didn't happen to Mary Cleave, just about everything did happen to a real person in the course of getting her off planet Earth... and back home again.

REFERENCES / BIBLIOGRAPHY

PEOPLE

Our best, and favorite, sources of information were people. We spent hours talking with Mary, and she answered every question we asked with patience, candor, and humor. She also put us in touch with Carolyn Huntoon, who was generous with her time and thoughts and stories.

NASA

The great thing about doing a book about space is that NASA has resources about almost everything, including—especially!—the people who did the science and exploration. The following are from the NASA Johnson Space Center (JSC) Oral History Project. As you can see, even though when Jim first read Mary's interview he knew he wanted to meet her and write a book about her, we read many more than just hers. And there are even more for you to discover at historycollection.jsc.nasa.gov/JSCHistoryPortal/history/oral_histories/oral_histories.htm.

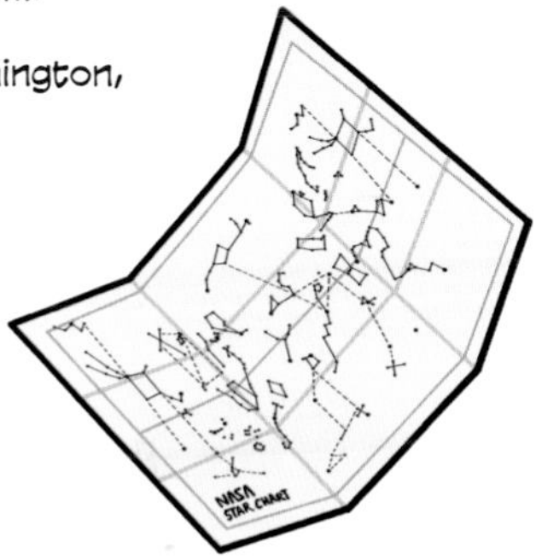
NASA
STAR CHART

Mary L. Cleave, interviewed by Rebecca Wright, Washington, D.C.—5 March 2002

Anna L. Fisher, interviewed by Jennifer Ross-Nazzal, Houston, TX—17 February 2009 and 3 March 2011

Ivy F. Hooks, interviewed by: Jennifer Ross-Nazzal, Houston, TX—5 March 2009; Rebecca Wright, Boerne, TX—24 March 2009

Dorothy B. Lee, interviewed by Rebecca Wright, Houston, TX—10 November 1999

Jon A. McBride, interviewed by Jennifer Ross-Nazzal, Kennedy Space Center, FL—17 April 2012

Bryan D. O'Connor, interviewed by Sandra Johnson, Washington, D.C.—17 March 2004

Sally K. Ride, interviewed by Rebecca Wright, San Antonio, TX—6 December 2002

Jerry L. Ross, interviewed by Jennifer Ross-Nazzal, Houston, TX—4 December 2003

Margaret Rhea Seddon, interviewed by Jennifer Ross-Nazzal, Murfreesboro, TN—21 May 2010

Brewster H. Shaw, Jr., interviewed by Kevin M. Rusnak, Houston, TX—19 April 2002

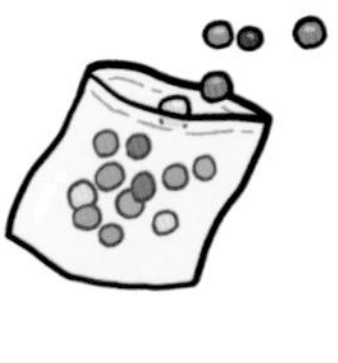

Sherwood C. "Woody" Spring, interviewed by Jennifer Ross-Nazzal, Arlington, VA—18 November 2003

Kathryn D. Sullivan, interviewed by Jennifer Ross-Nazzal, Columbus, OH—10 May 2007 and 28 May 2009

Charles D. Walker, interviewed by: Sandra Johnson, Houston, TX—14 April 2005; Jennifer Ross-Nazzal, Washington, D.C.—17 Mar 2005; Sandra Johnson, Springfield, VA—7 November 2006

We didn't stop there, of course, and consulted the following as well.

NASA Audio Collection at archive.org, STS-61-B EVA 2 audio digitized, cataloged and archived by the Houston Audio Control Room, at the NASA Johnson Space Center, archive.org/details/STS-61B

Space Shuttle Flight 23 (STS-61-B) Post Flight Presentation by The National Space Society, space.nss.org/space-shuttle-flight-23-sts-61b-post-flight-press-conference-video/

Space Shuttle Mission STS-30 Press Kit, November 1985, Release No. 85, science.ksc.nasa.gov/shuttle/missions/sts-30/sts-30-press-kit.txt

Space Shuttle Mission STS-61-B Press Kit, April 1989, www.jsc.nasa.gov/history/shuttle_pk/pk/Flight_023_STS-61B_Press_Kit.pdf

STS-7 Air Ground Transcript, Vol. 1: Launch through MET 02:05:00 (Public Information Office, NASA Johnson Space Center, Houston TX 77058, 1983)

ARTICLES

Here are a few of the many articles on spaceflight, and women in space, that were the most helpful.

"An extraterrestrial sandwich: the perils of food in space" by Jane Levi, *Endeavour*, vol. 34 no. 1, 2010, 6-11, doi.org/10.1016/j.endeavour.2010.01.004

"The first woman in Earth orbit: Part 1" by Asif A. Siddiqi, *Spaceflight*, vol. 51, January 2009, 18-27

"The first woman in Earth orbit: Part 2" by Asif A. Siddiqi, *Spaceflight*, vol. 51, February 2009, 64-71

Jane Briggs Hart papers: circa 1925-1996, Bentley Historical Library, University of Michigan, Ann Arbor

"Q & A: Nichelle Nichols, AKA Lt. Uhura, and NASA" by Arcynta Ali Childs, *Smithsonian*, June 23, 2011, smithsonianmag.com/smithsonian-institution/q-a-nichelle-nichols-aka-lt-uhura-and-nasa-180943982

"Sally Ride, Astronaut: The World is Watching" by Sara Sanborn, *Ms.*, January 1983, 45-52; 87-88

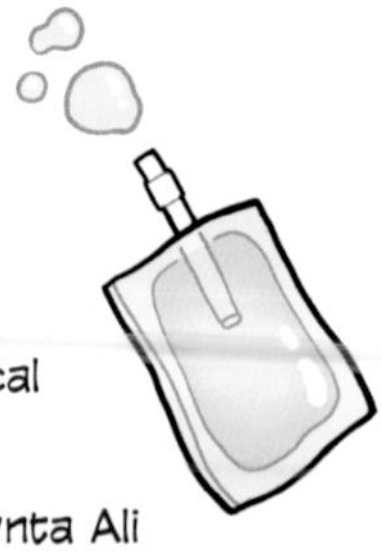

BOOKS

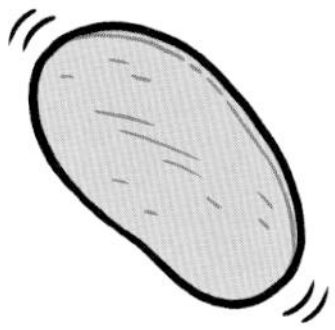

Finally, you can't make a book like this without reading other books. Here are our favorites from the stacks (and stacks of stacks) of books near our writing desk and drawing table.

Almost Heaven: The Story of Women in Space, by Bettyann Holtzmann Kevles (Cambridge, MA: MIT Press, 2006)

The Astronaut's Cookbook, by Charles T. Bourland and Gregory L. Vogt (NY: Springer, 2009)

Beyond Uhura: Star Trek® and Other Memories, by Nichelle Nichols (NY: G.P. Putnam's Sons, 1994)

Challenge to Apollo: The Soviet Union and the Space Race, 1945-1974, by Asif A. Siddiqi (NASA SP-2000-4408, 2000; history.nasa.gov/SP-4408pt1.pdf)

Lovelace's Woman in Space Program, by Margaret Weitekamp, history.nasa.gov/printFriendly/flats.html

The Mercury 13: The Untold Story of Thirteen American Women and the Dream of Space Flight, by Martha Ackmann (NY: Random House, 2003)

Promised the Moon: The Untold Story of the First Women in the Space Race, by Stephanie Nolen (NY: Four Walls Eight Windows, 2002)

Qualifications for Astronauts: Hearings Before the Special Subcommittee on the Selection of Astronauts of the Committee on Science and Astronautics, U.S. House Of Representatives, Eighty-Seventh Congress, Second Session, July 17-18, 1962

Right Stuff, Wrong Sex: America's First Women in Space Program, by Margaret A. Weitekamp (Baltimore, MD: The Johns Hopkins University Press, 2004)

Tethered Mercury: A Pilot's Memoir: The Right Stuff...But the Wrong Sex, by Bernice Trimble Steadman, with Jody M. Clark (Traverse City, MI: Aviation Press, 2001)

Valentina: First Woman in Space, by A. Lothian (Edinburgh, UK: The Pentland Press, 1993)

Women in Space: Following Valentina, by David J. Shayler and Ian Moule (Chichester, UK: Springer/Praxis, 2005)

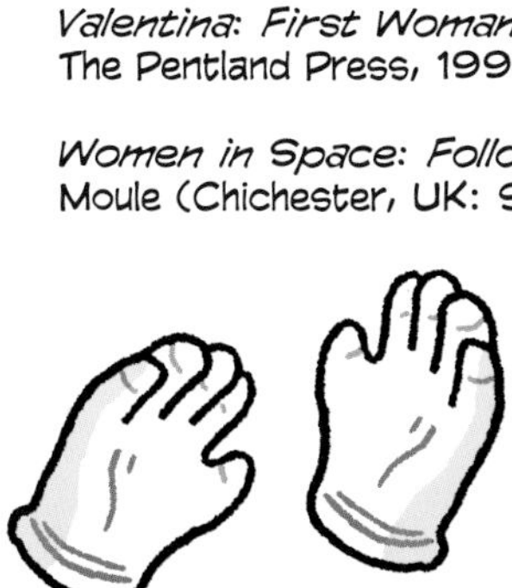

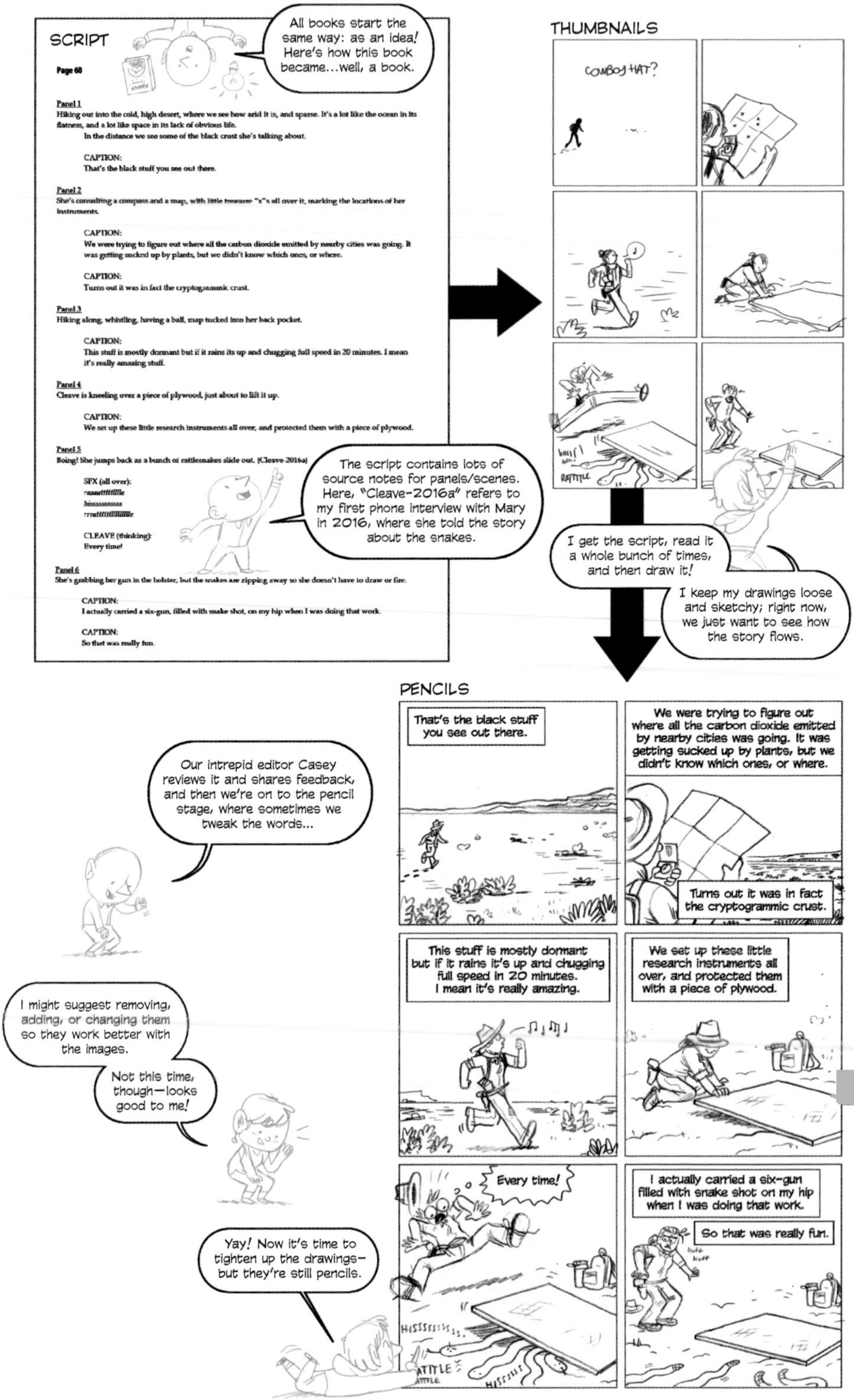
SCRIPT
All books start the same way: as an idea! Here's how this book became...well, a book.
Page 60
Panel 1
Hiking out into the cold, high desert, where we see how arid it is, and sparse. It's a lot like the ocean in its flatness, and a lot like space in its lack of obvious life.
In the distance we see some of the black crust she's talking about.
CAPTION:
That's the black stuff you see out there.
Panel 2
She's consulting a compass and a map, with little treasure "x"s all over it, marking the locations of her instruments.
CAPTION:
We were trying to figure out where all the carbon dioxide emitted by nearby cities was going. It was getting sucked up by plants, but we didn't know which ones, or where.
CAPTION:
Turns out it was in fact the cryptogrammic crust.
Panel 3
Hiking along, whistling, having a ball, map tucked into her back pocket.
CAPTION:
This stuff is mostly dormant but if it rains its up and chugging full speed in 20 minutes. I mean it's really amazing stuff.
Panel 4
Cleave is kneeling over a piece of plywood, just about to lift it up.
CAPTION:
We set up these little research instruments all over, and protected them with a piece of plywood.
Panel 5
Boing! She jumps back as a bunch of rattlesnakes slide out. (Cleave-2016a)
SFX (all over):
hissssssssss
CLEAVE (thinking):
Every time!
Panel 6
She's grabbing her gun in the holster, but the snakes are zipping away so she doesn't have to draw or fire.
CAPTION:
I actually carried a six-gun, filled with snake shot, on my hip when I was doing that work.
CAPTION:
So that was really fun.
The script contains lots of source notes for panels/scenes. Here, "Cleave-2016a" refers to my first phone interview with Mary in 2016, where she told the story about the snakes.
THUMBNAILS
COWBOY HAT?
RATTLE
I get the script, read it a whole bunch of times, and then draw it!
I keep my drawings loose and sketchy; right now, we just want to see how the story flows.
PENCILS
That's the black stuff you see out there.
We were trying to figure out where all the carbon dioxide emitted by nearby cities was going. It was getting sucked up by plants, but we didn't know which ones, or where.
Turns out it was in fact the cryptogrammic crust.
This stuff is mostly dormant but if it rains it's up and chugging full speed in 20 minutes. I mean it's really amazing.
We set up these little research instruments all over, and protected them with a piece of plywood.
Every time!
HISSSSSSSS
ATTLE
I actually carried a six-gun filled with snake shot on my hip when I was doing that work.
So that was really fun.
HUFF HUFF
Our intrepid editor Casey reviews it and shares feedback, and then we're on to the pencil stage, where sometimes we tweak the words...
I might suggest removing, adding, or changing them so they work better with the images.
Not this time, though—looks good to me!
Yay! Now it's time to tighten up the drawings—but they're still pencils.

INKS

REFERENCES

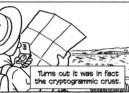

COLORS

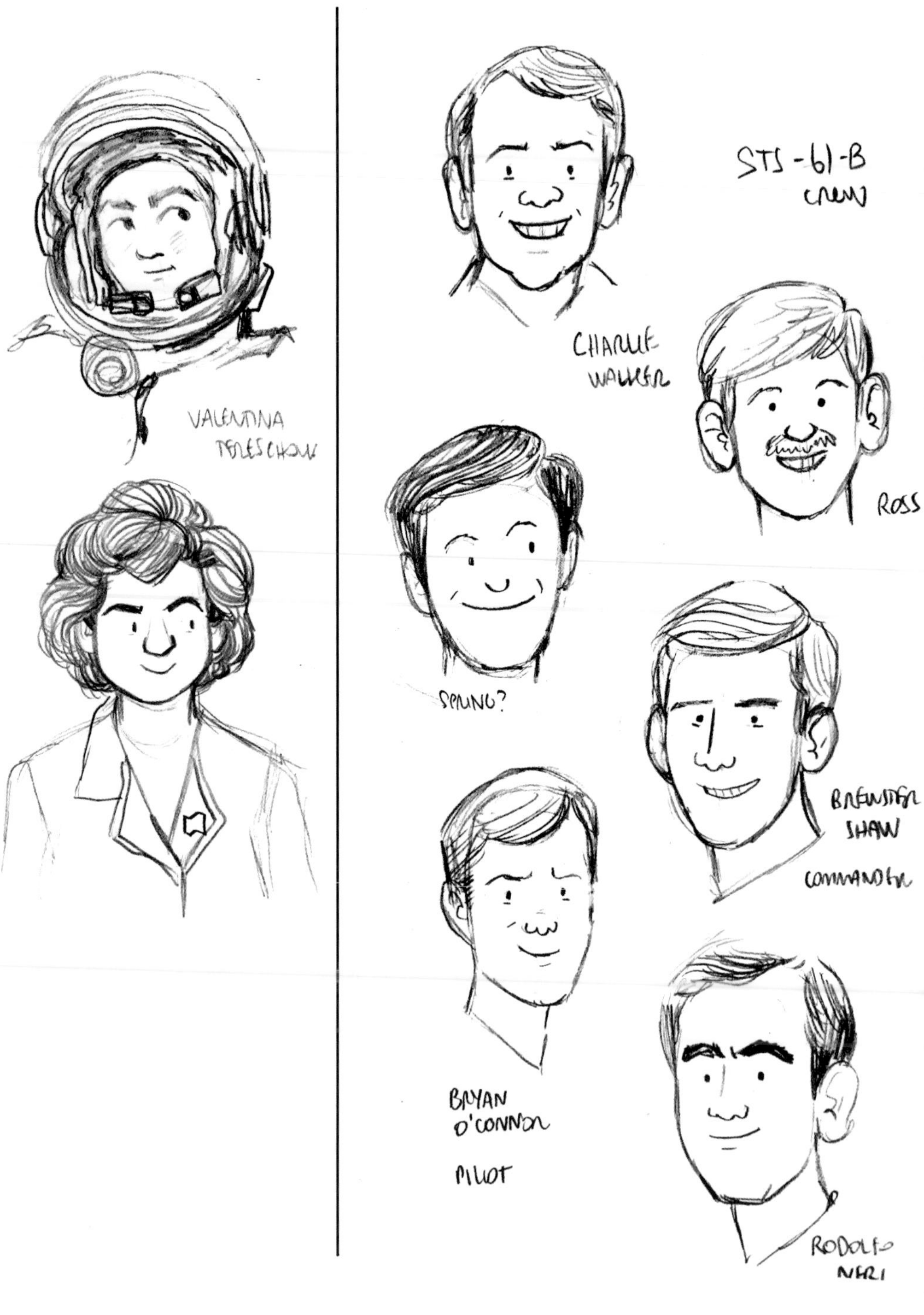
VALENTINA
TERESCHKOV
STS-61-B
CREW
CHARLIE
WALKER
ROSS
SPRING?
BREWSTER
SHAW
COMMANDER
BRYAN
O'CONNOR
PILOT
RODOLFO
NERI

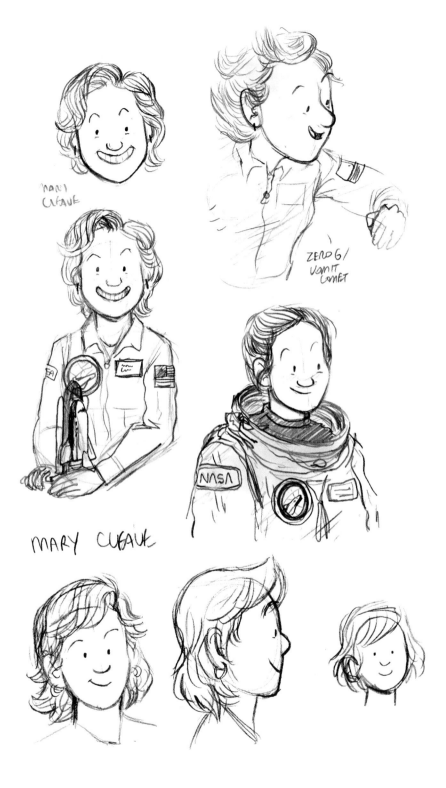

MARY CLEAVE

ZERO G/
VOMIT
COMET

NASA

First Second

Published by First Second
First Second is an imprint of Roaring Brook Press,
a division of Holtzbrinck Publishing Holdings Limited Partnership
120 Broadway, New York, NY 10271

Don't miss your next favorite book from First Second! For the latest updates
go to firstsecondnewsletter.com and sign up for our enewsletter.

Library of Congress Control Number: 2019930757
Paperback ISBN: 978-1-250-76003-6
Hardcover ISBN: 978-1-62672-877-6

Our books may be purchased in bulk for promotional, educational, or business use.
Please contact your local bookseller or the Macmillan Corporate and Premium Sales Department
at (800) 221-7945 ext. 5442 or by email at MacmillanSpecialMarkets@macmillan.com.

FIRST

EDITION

First edition, 2020

Edited by Calista Brill and Casey Gonzalez
Cover design by Andrew Arnold
Interior book design by Chris Dickey and Molly Johanson

Printed in China by Toppan Leefung Printing Ltd., Dongguan City, Guangdong Province

Photo of Valentina Tereshkova on page 155 by Keystone-France, © Getty Images
All other photos credited to NASA

Astronauts was penciled digitally in Photoshop. Inked with .7 mm and .5 mm
Uni-ball Vision Rollerball pens on Strathmore 300 Series Smooth Bristol Board.
Scanned and then colored digitally in Photoshop.

Paperback: 10 9 8 7 6 5 4 3 2 1
Hardcover: 10 9 8 7 6 5 4 3 2 1